THE
DISASTER
ARTIST

MY LIFE INSIDE *THE ROOM*,
THE GREATEST BAD MOVIE EVER MADE

GREG SESTERO
&
TOM BISSELL

SIMON & SCHUSTER
New York   London   Toronto   Sydney   New Delhi

Simon & Schuster
1230 Avenue of the Americas
New York, NY 10020

First Simon & Schuster hardcover edition October 2013

SIMON & SCHUSTER and colophon are registered trademarks of Simon & Schuster, Inc.

For information about special discounts for bulk purchases, please contact
Simon & Schuster Special Sales at 1-866-506-1949 or business@simonandschuster.com.

The Simon & Schuster Speakers Bureau can bring authors to your live event. For more
information or to book an event contact the Simon & Schuster Speakers Bureau at
1-866-248-3049 or visit our website at www.simonspeakers.com.

Designed by Akasha Archer

Manufactured in the United States of America

10 9 8 7 6 5 4 3

Library of Congress Cataloging-in-Publication Data
  The disaster artist : my life inside the room, the greatest bad movie ever made /
Greg Sestero, Tom Bissell.
     pages cm
1. Room (Motion picture) I. Bissell, Tom. II. Title.
  PN1997.R57565S47 2013
  791.43'72—dc23
                              2013008798

ISBN 978-1-4516-6119-4
ISBN 978-1-4516-6120-0 (ebook)

Photo Credits:
Photograph courtesy of the author: 1, 2, 3, 4, 5, 6, 7, 8, 9, 10, 11, 12, 13, 14, 15, 16, 17, 20,
21, 22, 23, 24, 25, 26, 27, 28, 29, 32, 37, 38, 39, 40, 41, 42; Photograph courtesy of Kyle Vogt:
18; Photograph courtesy of Greg Ellery: 19; Photograph courtesy of Michael Rousselet: 30;
Photograph by Shawn D. James: 31; Photograph courtesy of Alex Pardee, http://eyesuck-
ink.com: 33; Photograph by Theo Lyngby: 34; Photograph by Elias Eliot: 35; Photograph
courtesy of Francis Sheil: 36

To my family,
with my love and gratitude

Joe Gillis: Maybe it's a little long, and maybe there's some repetitions . . . but you're not a professional writer.

Norma Desmond: I wrote that with my heart.

Joe Gillis: Sure you did. That's what makes it great.

—*Sunset Boulevard* (1950)

I always thought it would be better to be a fake somebody than a real nobody.

—Tom Ripley, *The Talented Mr. Ripley* (1999)

This play can be played without any age restriction. It will work if the chemistry between all the characters makes sense. Human behavior and betrayal applies to all of us. It exists within ourselves. You love somebody. Do you? What is love? You think you have everything, but you don't have anything. You have to have hope and spirit. Be an optimist. But can you handle all your human behavior or other's behavior? You don't want to be good, but great.
—Director's Note, *The Room* (2001), by Tommy P. Wiseau

Contents

The Players

Tommy Wiseau .... *Johnny / writer, director, producer*

Don [*sic*].. *the other Mark*

Brianna Tate.. *the other Michelle*

Philip Haldiman... *Denny*

Dan Janjigian .... *Chris-R*

Scott Holmes... *Mike*

Juliette Danielle... *Lisa*

Carolyn Minnott.. *Claudette*

Robyn Paris .... *Michelle*

Kyle Vogt.. *Peter*

Greg Ellery... *Steven*

Bill Meurer... *Birns & Sawyer owner*

Peter Anway... *Birns & Sawyer rep*

Raphael Smadja................................. *director of photography no. 1*

Sandy Schklair .... *script supervisor*

Safowa Bright... *costume designer*

Amy Von Brock.. *makeup artist*

Zsolt Magyar .... *sound mixer*

"Merce" .... *art department*

Graham Futerfas... *director of photography no. 2*

Todd Barron .... *director of photography no. 3*

Byron .... *stagehand / director of yelling*

Joe Pacella... *camera assistant*

Author's Note

Imagine a movie so incomprehensible that you find yourself compelled to watch it over and over again. You become desperate to learn how (if) on earth it was conceived: Who made it, and for what purpose?

This book is about what might be the world's most improbable Hollywood success story. At its center is an enigmatic filmmaker who claims, among many other things, to be a vampire. This man speaks with a thick European accent, the derivation of which he won't identify. He also refuses to reveal his age or the origins of his seemingly vast fortune. His name is Tommy Wiseau; and the film he wrote, directed, produced, starred in, and poured $6 million into is a disastrous specimen of cinematic hubris called *The Room*.

The Room is—despite its ostensibly simple plot—perhaps the most casually surreal film ever made. To put it simply, *The Room* doesn't work in any way films have evolved to work over the last century of filmmaking. It's filled with red herrings, shots of locations that are never visited, and entire conversations comprised of non sequiturs. It is, essentially, one gigantic plot hole. For many, experiencing *The Room* is both wildly exhilarating and supremely dislocating. The film engenders an obsessive fascination, instantly luring you into its odd, convoluted world. Tommy Wiseau intended *The Room* to be a serious American drama, a cautionary tale about love and friendship, but it became something else entirely—a perfectly literal comedy of errors.

Yet since its 2003 release, *The Room* has spread across the United States, and now the world, with viral unstoppability. Many believe that *The Room*'s unfathomable incompetence elevates it to something like Bizarro-world brilliance. It's revered for its inadequacy and its peerless ability to induce uncontrollable laughter from beginning to end. It may be the most wonderfully terrible one hour and thirty-nine minutes ever committed to celluloid.

And I was in it.

In 1998, as a nineteen-year-old aspiring actor, I enrolled in an acting class in San Francisco. It was there that I met Tommy Wiseau, an encounter that had an unforeseeable impact on the direction of my life. Tommy and I were opposites in every conceivable way, though we shared a common dream: a career in entertainment. This chance meeting inspired a journey neither I nor anyone else could have imagined.

This book is a personal account of that journey—the one that led to the phenomenon that is *The Room*. It is, I hope, a tale of heart, sadness, and blind artistic courage. The story it tells is as much about the power of believing in oneself as it is about the perils that can arise in conquering self-imposed limitations.

The conversations and events depicted herein are true and have been rendered as I recall them. The material in this book not derived from my observations and experience is the documented result of on-the-record interviews with Tommy and other persons concerned. I have also used as reference *The Room*'s original script, photographs, and hours of behind-the-scenes production footage. The footage in particular was used to accurately describe scenes related to the filming process. Minimal liberties have been taken to streamline the narrative. In combining and condensing some conversations or events, I have done so with the hope of maintaining their integrity while also accurately capturing their mood and spirit.

Upon its debut, *The Room* was a spectacular bomb, pulling in all of $1,800 during its initial two-week Los Angeles run. It wasn't until the last weekend of the film's short release that the seeds of its eventual cultural salvation were planted. While passing a movie theater, two young film students named Michael Rousselet and Scott Gairdner noticed a sign on the ticket booth that read: NO REFUNDS. Below the sign was this blurb from a review: "Watching this film is like getting stabbed in the head." They were sold.

The Room mesmerized Rousselet and Gairdner. They rallied others to experience the film and soon enough a cult was born. These young men and women created many of *The Room's* now famous audience participation rituals, and for several years served as the vanguard of an unofficial underground fan club. They simply wouldn't let the film die, going so far as to camp outside one theater to demand its continuance. The combination of their enthusiasm and Tommy's hapless guerrilla marketing made the film an L.A. in-joke and an entertainment industry curiosity. Before long, the cream of Hollywood's comedy community developed a particular affinity for Tommy's film, hosting private *Room* parties and parodying it in their work. Slowly, the film's cult status gained momentum, and by 2009, *The Room* had entered the mainstream. It was featured in *Entertainment Weekly, Time,* and *Harper's* and covered on CNN, FOX News, and ABC *World News;* it also began airing annually on national television. Following the media blitz, *The Room* emerged as a top-selling independent film, and to this day it screens to sold-out crowds worldwide.

The magic of *The Room* derives from one thing: No one interprets the world the way Tommy Wiseau does. He is the key to *The Room's* mystery as well as the engine of its success. Tommy had always predicted his film would become a classic, embraced worldwide—a notion that could not have seemed less likely. Yet he was right. *The Room* became every bit the blockbuster that Tommy had envisioned, though not, of course, in the *way* he envisioned. Despite *The Room's* reputation as "the *Citizen Kane* of bad movies," Tommy continues to believe that his is the greatest film of all time.

In the end, the phenomenon of *The Room* has allowed me to realize that, in life, anything is possible. *The Room* is a drama that is also a comedy that is also an existential cry for help that is finally a testament to human endurance. It has made me reconsider what defines artistic success or failure. If art is expression, can it fail? Is success simply a matter of what one *does* with failure?

Many of us want to embark on a creative life and never take the chance—too stifled by our self-awareness or fear to try. All the odds were against Tommy Wiseau becoming a filmmaker, yet something pushed him to go for it—something powerful enough to inspire a global phenomenon. Ten years after wrapping *The Room,* and living my life in its strange wake, I realize how much the experience has changed me, and how grateful I am for that. By now millions of people have stood before the great, mysterious closed door that is *The Room,* peering through its keyhole with a mixture of joy and bewilderment. My hope is that I have unlocked this door and welcomed everyone, at long last, inside.

Greg Sestero
South Pasadena, CA
October 2012

one

"Oh, Hi, Mark"

Betty Schaefer: I'd always heard you had some talent.
Joe Gillis: That was last year. This year I'm trying to earn a living.
—*Sunset Boulevard*

Tommy Wiseau has always been an eccentric dresser, but on a late-summer night in 2002 he was turning the heads of every model, weirdo, transvestite, and face-lift artist in and around Hollywood's Palm Restaurant. People couldn't stop looking at him; *I* couldn't stop looking at him. Even today, a decade later, I still can't unsee Tommy's outfit: nighttime sunglasses, a dark blazer as loose and baggy as rain gear, sand-colored cargo pants with pockets filled to capacity (was he smuggling potatoes?), a white tank top, clunky Frankenstein combat boots, and two belts. Yes, two belts. The first belt was at home in its loops; the second draped down in back to cup Tommy's backside, which was, he always claimed, the point: "It keeps my ass up. Plus it feels good." And then there was Tommy himself: short and muscular; his face as lumpy and white as an abandoned draft of a sculpture; his enormous snow-shovel jaw; his long, thick, impossibly black hair, seemingly dyed in Magic Marker ink—and currently sopping wet. Moments before we walked in, Tommy had dumped a bottle of Arrowhead water over his head to keep "this poofy stuff" from afflicting his considerable curls. He had also refused to let the Palm's valet park his silver SL500 Mercedes-Benz, worried the guy would fart in his seat.

At this point I'd known Tommy for almost half a decade. Tommy and I looked more like Marvel Comics nemeses than people who could be friends. I was a tall, sandy-blond Northern California kid. Tommy, meanwhile, appeared to have been grown somewhere dark and moist. I knew exactly where Tommy and I fit in among the Palm's mixture of Hollywood sharks, minnows, and tourists. I was twenty-four years old—a minnow, like Tommy. That meant we had at least thirty minutes to wait for a table. Upon entering the restaurant, I could see various diners consulting their mental Rolodexes, trying to place Tommy. Gene Simmons after three months in the Gobi Desert? The Hunchback of Notre Dame following corrective surgery? An escaped Muppet? The drummer from Ratt?

"I don't wait in the line," Tommy said, speaking to me over his shoulder. He marched up to the Palm's hostess. I kept my distance, as I always did at times like this, and waited for the inevitable moment in which Tommy spoke and the person to whom he was speaking tried to make geographical sense of his pronunciation, which sounded like an Eastern European accent that had been hit by a Parisian bus. The hostess asked Tommy if he had a reservation.

"Oh, yes," he said. "We have table reservation."

"And what's the name?" she said, slightly sarcastically, but only slightly, because who knew whether Ratt was on the verge of releasing a Greatest Hits album? Her job required carefully hedging one's fame-related bets.

"Ron," Tommy said.

She checked her list. "Sorry," she said, tapping her pencil on the page. "There's no Ron here."

"Oh, sorry," Tommy said. "It's Robert."

She looked down. "There's no Robert here, either."

Tommy laughed. "Wait, I remember now. Try John."

The hostess found the name John near the bottom of her list.

"John," she said. "Party of four?"

"Yes, yes," Tommy said, summoning me over to bring him one party member closer to accuracy.

I don't know who "John, party of four" actually was, but the hostess snagged a wine menu and began walking us to our table.

I followed Tommy and the hostess through the Palm's dim interior and looked at the dozens of movie-star caricatures that lined its walls. There was Jack Nicholson, Bette Davis, O. J. Simpson—which made me wonder: What, exactly, did you have to do to get banished from the wall of the Palm? I noticed some starry faces sitting at the tables, too. Well, maybe not starry, but midsize astral phenomena: sports broadcaster Al Michaels, colleague to my beloved John Madden; *Sports Illustrated* swimsuit model Josie Maran; the cohost on our local ABC News. There were also lots of faces unknown to me but obviously connected. These mostly middle-aged men and women talked show business at conversational levels, and *real* show business sotto voce. The waiters were all older, beefy guys who smelled of expensive aftershave and had big, white, manicured nails; they were such smooth operators, they almost managed to convince you it didn't matter that you weren't famous. The air in the Palm was very expensive. Everything, other than the food, tasted like money.

"Excuse me," Tommy said indignantly, after the hostess showed us to our table. "Excuse me but no. I don't sit here. I want booth." Tommy always insisted on a booth.

"Sir, our booths are reserved."

But Tommy was nothing if not unrelenting. I think the hostess figured she had two options: Give Tommy a booth or call animal control to tranq him. Through a combination of lying, grandstanding, and bullying, Tommy and I were now seated in a booth in the nicest section of the Palm. As soon as Tommy sat down he flagged someone down and said he was "starving" and ready to order.

"I don't work here," the person said.

Whenever Tommy is in a restaurant, he always orders a glass of hot water. I've never seen a waiter or waitress do anything but balk at the request.

Here's how the Palm's waiter handled it: "I'm sorry. Did you say a glass of—?"

Tommy: "Hot water. Yes. This is what I am saying."

"A lemon maybe or—?"

"Look, why you give me hard time? Do I speak Chinese? This is simple request, my God. Are you tipsy or something? And more bread with raisin stuff."

We were at the Palm to celebrate. The following morning, official production would begin on *The Room,* a film Tommy had conceived, written, produced, cast, and was now directing and set to star in. If you'd known Tommy as long as I had, the beginning of *The Room*'s production was a miracle of biblical significance. I'd worked on the film with him, on and off, since its inception. My most recent and intense job on the film was working as Tommy's line producer. When we began, I had no idea what a line producer was. Neither did Tommy. Basically, I was doing anything that needed to be done. I scheduled all auditions, meetings, and rehearsals; ran the casting sessions; helped find equipment; and, most challenging, made sure Tommy didn't sabotage his own film. In a sense I was his outside-world translator, since no one knew him better than I did. I was also in charge of writing the checks that were flying out the door of Wiseau-Films like doves in search of dry land. For all this, Tommy was paying me a decent wage, plus "perks," which was what Tommy called food. With Tommy's vanity project about to begin, my plan was to walk into my eight-dollars-an-hour retail job at French Connection the next day and quit. I hoped never again to fold something I wasn't going to wear myself.

"So," Tommy said, taking off his sunglasses. His eyes were red with veiny lightning. "We are in production. How do you feel?" He started to wrangle his hair into a scrunchie-secured ponytail.

"It's great," I said.

Tommy was looking at me directly, which didn't happen that often. He was sensitive about his left eyelid, which drooped noticeably, and he rarely held anyone's gaze. When he did talk to someone he'd try to hold his face to the left, which he thought was his best angle.

"Are you nervous little bit?" Tommy asked.

"For what?"

"For big day tomorrow."

"Should I be nervous?"

He shrugged. As we ate, we talked a little more, and things in the Palm started to wind down. Nine p.m. is, however, Tommy's noon, so as the Palm became emptier and more sedate, Tommy grew more and more energetic. I had to get home for a number of reasons, not the least of which was my girlfriend, Amber. She wasn't a fan of Tommy's and hated it when I wasn't with her on her nights off.

Tommy leaned forward. He'd never touched his hot water. "What you think now about *The Room*?"

I'd told Tommy what I thought about *The Room* several times, which was that the script didn't make any sense. Characters' motivations changed from scene to scene, important plot points were raised and then dropped, and all of the dialogue sounded exactly the same, which is to say, it sounded exactly like Tommy's unique understanding of the English language. But nothing I said would ever change his view of *The Room,* so what did it matter? I thought the film offered a fascinating glimpse into Tommy's life. But I couldn't imagine anyone anywhere would be able to decipher it, let alone pay money to see it.

"You know what I think about *The Room,*" I said. "Why are you asking me this now?"

"Because tomorrow is very important day. It will go to the history. Touchdown. No one can take away. Our top-of-mountain day! We begin to shoot." He smiled and leaned back. "I can't *believe* this, if you really think about it."

"Yeah. Congratulations. You deserve it."

Tommy looked at me, his face slack. "This 'yeah' is not convincing. You are not happy?"

I *was* happy. I was also, at that moment, distracted. I'd accidentally caught eyes with a young brunette across the restaurant, which I think she mistakenly took as an invitation. She and her blond friend were checking out our table. And now, suddenly, they were coming over. Dressed up, both of them. Heels, both of them. Young, both of them. The blond woman looked like an agent's assistant maybe meeting her slightly racier, less securely employed friend for a night of whatever they felt like they could get away with. They had sparkly eyes and hello-there smiles and were holding half-drunk glasses of wine, which were clearly not their first drinks of the evening.

They motioned for Tommy and me to scoot in so they could join us.

"Just wanted to come over and say hey," the brunette said. "Thought you were cute."

We awkwardly shook hands, introduced ourselves. Greg. Tommy. Miranda. Sam. Our booth smelled like it had been hit with a precision strike of apples-and-vanilla perfume.

Conversation, haltingly, began. Yeah, the food was great. Oh, that's so funny! My bare arm was touched once, twice. Tommy was glowering, backing away into some small, irritated corner of his mind. He stayed there for a bit, before, out of nowhere, he asked the girls, "So what do you do besides drink?"

They exchanged a quick, decisive look. I could almost see the mischief in their eyes flicker out at the same time. "Excuse me?" Miranda said.

Tommy sighed. "I ask what do you do? Any job or anything? What do you offer besides the vodka?"

Miranda looked into her wineglass questioningly, and then over at me. There was nothing I could say. Miranda and Sam stood up. Yes. Well. It was nice meeting you, Greg. Yeah, thanks. You, too. We'll see you around. Sure. Take care, then. Absolutely.

After they left, I looked at Tommy and shook my head. "Girls are crazy," he said.

The waiter arrived and asked to see Tommy's identification. This wasn't unusual. Our bill was huge, and Tommy was paying with his credit card, which wasn't reading. Tommy, however, refused to show the waiter identification, eventually announcing, "I have a right under law of California!" Then the waiter made it clear to Tommy that the Los Angeles Police Department was only a phone call away. Tommy got angry and allowed the waiter to glimpse his driver's license beneath a murky plastic lining in his wallet. The waiter said he was sorry, but Tommy had to remove the identification. "Very disrespectful!" Tommy said. "I'm sorry but you are completely off the wall." The waiter, finally, acceded.

Tommy stormed out. I lingered behind, apologizing to every member of the staff I saw. I'd become accustomed to this; it was how *I* paid for our dinners.

Outside the Palm, we waited for the valet to drive Tommy's Benz around. (He had apparently forgotten about the dangers of valet farting.) I dreaded the look on the valet's face when Tommy tipped him. On a hundred-dollar dinner tab, Tommy would often tip five dollars. Sometimes the recipients of Tommy's tips would come back to him, with an air of wounded dignity, and ask, "Have I done something wrong?" And Tommy would say, "Be happy with what you have." Tommy must have been feeling a little guilty about what went down inside the Palm, because the valet didn't seem scandalized by the tip Tommy gave him.

We headed east on Santa Monica. Traffic was light, but Tommy was nevertheless driving at his standard speed of twenty miles below the legal limit. I wondered, sometimes, what drivers on the freeways of Greater Los Angeles thought when they passed Tommy. Expecting to see some centenarian crypt keeper behind the wheel, they instead saw a Cro-Magnon profile, wild black hair, and *Blade Runner* sunglasses.

Coincidentally, at the first stoplight, Miranda and Sam from the Palm pulled up beside us. I looked over and smile-waved. They, of course, burst out laughing. Tommy powered down the passenger window and said, as loud as he could, "Ha! Ha ha ha ha ha ha ha. Ha! Ha! Ha!" Horrified, they pulled away from the stoplight as though from a terrible accident. I sank into my seat. This was another way in which I passed the time in Tommy's company: trying to disappear.

Tommy looked over at me and said, "You look great, by the way. Like Spartacus."

Tommy loved movies, though I wasn't sure he'd seen anything made after 1965. I think he thought I looked like Spartacus because for the first time in my life I was wearing a beard. While working on the casting of *The Room,* which took months longer than it should have, I had let the beard—along with my relationship—just sort of *go.* Though Amber hated it, I'd grown to like the beard. There was something invigoratingly Viking about it.

"Spartacus?" I said. At that point, I had never seen *Spartacus,* but I gathered Tommy's observation was accurate. A few years later I finally watched it. Spartacus does not have a beard.

The car began to roll forward again. "So listen now," Tommy said. "This is *very* important. You have to do *The Room*."

"I am doing *The Room*."

"This is not what I mean. I mean you must act in *The Room*. Perform. You *have* to play Mark."

We'd been over this. Many, many times. Tommy claimed that he'd written the part of Mark—who in the script betrays his best friend, Johnny (Tommy's character), by sleeping with Johnny's future wife, Lisa—for me. I was never sure how to take this.

In the four years that I'd known Tommy, he'd come to my aid on numerous occasions. If it weren't for Tommy, I never would have moved to Los Angeles. Now he was making a film—a film that meant the world to him. So I was happy to help him. But act in it? That was an entirely different level of obligation. I knew what good films looked like. *The Room* was not going to be a good film. It was probably going to require divine intervention just for Tommy to *finish* the thing.

This was to say nothing of the fact that the role of Mark had already been cast.

"What do you think about this?" Tommy asked.

"I think," I said, "that Don is already playing Mark." The actor's name was Dan, but Tommy always called him Don, so I had to call him that, too.

Tommy was quiet for a block. Gobs of oncoming headlight filled the car and withdrew. We were now traveling ten miles below Tommy's standard twenty miles below the speed limit, all while he veered into other lanes. Men on bicycles were passing us. The cars not honking at us should have been.

"What if we do something?" Tommy said. "What if *we* give you very good money?"

We? The leadership structure of Wiseau-Films was simple: Tommy was the founder, president, chief executive officer, treasurer, legal department, brand manager, administrative assistant (under the pseudonym of "John"), phone answerer, and mail opener. He claimed to have four other producers backing him on *The Room*, but no one, including me, had met them. A few months before, Tommy had offered me the salary-less title of "Vice President of Wiseau-Films," and even gone so far as to print business cards with my name on them. I had politely declined.

Tommy was now stopped at a green light with his brights on. I motioned for him to drive, but he was busy being incredibly determined to convince me to play Mark. "Just listen what I say; forget these honking people. What if we give you good money to play Mark? What do you say about that?"

What, I wondered, was up his sleeve here?

I had called Don in when he responded to an ad Tommy placed in *Backstage West*. During the audition process, Tommy had made Don expose his bare backside, which was humiliating for him and deeply uncomfortable for the cameraman (me). For reasons that were never completely clear, Tommy didn't like Don, possibly due to his vaguely entitled rich-kid vibe. (Tommy was rich now, but he hadn't always been, and no one dislikes each other more than the circumstantially different rich.) Regardless, two months ago Tommy had Don sign a contract; Don had been rehearsing ever since. He'd even finagled a part in the film for his roommate. As far as Don or Don's roommate or anyone else involved in *The Room*'s production knew, I was a "summer intern" at Wiseau-Films.

Tommy's car was still stranded at the La Cienega stoplight. I couldn't believe he would spring this on me hours before filming began. Things were finally simple: *The Room* was being made. But Tommy *had* to make things unsimple. He couldn't proceed unless he was under heavy fire.

To make matters worse, Don had also made friends with other cast members—especially Brianna, who was playing a character named Michelle. If Tommy got rid of him, for no reason, on the day filming began, I felt certain everyone would revolt. These were the kinds of details that tended to escape Tommy's notice.

Tommy, finally, pulled away from the light. Within moments he was serenely piloting his Benz down Santa Monica, waiting for me to say something. "I can't do it," I said.

He didn't look over at me. "I always intended you to play the Mark.

Okay. So you have to do it, you see. This is your chance. Don't blow it. You will miss the boat." Now he looked over at me. "What is your problem?"

"Don is Mark. End of conversation."

Tommy turned away. "Forget this guy. He can't perform shit. The love scenes? He's plastic. There's nothing there. Everything is flat."

"Love scenes? Tommy. Are you kidding me?"

"I say there's nothing there. I would fire this guy. No matter what I fire this guy. So this is your chance."

"There's no way I'd ever do a love scene the way you've rehearsed them. I won't do it."

"Fine, then. I make special arrangement for you. During love scene, you don't have to show your ass. You keep your pants on. We do the way you feel comfortable. But this is your last chance. We pay you some very good money."

Tommy kept hitting the "very good money" point because he knew I didn't have any. Out of curiosity—but also, I suppose, out of greed—I asked Tommy what he would pay.

And Tommy told me.

"Huh" is what I said. *Holy shit* is what I thought. This could put me back in the game. I could stay in L.A. once the movie was done and not have to go back home to San Francisco a failure. This could be the thing I had to do so I could do what I wanted to do. "That's a lot of money. Are you sure?"

"Yes, we pay very well."

"What would you do about Don?" As much as I needed the money, I was trying to push away this . . . *number* Tommy had dropped in my lap. "Everyone likes Don. If you fire him, you'll piss everyone off. People might quit." I wanted to avoid another casting ordeal. The fact is dams have been built in the time it took to cast *The Room*—a film with only eight parts to be cast.

Tommy finally turned onto my street, Flores, where I could see my car—a 1991 Chevy Lumina a grandfather would have felt square driving—parked beneath the smeary light of a streetlamp. Amber's car was parked behind mine. I was thinking of the car I could finally buy with the money Tommy had just offered me, when he said, "What about we also get you new car?"

The week before I'd tried to drive a few blocks to buy some groceries and my car broke down halfway there. My Lumina was keeping half of Hollywood's mechanics employed. "Tommy," I said, "I just don't know. Let me think about it." My voice was weak, small, and therefore revealing. Tommy had me now, and he knew it.

He pulled up to my place. "Don't worry about this Don guy. We take care of him, okay?"

"You're talking like a mobster."

"No, not mobster. So this is my idea. You show tomorrow, and we tell everyone producers want to see you on the camera for future project. And we shoot you on the 35mm film. For him we say we roll the film but we shoot the video. No worry. We delete everything. It's over. Very simple."

It was just crazy enough not to work at all.

"Don," I told Tommy, "will figure out in ten minutes what's really going on."

"Don't worry about that. We take care of it."

At that point I told myself a few things. I told myself (a) Tommy wanted Don out, and I couldn't do anything to stop that; (b) a new car meant new confidence, and new confidence meant better auditions, and better auditions meant booking work; (c) this movie was, probably, never going to be finished, and it *certainly* wasn't going to be released; and (d) pushing Don out of the film would be doing him a favor. Really. "Greg," Tommy said, "I don't have time for games. I need response."

"Give me an hour," I said, and got out of the car. Immediately I noticed Amber standing by the front door of my building. I could tell from her expression that she was about to leave because she was sick of waiting for me, sick of Tommy, sick of *The Room,* and sick of my beard. It occurred to me, as I walked toward her, that I'd let my beard come in not only because *The Room*'s casting process had overwhelmed me, but maybe also because I liked having another barrier between her and me. Which was surely why Amber hated it so much.

Amber was a makeup artist from San Diego who prided herself on being a cool chick, and she *was* a cool chick. She had dark, wavy hair, and was feisty in the way short girls with confidence can be feisty. Spicy feisty. Stare-you-down feisty. She stared me down all the time, even though I had almost a foot on her.

We'd been dating for a year and a half; it was time to either move in together or move on. Unhappily, I didn't want to do either. A month previous I'd sort of preempted the move-in-or-move-on conversation by using the money Tommy was paying me to lease an apartment in an Old Hollywood building with a dense palm-tree perimeter and a great view of the Hills. Amber loved the place so much that she started spending all of her time there.

"Well, hello," she said coolly. "What took you so long?"

"Guess."

Tommy was pulling away now, after awkwardly staring for too long. He beeped. Not a fun little bye-bye beep, but a long, sustained *beeeeeeep*.

"So," she said, arms folded, "how's Tommy?"

Whatever Amber and I had, she was obviously as close to being over it as I was. Which hurt, oddly.

Tommy was now at the end of the street, beginning an agonized turn, still beeping. At least, now, they were little beeps. *Beep beep. Beep beep.* 'Bye, Tommy. Amber watched with an expression of disgust as his Benz disappeared around the corner.

"Greg," she said, "what is this Tommy thing getting you? He's taking over our lives. Try something else. Get that job at EA Sports you're always talking about. Being around Tommy is just too hard on you."

"Tommy," I said, "just offered me the role of Mark."

Her head was shaking; she was still on guard. "So? He's offered you that part, like, a hundred times."

"Yeah, but this time he offered to pay me for it."

Her head was no longer shaking. "How much?"

I told her, after which she became very quiet. Above us, wind flapped in the palms.

"And a car," I said. "He also offered to buy me a new car."

Amber looked puzzled. "Isn't somebody already playing Mark?"

I described Tommy's absurd scheme. We stood there, looking at each other. I assumed she thought I was a terrible person for even considering it. I decided to tell Tommy no thanks. "Okay," I said, turning to go inside. "I'll go tell him."

Amber was still looking at me. "Tell him what?"

I froze in midstep. "What do you think I should tell him?"

"I think you should tell him yes. You're going to be on set all day anyway, right? Fuck it. Do it."

I was shocked. "You want me to do it?"

"Yeah. Do you think the other guy would give a shit about you if the situation was reversed?"

I didn't know, honestly. Maybe he would have.

"I don't know. Nothing about it feels right."

"It's a lot of money."

Amber was right about that; we'd been struggling. *And remember,* I thought to myself, *Don is a rich kid.* Actually, I had no idea if Don was a rich kid. It just seemed like he was, and right now I was very fond of that impression. "You're right," I said. "I'll do it."

"Good," Amber said—there was, I noticed, no joy or victory in her voice—and we walked inside. The phone was heavy in my hand as I dialed Tommy's number. While Tommy's cell rang, I imagined him making one of his semi-truck-slow turns onto another street. No. He was probably still driving down Fountain, the next street over. When Tommy picked up I asked him where he was. "I am on the Fountain," he said. "So what's the story? I have no time to beat the bush."

"I'll do it."

"Greg," Tommy said, "I think you make great decision."

two

La France a Gagné

Everybody should have one talent.
—Dickie Greenleaf, *The Talented Mr. Ripley*

I saw *Home Alone* in Walnut Creek, California, on Christmas Day 1990, when I was twelve. After the movie I immediately got to work on writing the sequel, *Home Alone 2: Lost in Disney World*. The plot hinged on Kevin McCallister (Macaulay Culkin) boarding the wrong plane and winding up in Disney World, where he runs into his slightly older neighbor Drake (Greg Sestero). There, Drake and Kevin get into various monkeyshines while avoiding a crack team of bandits recently escaped from a Florida state penitentiary. I created a soundtrack, drew up a poster, and threw together a marketing campaign. When I finished the script, I remember thinking that soon I'd be on set in Orlando and skipping eighth grade.

Next, I did what all twelve-year-old screenwriters do, which was call information and ask for the phone number of 20th Century Fox. I got through to someone at Fox, though for some reason I was given the runaround. Incensed, I called information again and asked for the address of John Hughes's production company in Chicago. Then I sent Hughes my screenplay directly.

My mother teased me about my dream of getting my movie made, but that only fueled my aspirations. I checked the mail every day after school, hoping to prove her wrong.

A month later my mom walked into my bedroom holding a brown envelope. She looked stunned. "It's from Hughes Productions," she said.

I tore open the package like I was about to find Wonka's Golden Ticket. Sad news—my screenplay was being returned—but attached to the pages was a handwritten note from John Hughes himself. "Believe in yourself," he told me in closing, "have patience, and always follow your heart." Writing a random little boy a note of encouragement was merely a small, dashed-off kindness on Hughes's part, but at the time it meant a lot to me. It still does. In the intervening years, I've learned that many people can afford to be that kind, but of those who can, most don't.

After reading Hughes's letter, I knew I'd found my calling.

I love my mother. She is a wonderful human being: strong, tough, loving, practical, and beautiful. We get along and have always gotten along, save for one key area: my choice of career.

The first thing to know about my mother is that she's French-Sicilian. I'd like you to think for a moment about the temperamental implications of that genetic combination. My mother wanted me to become a Rhodes scholar, a lawyer, a doctor. For my mother, "I want to be an actor" was roughly analogous to "I want to be homeless." Oddly—or not oddly at all—my mom had once wanted to be an opera singer. "If it were that easy," she said when I asked about this, "I would have done it."

In retrospect, the way my mother went about discouraging me from acting was, tactically speaking, all wrong. She could have sat me down and said, "Greg, look. This is an incredibly hard thing to do, and even many of the most talented actors barely survive. You might be great and still not make it. Is that the kind of chance you want to take?" But she didn't say that. What she said was, "You are going to learn the hard way, and the worst part of it is you had your parents to warn you, unlike all those loser Hollywood runaways you see in the streets." It was hard to hear this from her. My mother was the one person I wanted to be proud of me.

With my dad it was different. His idea of solid parenting has always been to say, "Just do what you can to enjoy life, because it sure goes by fast." But with my father so low-key, my mother's voice dominated.

"Most people have nothing to lose," she would tell me. "Gregory, you have a lot to lose." It wound up feeling like that, which meant I lost a lot. I didn't go out for high school drama, for instance, because I was afraid of not being good. I persisted in reading about acting, though, and remember my stomach dropping when I learned that Jack Nicholson stumbled through 350 auditions before getting his first small part. By the end of my junior year, I was fear-stifled and I had no idea what I wanted to do. I didn't apply to colleges; I didn't have a plan. Nothing felt right.

It was around this time that I watched another movie that had a huge influence on me: *Legends of the Fall*. I believed that Tristan Ludlow (Brad Pitt) was on a quest for self-understanding similar to mine, though mine, I hoped, would have fewer bear attacks. The morning after I saw the film, I noticed an ad in the *Contra Costa Times* for Stars, a San Francisco talent agency, that was seeking new clients. I decided to send them photos, and after a couple of weeks, someone from Stars called me in for a meeting.

A month and a half later, Stars had gotten me a gig to model in Milan. This overlapped with what would have been the beginning of my senior year of high school. I worked out an ad hoc "independent study" with my school, and suddenly I was landing at Malpensa Airport and blinking in the glorious Italian sunshine.

I got off to a frantic start, attending castings all over the city, many of which had four hundred models waiting for hours in line to be seen. This was about as intimidating as anything I could imagine. For the first time, though, I didn't let my fear control me. Just because I was sheltered didn't mean I wasn't good; it didn't mean I should quit. That said, I was greatly rattled by the beauty of the Italian women and by the alien qualities of the fashion world as seen through the eyes of a seventeen-year-old California boy who wanted to act. I made the mistake of voicing this aspiration to fashion people: "I'm doing this to act," I'd say. "You should be doing this to model," I was told (rightly, too, I now know).

Every moment of every day felt newly, freshly incredible. I did shoots in Florence and Venice and Lake Como. On my off days I hung out with other young models near the Duomo. In Paris I got the chance to work for Jean-Paul Gaultier. I met the fashion editor of *Vanity Fair,* who playfully asked me, "Your mom let you out of the house?" (*Not exactly,* I didn't say.)

After six months in Europe I returned home to San Francisco. I didn't plan on modeling again because I wanted to focus on acting exclusively. Models, I knew, had a hard time being taken seriously as actors—sometimes for very good reason. I asked my print agent, Lisa, if she would submit me for whatever movies or television shows were filming in the Bay Area. Lisa found this request amusing: "It sort of sounds, Greg, like you want to fly up the ladder."

Lisa reminded me of the many things I didn't have: an acting résumé, an acting headshot, or any training. But I was adamant that she try anyway. To Lisa's and my shock, I quickly scored a bit part in *Nash Bridges* as Joel, an upset guy who'd seen a murder. After I got sides, I spent three days throwing everything I had into them. My two lines in the scene were "Yes" and "No." *This is it,* I thought. *My break. My rocket start up the ladder.* Except that it wasn't. Phil Jackson, my sports hero, once said, "It wasn't the last hit that broke the rock but the thousands of hits that came before it." My part on *Nash Bridges* was one tiny hit.

I shot the part in Oakland with Don Johnson himself. During the shoot, I met an actor named Peter Gregory, who was up from Los Angeles doing a guest-star turn on the show. We talked a bit on set. Gregory offered me some big brother–type advice. He told me I had a "young Rob Lowe" thing going in my favor, a kind of likable innocence, and that if I wanted to do well, I had to figure out a way to give that aspect of myself some kind of edge. "You don't want to be just another pretty face," he said. "Pretty boys are a dime a dozen in L.A." The most helpful thing Peter mentioned was the name of his agent, Judy Schoen, which I filed away for immediate use. My scheme: Call Judy Schoen and say, "Hello, Peter Gregory recommended you to me." Which was only slightly a lie. Peter told me I shouldn't have any trouble attracting a Los Angeles agent, so why not start with his?

When I came home and told my mother I was going to send out

feelers with L.A. agents, she said, "If you do that, if you go to L.A., *mon cher,* then you are on your own. I'm not helping you at all."

Before I could contact Judy Schoen, I booked a few things you would have needed a high-powered microscope to see me in. These parts are called "being a background performer" in polite company and "being a fucking extra" if you're talking to other actors. One such gig was *Gattaca,* the Ethan Hawke and Uma Thurman sci-fi movie directed by Andrew Niccol, in which a brief flash of my face can be seen among wanted Gattacan citizens. I was also a "featured extra" (my favorite movie-language contradiction in terms) in *Metro,* which starred Eddie Murphy and Michael Rapaport. The on-set casting person plucked me from a teeming mass of extras and stuck me right behind Murphy for a scene in a tavern that wound up getting cut.

Shortly after my background performing triumph in *Metro,* I called Judy Schoen. To her credit, she actually took my call. I explained that I'd recently done *Nash Bridges* with her client Peter Gregory. Soon I'd be coming down to Los Angeles; I'd love to meet with her.

"Well," she said in a hard-ass, cigarettey voice, "don't come down here just for me."

I drove down, a few days later, just for her.

Judy turned out to be unexpectedly kind in person. "The first thing you need," she told me, "is to get tape. Also training. You need good training." She put her cigarette down and looked at me. "What if I asked you to intensify a scene? Would you know what I meant?" I didn't answer. "I thought so," she said. "Come back to me with tape and training under your belt and we'll talk." I went back to San Francisco with *I've got to get tape, I've got to get training,* running through my head like numbers on a stock-exchange ticker.

I enrolled in classes at the American Conservatory Theater in San Francisco, whose alumni included Denzel Washington, Teri Hatcher, Winona Ryder, and Danny Glover. Then I got as many jobs as possible, because my eventual move to Los Angeles was not going to be cheap. I ushered at Golden Gate Theatre in the Tenderloin; I shuffled papers at an investment firm; I filed documents at my father's land-development company.

I'd been studying at A.C.T. for six months when I called Judy Schoen again to update her on my progress. I didn't get her directly, so I left a message. The next day I walked by my father's office and saw him talking on the phone. From the startled way he looked up, I knew the conversation he was having somehow involved me. "Yeah," my father kept saying. "Yeah, I know. She's screwed up. I agree. I wouldn't deal with her. I'll let him know." He put the phone down. Whatever this was, it was bad.

"Dad?" I said.

His eyes lifted heavily to meet mine. "Your mother talked to that agent. She said Mom was rude or harassing to her assistant, so now she doesn't want to hear from you anymore. So it's over. You need to let it go."

My mother, being French, can ruffle and alarm people not accustomed to more, shall we say, Gallic forms of no-nonsense directness. It's not rudeness, or not intended as rudeness, but try telling that to Judy Schoen's assistant, who called me back and got my mother. She pretty rapidly found herself being shouted at—and then shouting right back. The whole debacle ended, I later learned, with Judy Schoen herself getting on the phone and telling my mother, "Don't ever fucking call my office again. I'm not interested in your son."

I'd spent the last six months doing everything I could to get represented by Judy Schoen and it had all collapsed in one thirty-second conversation. I went home immediately and confronted my mother, who had an interesting appraisal of the day's events. Her first point was that Hollywood people, as she'd long argued, were "flakes and thieves." Her second point was that this was exactly the sort of thing she'd been warning me about. Her third point was that Hollywood didn't work in the way the rest of the world worked. You needed to have connections, rely on the casting couch, or be rich. I, in turn, had one point, which I repeated to her again and again: She should have let me return that phone call and not taken it upon herself to torch the one connection I had. Other than that I had nothing to say; soon enough, neither did she.

Several weeks later, my mother was driving my brother to Los Angeles for a dental school interview. She offered a spot in the car for me, too, so I could meet with some Hollywood agents. I knew this was her way of apologizing.

I went despite having been unable to make any appointments with agents. "By referral only" is basically the model of every legitimate agency in Los Angeles. Thus, operating out of complete hopelessness, I decided to crash the offices of Cunningham-Escott-Dipene, a prominent talent agency I knew of mainly because they represented Mark Hamill. My hope was that every law known to govern the entertainment industry would cease to exist for the few minutes I was there.

My crash of CED's offices went exactly as it should have gone. Did I have an appointment or referral? I didn't and was asked to leave. I began to make a case for myself and heard my voice develop a worrying quiver, so I stopped, nodded, and walked out.

A month later I got an unexpected bit of good news when my San Francisco agency booked me for two commercials. One of them was for Ford, in which I portrayed a college guy hanging out with his girl. A Ford truck goes by and it's so amazing, we wave at it. It made no sense, but it got me my SAG card and a few residual checks—which was helpful.

Less helpful were my classes at A.C.T. Students didn't get a lot of time onstage and the place had an intimidating vibe. So I asked around: Where else did people seek training in San Francisco? One name that kept coming up was Jean Shelton. I went to see her and, after a short conversation, she let me in.

It was now April 1998. I was almost twenty years old. After a week in Shelton's class, the good news kept coming: I got a call from a casting director working with Tom Shadyac on a film called *Patch Adams;* Robin Williams was the star. The casting director had seen my headshot and thought I might be right for a character who didn't have any dialogue but would be prominently featured in several funeral-scene close-ups as the dead girl's grief-stricken brother. I was cast and drove out to Napa Valley. My mother didn't understand why I was driving so far to shoot a scene in which I had no lines.

I arrived in St. Helena—the town where we were shooting—

around seven in the morning. I was given my funeral wardrobe and then waited around like everyone else. Out of nowhere, my name was called over the loudspeaker. The line producer, incredibly, wanted to speak to me. She said she thought it would be good for me to talk to Robin, because I was a member of his on-screen family. A little intimacy, she said, might be nice.

Robin Williams is a longtime resident of San Francisco; I grew up watching him on local television. I thought he might find it funny if I greeted him by referencing one of his local bits: an odd character named Handsome Williams, whom he created right around the time of *Mork & Mindy*. When I approached Williams he was slowly pacing a few feet from his trailer. The line producer, walking ahead of me, sped up to prepare Williams for my arrival. I was about to talk to an actor whose work I admired and who had only weeks ago won an Oscar for *Good Will Hunting*. When I got close he smiled and stuck out his hand.

"Handsome Williams," I said, excited, smiling, as I shook his large, hairy loaf of a hand.

Williams stared at me blankly. "Handsome?" he said. He'd stopped shaking my hand. He had no idea what I was referring to. He was too focused on the scene he was about to shoot to remember some goofy old bit he'd done.

"Handsome Williams," I said again, unhelpfully. I felt all the soft parts of my face get blood-gushingly warm. Williams let go of my hand, gracefully putting the misunderstanding behind us. He began to explain to me, in a very calm voice, that the scene we were shooting today was an intensely emotional part of the film for him. My job, consequently, was to stand there and radiate sadness. He was very kind, and actually pretty helpful, and after some polite chitchat he thanked me for being part of the film and walked off.

I was shown to the mark on which I was supposed to stand for the duration of the scene. Next to me was a guy I mistakenly assumed was another extra. In fact, he was a young actor I hadn't yet heard of, though he'd already done terrific work: Philip Seymour Hoffman. I tried to make a little small talk with him, but he was also in the zone or trying to get there and sent back my way some palpable energy indicating that I should just shut the fuck up already, which I did.

Tom Shadyac, the director, suddenly appeared, and walked back and forth in front of us, occasionally suggesting a few microarrangements. Shadyac was very cool, in a rich-hippie kind of way. He'd already done a few huge movies, *Ace Ventura* among them, but carried himself in such a manner that his authority always seemed pleasant and gentle. Eventually he zeroed in on me. "I'm going to go a little bit tighter on him," he said to someone trailing him, "and then we're going to do a little bit more with him later." Then he spoke to me directly: "Really great, Greg," he said. "Thank you." By now I knew enough not to say anything. Not even a thank-you for remembering my name, which truly was above and beyond. I just nodded.

After we finished shooting, I drove around instead of going home. I had been a competent featured extra—nothing more, nothing less—but it was enough to feel like I'd done something real. I'd stood still and looked appropriately grief-hammered and Shadyac got exactly what he'd wanted from me. A few weeks before, I'd been ready to give up. Maybe I wasn't crazy to need to do this.

As if in validation of my reborn drive, a bunch of auditions came in at once, including one for Trip Fontaine in *The Virgin Suicides,* the character Josh Hartnett wound up playing. My audition tape was forwarded on to a Los Angeles casting director, who told my agent she thought I had something she could use down the line. Shortly after this, a San Francisco casting director whom I'd read for a few times brought me in for another part and said, "I don't know what you're doing, but every time you come in here, you're getting better. Keep it up." But nothing happened and nothing kept on happening, and I could only live on the supportive words of a couple of casting directors for so long.

You know you're in somewhat dire personal straits when the best news of the month is that France has won the World Cup. On July 13, 1998, two days before my twentieth birthday, I walked into Jean Shelton's class. I was still buzzing: France had won the World Cup! Why wasn't anyone else as excited as I was about this?

It turned out that someone was—my classmate Murad, a young

French-speaking Tunisian guy. After class started, I heard Murad say, in a whisper, *"La France a gagné." France won*. I had spoken French with Murad a few times and figured he was talking to me. I winched around in my seat but Murad wasn't speaking to me. He was addressing, or rather trying to address, another guy to his left, who was sitting alone, several seats away. This guy had a rather piratical face and presence, with a sour expression and long, messy black hair. The pirate just stared at Murad. That France had won was evidently of no immediate concern to him. "Yeah, right," the pirate said finally. *"La France a gagné."* Then he looked back at the stage.

It was such a strange reaction. His accent, at least from what I could hear, didn't quite sound French, which he obviously knew and spoke. He looked older in everything but his attitude; he sat in his seat like a slouchy teenager in detention. The more closely I studied him, the odder he appeared. He seemed half comic book character, half hair-metal icon. Was this guy French? If so, why was he so indifferent about France's victory?

I had no idea how significant this moment would be in my life. This was the first time I saw the man who called himself Tommy Wiseau.

three

"Do You Have Some Secrets?"

Audiences don't know somebody sits down and writes a picture;
they think the actors make it up as they go along.
—Joe Gillis, *Sunset Boulevard*

On the first day of *The Room*'s production it was my job to make sure Tommy got up and to the set on time. This would remain my job for the entirety of filming, during which Tommy was routinely three to four hours late. In my defense, Tommy's interior clock is more attuned to the circadian frequencies of a bat or possum than a man. He typically goes to bed around six or seven in the morning and gets up at three or four in the afternoon. Yet he was insisting on morning shoots for *The Room*.

After quitting my job at French Connection I parked my Lumina in Tommy's driveway. I walked through his front door, which was ajar, and called his name. No answer. There was a kettle of boiling water on his stove, whistling away. I took the nearly empty kettle off and went upstairs. Tommy's bedroom door was closed but I heard him make a few grumbly noises, one of which sounded like "Five minutes." I went back downstairs and sat on his couch, where I found a note from him to me that said: "You will receive majority of candy (95%) when completion of production. I'm not Santa Claus."

"Candy" was Tommy's unusually creepy slang for money. It was typical Tommy behavior to delay revealing an agreement's fine print until after the handshake.

After twenty minutes, I went back upstairs and knocked on his door. "Five minutes," Tommy said again.

I realized, sitting there on his couch, that there was a pretty significant loophole in Tommy's payment plan: What if we *never* completed production?

Tommy briefly appeared on the staircase, looking disheveled. "We take your car, okay?"

"Okay," I said. "But why?"

"Because these people talk if they see my car." He started heading back to his room.

"We're late," I said. "When will you be ready to go?"

"Five minutes," he said.

Soon I was lying down on the couch. Tommy's plan was kind of ingenious when I thought about it. How better to incentivize my involvement in the film? How else to convince me to wait on his couch for an hour after he told me he'd only be five minutes?

What was Tommy doing? Primping, getting dressed, getting undressed, reprimping, doing pull-ups, getting dressed, primping again, falling asleep. At one point I marched up the stairs to inform Tommy that he couldn't be two hours late on the first day of filming his own movie. But before I could give him this blast of tough-love truth, Tommy walked out of his bedroom wearing white surgical gloves stained to the wrist with black hair dye. Tommy had actually decided to redye his hair before heading over to the set. I went back downstairs and started watching *Spy Game*. Tommy had hundreds of DVDs scattered all over the floor, though I'm not sure he watched many of them. By the time *Spy Game* was over, Tommy was ready to go. We were four hours late now—and we hadn't even stopped at 7-Eleven for Tommy's customary five cans of Red Bull. I think this could be deemed an inauspicious beginning.

The Room was being filmed on the Highland Avenue lot of Birns & Sawyer, which over the last five decades had become a legendary provider of cameras and equipment to mainstream Hollywood film and television productions. Birns & Sawyer's owner, Bill Meurer, had made the unusual decision to let Tommy use the company's parking lot and small studio space because Tommy had made the breathtakingly expensive decision to purchase, rather than rent, all his equipment. This was a million-dollar investment that not even a large Hollywood studio would dare. Camera and filmmaking technology is always improving and anything regarded as cutting-edge will be obsolete within twelve months. Tommy's purchases included two Panasonic HD cameras, a 35mm film camera, a dozen extremely expensive lenses, and a moving truck full of Arriflex lighting equipment. With one careless gesture Tommy threw a century of prevailing film-production wisdom into the wind.

Probably the most wasteful and pointless aspect of *The Room*'s production was Tommy's decision to simultaneously shoot his movie with both a 35mm film camera and a high-definition (HD) camera. In 2002, an HD and 35mm film camera cost around $250,000 combined; the lenses ran from $20,000 to $40,000 apiece. And, of course, you had to hire an entirely different crew to operate this stuff. Tommy had a mount constructed that was able to accommodate both the 35mm camera and HD camera at the same time, meaning Tommy needed two different crews and two different lighting systems on set at all times. The film veterans on set had no idea why Tommy was doing this. Tommy was doing this because he wanted to be the first filmmaker to ever do so. He never stopped to ask himself why no one else had tried.

I navigated my loud, coughing Lumina through the parked trucks and construction equipment toward Tommy's reserved spot, which had been ostentatiously blocked off with large orange cones. Guess who put them there?

The best description I ever heard of Tommy was that he looks like one of the anonymous, Uzi-lugging goons who appeared for two seconds in a Jean-Claude Van Damme film before getting kicked off a catwalk. That's what Tommy looked like now, sans Uzi. This particular day, he was wearing tennis shoes, black slacks, a loose and billowy dark blue dress shirt, and sunglasses, his hair secured in a ponytail by his favorite purple scrunchie. As we walked from the car to the set, he was yelling in every direction: "Why are you standing around like Statue of Liberty? You, do your job! You, move those here! And you film operators, don't touch anything for HD. Be delicate! We need to hurry! There is no time for waste!" Everyone stared back at him with expressions that said, *Are you fucking kidding me?* Tommy was ludicrously late for his own shoot and his first leadership step was to hassle the crew? It was not a hot day, but already I was sweating.

The Room's crew had been provided by Birns & Sawyer, largely thanks to Bill Meurer and his sales rep, Peter Anway, who realized Tommy was going to need help operating all this expensive equipment that he knew less than nothing about. Meurer and Anway's ultimate motive was to keep this production afloat for at least thirty days, which was the period Tommy had to return the pricey equipment he'd bought from them. Still, providing Tommy with a crew was an act of legitimate kindness on Meurer's part. It gave Tommy access to some cinematic veterans, among them Raphael Smadja, a French-born director of photography who'd done a ton of work in reality television. These were savvy and competent professionals, which meant they were completely unprepared for dealing with someone like Tommy.

Peter Anway had worked hard to convince Tommy that the production would need a script supervisor. In terms of emotional coherence and dramatic logic, Tommy's script may as well have been written in crayon. Tommy wanted to make sure that *The Room* was legitimate in the eyes of Birns & Sawyer, so Raphael Smadja brought his old friend Sandy Schklair in to meet Tommy.

Sandy had twenty-five years of experience in film and television, most of it in a script-supervising capacity. With his untucked flowered shirt, Selleck mustache, and hefty glasses, Sandy looked about as non-L.A. as it was possible to look. He was friendly and funny most of the time—though his work on *The Room* nearly drove him mad. Years later Sandy would claim to have directed the lion's share of *The Room*, which is a bit like claiming to have been the *Hindenburg*'s principal aeronautics engineer.

Sandy later told me his first thought when he met Tommy was to wonder why his arctic skin didn't sizzle when it came into contact with direct sunlight. He figured Tommy was probably some spoiled wild child from an oil-rich Bulgarian family who'd been paid by his parents to vacate the motherland and never come back. In their meeting, while Tommy described *The Room* to Sandy, Raphael—who had already signed on—was standing off to the side, out of Tommy's line of sight, with his hands pressed prayerfully together, silently begging Sandy to come aboard. To Sandy, Tommy seemed delusional, inexperienced, and rich, so why not?

Sandy was the only person on set, besides me, who'd been given a complete script of *The Room*. He'd done considerable work on it, mostly turning its dreadful dialogue ("Promotion! Promotion! That's all I hear about. Here is your coffee and English muffin and burn your mouth.") into linguistic units human beings could exchange. Beyond that, Sandy couldn't do more without rewriting everything from scratch, which Tommy would not tolerate and which Sandy had no stomach for. Sandy saw the script for what it was: unintelligible and shot to the core with a curiously unexamined homoeroticism. But a job was a job.

One of the first things Tommy did after arriving on set was check in with Raphael, who was clearly puzzled as to why Tommy was so late. His wan smile was balanced atop his little silver soul patch. Raphael was standoffish, the opposite of the gregarious, talkative Sandy. He seemed to take the fact that he was working on something as low grade as *The Room* personally. But he softened to me considerably when he found out I spoke French, and became more open as production wore on.

Once it was established that Raphael was eager to get going, Tommy checked in with *The Room*'s costume designer, Safowa Bright, another decent and conscientious on-set presence. Tommy had given her a minuscule budget and so she spent much of her time despairingly combing through L.A. thrift stores to piece together outfits. The result was a "Wardrobe" unit consisting of a single homeless-shelter rack of clothing and a few plastic laundry tubs. Safowa also had to deal with Tommy's eccentric design whims. Unsurprisingly, many of *The Room*'s costumes would turn out to be baffling at best and catastrophic at worst.

Tommy's final stop was to see Amy Von Brock, *The Room*'s makeup artist, who'd been assigned a dusty, pathetic station to the immediate right of the stage door. Amy had no place for a mirror or a table on which to set her many brushes. After seeing Catering's table, monopolized by Tommy's hot-water keg, she was already deeply frustrated, when Tommy plunked himself down in her chair, demanding that none of his "nest" show. I had to translate that: In Tommyese, *nest* means *scalp,* though I couldn't begin to tell you why. While Tommy's nest was being covered up, he told Amy that he wanted every actor's moles to be concealed, too. Amy looked at me. I shrugged. This experience was not going to be easy on her.

I hadn't seen *The Room*'s interior sets in anything resembling finished shape, so I headed over to Birns & Sawyer's small studio space to have a look. Several crew members—who, as a favor to Anway, were working below their normal rates under the assumption that the film was low budget—were staring daggers into the $6,000 private bathroom Tommy had constructed for himself near the back of the stage. This bathroom had everything: separate plumbing, extrasoft toilet paper, a vanity mirror, a sink. One thing it didn't have: a door. Instead it had a little blue curtain for a partition.

This was weird for so many reasons. For one, Birns & Sawyer had a clean, roomy bathroom facility eighty feet away from Tommy's little toilet ego shrine. For another, was he really going to void his bowels in the middle of the studio, separated from the people with whom he was working only by a flimsy curtain?

One of the crew hissed, "What is a private bathroom doing in here?"

"This guy had enough money to build his own bathroom? Why doesn't he just use the normal bathroom, like everyone else?"

"That's fucking ridiculous. With what we're being paid? That. Is. Fucking. Ridiculous."

"I am totally shitting in that thing every time he's not looking."

The studio door opened behind us. "Greg!" Tommy shouted from the doorway. "Greg, I need you here. We do rehearsal!" Some crew members had stuck around and were staring at Tommy with openly mutinous expressions. "Don't talk to Greg," Tommy said to them. "Leave him alone. *I* talk to Greg."

Tommy dragged me outside, where he spotted the man operating the 35mm camera. He proceeded to give him the secret lowdown as to how he wanted to film Don and me today. In the ten seconds Tommy spoke to him, the camera operator's face underwent at least five distinct changes of expression: puzzlement, dismay, shock, incredulousness, and finally bleak acceptance.

I hated myself for having any part in this. I knew if I did the right thing and walked away from being Mark, it also meant walking away from a life-changing amount of money—and at the time I didn't believe enough in myself to feel I could have earned that amount another way. I felt my weaknesses were being exploited—and I was letting it happen. Maybe that's why I was dispirited: Tommy had made me realize that I had a price. I knew what Tommy was doing to Don was duplicitous and even cruel. But now I was struck afresh by how incredibly wasteful an idea this was. Tommy was wasting the cameramen's time, and obviously Don's time, but also the lighting people's time, and the sound guy's time, and the makeup person's time, and the costume designer's time—all because he didn't want to engage Don directly. It was strange: Tommy normally thrived within the black light of confrontation.

The actors were all waiting around for Tommy to start doing *something*. It was, after all, hours past their call time. Tommy was insistent that the entire cast, even those who weren't shooting that day, be on set, all day, every day of filming. He loved to spontaneously include actors in scenes they were not originally written into. If you were an actor on *The Room,* every day was a surprise.

"Everyone," Tommy said, waving his arms, "now please listen. I need crew here, too." With everyone gathered around, I looked at the actors with whom I'd grown so familiar over the last few months: Scott Holmes (who was playing Mike—and who was eventually credited as "Mike Holmes" because Tommy forgot his real name), Philip Haldiman (Denny), Juliette Danielle (Lisa), Carolyn Minnott (Lisa's mother, Claudette), Brianna Tate (Lisa's friend Michelle), Dan Janjigian (the uniquely named Chris-R), and Don himself, who already looked suspicious. Everyone seemed wiped out. Months of Tommy's drama, loony rehearsals, vicious arguments, and a blowout between Tommy and the cast just days before had left us all on edge.

"So," he said, "Greg is here, as you know. And I have news that we want to see him—producers want to see Greg—for future project. So he's going to do couple scenes today on film with you guys. Producers want him on the film, okay. That's what they say"—he shrugged—"so we need to organize cameras, et cetera, et cetera."

The cast tried to wrap their minds around this odd announcement. "Who's he playing?" Brianna asked.

Tommy answered: "He's going to be playing the Mark for rehearsal process. The producers want to see him as the Mark."

Don turned to Brianna—no one was aware then that they'd been secretly dating—and exchanged a pregnant look with her. Then Don's eyes found mine. I shrugged at him.

Tommy dismissed us with the promise that rehearsals would begin in twenty minutes. I tried to go find someplace inside the Birns & Sawyer studio to hide but Don caught up to me. "Hey," he said, his head atilt.

I smiled at him with as much genuine, non-back-stabby warmth as I could muster.

"Weren't you . . . weren't you going out for a soap or something?" A week or so before I'd had to take off during rehearsal to audition for *The Young and the Restless,* a part I didn't land. I'd only told Brianna about it, but word had obviously wended its way back to Don.

"Yeah," I said.

Don's eyes filled with jumpy, piqued alertness. "So did you get it?"

"Uh, yeah." I still don't know why I said yes. I think Don's manic newfound interest in my career was freaking me out a little.

"Hey!" Now Don was smiling. "That's great. Congratulations." He looked back at Tommy for a moment, as though having finally made sense of the situation. "So," he said, assertively, "you're auditioning for some other thing for the producers? Or does this have anything to do with the soap?"

"No," I said. "It's something different." This was getting ridiculous. For all Don knew, I was an intern. Yet here I was, appearing to be effortlessly moving ahead in his field while he was stuck trying to get tape in *The Room.*

"What's your character's name?" Don asked suddenly.

I hesitated. "In the soap?"

"Yeah."

"Tristan."

"Well," Don said, drifting away from me now, "it sounds exciting. Good luck!"

Brianna, too, tracked me down to extend her congratulations, a thin cover for wanting to know what the hell was really going on. Brianna had not had a good experience with Tommy to date. A week before, in what turned out to be a disastrously intemperate cast meeting in the Birns & Sawyer office, Brianna had asked why Tommy was always hours late and why, since it was so hot, did he not have water available for them to drink? Tommy erupted, yelling, "Nobody in Hollywood will give you water!" before chucking a plastic water bottle at Brianna's head. Brianna and the rest of the cast walked out and almost quit the film entirely. I didn't blame them.

Brianna—an actress even if a camera wasn't pointing at her— looked like the sort of pretty blond earth-child who should have small colorful birds floating about her head and chipmunks sitting content- edly on her shoulders. She had asked me, several times, why I wasn't in *The Room*. Now she was saying, "I *told* you, Greg! I *told* you you should have been in front of the camera instead of interning!"

"Thanks," I said. "It's probably going to turn out to be nothing, though."

"*Producers,*" she said, turning the word into an implicit accusation.

The first scene we shot for *The Room* was on the remarkably fake "alley" set that Tommy had built in the studio space. Tommy's rationale for choosing not to film in the *real* alley that was literally right outside Birns & Sawyer's door? "Because we do first-class production. No Mickey Mouse stuff!"

The alley scene's major players were Johnny, Chris-R, Mark, and Denny, whom Sandy referred to as "the weirdest character I've ever encountered in twenty-five years of filmmaking." During the mak- ing of *The Room,* Tommy demanded that Philip Haldiman, who was playing Denny, enter some scenes singing his lines, asked him to "cry hysterically" while Juliette yelled, *"What kind of drugs?"* and made him lingeringly eat an apple early in the film because, Tommy explained, this was "very sexual symbol." Given the nature of the character Philip Haldiman was asked to play—a man-child Peeping Tom neighbor who has no purpose in the story other than to ambiguously propose a threesome and be saved from a drug dealer—he did about as well as any young actor could have.

Philip was twenty-six at the time—older than I, Scott, Brianna, or Juliette—but Tommy still cast him as the youngest character in the film. Tommy wasn't clear in the script about Denny's age (or anything else), but we all assumed Tommy wanted Denny to be between fifteen and eighteen. Philip looked young, but not that young, which makes every scene he's in that much more uncomfortable. In an attempt to make Philip appear more youthful, Safowa had fit him in a tunic-length Charlie Brown–goes–to–prep school rugby shirt. I felt for Philip. Everyone did.

Don, meanwhile, was warming up a few feet away from me. His spiky dirty-blond hair appeared to have been newly highlighted. He was wearing slacks and an off-white Abercrombie & Fitch collared shirt, which had been generously unbuttoned. Tommy was ready to go now, too, having changed into black Nike cross trainers and dress pants. He walked past Don and said, "Don't try to be Brando today because you will hurt yourself."

Dan Janjigian was playing Chris-R, *The Room*'s resident drug dealer. Despite having only ninety seconds of screen time, and having been cast as a complete fluke, he turned in what is commonly regarded as the single best performance in *The Room*.

Tommy had had a lot of trouble casting the part of Chris-R, probably because he chose to greet most of the guys auditioning for the part by jumping them when they walked through the door. At one point, Tommy wanted to have Scott Holmes (who'd been cast as Mike) also play Chris-R. Scott was supposed to pull this off by wearing what Tommy described as a "disguise"—a black Indiana Jones–style hat and horn-rimmed glasses—on the assumption that the audience wouldn't notice. Scott was no pushover physically, but in terms of attitude and aura he was about as menacing as an Ewok. When Don learned of Tommy's trouble finding a good Chris-R, he suggested that Tommy meet his stacked six-three roommate, Dan, who cut a nicely intimidating figure.

Prior to *The Room,* Dan was busy doing things like competing in the 2002 Olympics on the Armenian bobsledding team, working as a motivational speaker in Los Angeles's Armenian community, and starting successful Internet companies. Dan's audition for Tommy was his first audition ever. Not one to phone anything in, he read up on Stanislavsky and Uta Hagen beforehand, on the mistaken assumption that Tommy knew something useful about either.

On the first day of filming, Dan arrived on set in character and stayed in character. Trained or not, the guy had become a Hellfire missile of method. In his tight black tank top and even tighter black beanie, he was at times so frighteningly locked into Chris-R that no one dared talk to him. Between rehearsals, Dan would stalk back and forth along the set's edge, muttering and swearing, keeping himself angry.

Dan had some questions about Chris-R. We all did. Why the name "Chris-R," for instance? What's with that hyphen? Tommy's explanation: "He is gangster." What about this drug business, which never comes up either before or after Chris-R's only scene in the film? "We have big problem in society with the drugs. Chris-R is gangster and Denny takes drugs. So he must be rescued."

The original Chris-R scene opens with Denny playing basketball in an alley. Chris-R suddenly joins Denny and demands, "Where's my fucking money?" Apparently, Denny has bought drugs from Chris-R, which makes Chris-R's demand for money a little odd, in that drug dealers pretty much require up-front payment. Eventually, Chris-R pulls a gun on Denny, after which Johnny and Mark rush into the scene to disarm him.

Soon enough Don was being "filmed" running into the scene with Tommy to disarm Dan. They did several takes. "A lot of emotion!" Tommy kept saying. Zsolt, the Hungarian sound guy, was immersed in his sound equipment instruction manual and thus still unable to get the sound to synch. Raphael chimed in to say how strange it was that a guy the size of Chris-R, who's holding a gun to someone's head and is presumably prepared to fire it, could be jumped on and disarmed so easily. Tommy told Raphael not to worry, that when they got "more emotion" into the scene, it would all make sense.

Then it was my turn. "Be aggressive!" Tommy told me. "Really go to edge of your moment. This is drama! Show these people what you can do. Very powerful."

We rehearsed the scene a few times before Tommy announced he was ready to begin filming me. If anyone found it odd that the first thing *The Room*'s mysterious producers wanted to see me do was rush into a scene in which I had no lines, they kept it to themselves.

In between shots, Tommy noticed that Don had walked away to get a drink of water. This was a mistake: Brianna had already established that water was an issue guaranteed to make Tommy go berserk. When Don sidled back up to the edge of the stage, Tommy stopped the scene that was under way and pointed at him. "You stay here while we shoot! Okay? You do not leave set, I tell you right now. Follow instruction! Do you understand?"

At first Don laughed, unable to believe that stepping away from a scene he'd already shot to get a cup of water could possibly be an issue. When Don realized Tommy was serious, his face bunched up. "What's your problem, Tommy? I just stepped out to get water."

"No," Tommy said, "you stay here! You leaving is fucking up our set." Suddenly I realized that Tommy was creating a pretext to fire Don.

The alley scene finally wrapped. Sadly, none of its particular magic ever made it into the film; Tommy had the entire Chris-R scene reshot on another set a week later. The dreadfully unconvincing indoor alley set turns up in the finished film only once, during a scene in which Mike tells Johnny a long story involving wayward underwear.

I'm not sure when word got out on set that film hadn't been rolling on Don, but it did, and now several people were whispering about it. As everyone regrouped to shoot the next scene, I became increasingly worried about what would happen when Don found out. Tommy, sensing my discomfort, took me aside and said, "Don't worry about him. If he attacks you, I will protect you." Very reassuring.

Tommy chose to shoot next on the Rooftop set. Now, the logical thing to do would have been to shoot another of several planned alley scenes because everything was already set up there, and the Rooftop wasn't even completed. But Tommy went with his gut—his weird, inscrutable, unpredictable gut—and so the relevant crew members hurried to put their finishing touches on what has become *The Room*'s most famously incompetent cinematic element, deserving of its capital *R*.

To begin, the Rooftop wasn't a rooftop but rather three separate Styrofoam walls backed with cheap plywood, all of which had been hastily set up in the Birns & Sawyer parking lot. When shooting Rooftop scenes from alternate angles, the crew moved the three walls to create the illusion of four. (Unfortunately, they often failed to align these pieces, as you can see in the finished film.) Tommy had also determined that a convincing approximation of a fancy San Francisco condominium's rooftop access point would be a sheet metal shed. When this shed was included in Rooftop shots, the two Styrofoam walls were pulled apart and the shed was pushed into the gap: movie magic at its finest.

Behind the Rooftop was Tommy's coup de grâce: a green screen wall. Tommy had decided to add the San Francisco skyline to every Rooftop scene via postproduction digital trickery. As everyone who's seen the film now knows, this compositing process was not successful. Half the time the Mediterranean San Francisco skyline more closely resembles that of Istanbul; at other times, it looks as though the Rooftop is carrying its inhabitants through space and time itself.

The Rooftop scene Tommy now wanted to shoot involved two characters: Peter, Johnny's psychiatrist friend, and Mark. Mark has headed up to the Rooftop to evade his problems and smoke a joint when Peter arrives to confront him about his affair with Lisa, Johnny's future wife. Mark responds to Peter's accusation with an uncharacteristically abrupt burst of anger and tries to throw Peter off the roof. Then Mark immediately apologizes to Peter for trying to kill him, and Peter lets it slide. It's probably the most swiftly forgiven attempted murder in the history of film.

Safowa scrambled to throw together our costumes, presenting me with an all-denim getup complete with cowboy boots that made me look like a rejected concept drawing of the Marlboro Man. By now I noticed that Don was watching Tommy closely. Tommy still hadn't requested new wardrobe for him for the Rooftop scene, which must have seemed suspicious.

When the cameras started rolling, Tommy kept interrupting the scene. As per the original script, Tommy wanted Mark to knock Peter out and then wake him up by dumping a bucket of water on him. Kyle Vogt, who was playing Peter, sensibly pointed out he had only one suit. "Yeah," Sandy said, unable to believe Tommy was seriously proposing this. "Once Kyle's suit is wet, we can't shoot again until it's dry." Tommy ran his hands through his hair, as though whether or not to dump a pail of water over Peter's head was the most agonizing decision imaginable.

We tried the scene again, but Tommy remained unhappy. "There's no chemistry! Voice need to go up! Okay? Come on, Greg!" I have never been so aware of someone's eyes on me as I was of Don's at that moment. This was obviously way beyond anything some producer wanted to see.

Tommy was also mad because he thought I'd changed a line in the script. In the scene, Mark is supposed to ask Peter, "Why do you want to know my secret?" Tommy thought the line was: "Do you have some secrets?" But it wasn't. That's something Johnny says to Mark earlier in the film. Tommy didn't know his own script. By this point, Tommy was getting looks from just about everyone, especially Don. To deflect his embarrassment, Tommy yelled "More emotion!" and kicked a pail of water that turned over and splashed up near his $250,000 worth of cameras.

Sandy put his arms on Tommy's shoulders and guided him away, saying, "Whoa, whoa, whoa. We can't have any of that near the cameras."

Tommy was not hearing this. "It's boring!" he said. "No emotion!" Then he called me over to where he and Sandy were standing, put his arm on my shoulder, and said, quietly, "I know what you want to do."

I had no idea what he was talking about.

"Just do it," he said. "Don't be scared. Throw this stupid chair like your spy movie."

It occurred to me that Tommy was referring to *Spy Game,* which I'd watched that morning. In particular, he was referencing the scene in which Brad Pitt, while arguing with Robert Redford, throws a chair off a roof. Tommy, it turned out, had watched a good chunk of *Spy Game* from the stairs behind me. No wonder he was so late. "If you want to break chair or something," Tommy said, "break chair! I don't care."

In my next take, I kicked over a prop table and threw in an authentically frustrated "fuck," all to appease Tommy and bring this painful, awkward scene to an end—not only for me but also for Don. When Tommy watched the playback he decided that my ad-libbed "fuck" was his favorite take. He couldn't stop talking about how much he liked that take. It was now evident to anyone paying attention that I was being filmed for something more than a screen test. I looked over at Don and saw him talking with Brianna and Juliette. Brianna was animatedly throwing her hands around. Don was shaking his head. Juliette's hands were clasped over her mouth. Tommy's scheme was over. Don knew.

four

Tommy's Planet

He has so many realities—and he believes them all.
—Tom Ripley, *The Talented Mr. Ripley*

David and Donna were scene partners in Jean Shelton's class, and also extremely nice people, but they were in growing danger of raising Samuel Beckett from the dead and compelling him to stomp through San Francisco like Godzilla. I was sitting two rows back from Shelton, who was pinching the bridge of her nose and looking into her lap. When David and Donna came to the end of their scene from *Waiting for Godot,* Shelton was silent, as was everyone else. David and Donna stood on the stage like prey animals waiting to see which one of them would be eaten first.

Jean Shelton looked a little bit like Yoda's mother: short, glasses, frizzy white hair. Yet she seemed to us, her students, more like Darth Vader. When you got up onstage in front of her, you were pulled between feelings of terror and exhilaration. She was the best kind of teacher, in that you didn't care if she liked you personally; you just wanted her to respect you professionally.

Shelton's class was held in a basement studio space on Sutter Street, off San Francisco's Union Square. But for the stage, the room was kept very dark, though you could always see Shelton, thanks to the way the light illuminated her halo of white hair. When you were awaiting her judgment, as David and Donna were now, you dreaded the first few words from her mouth. Her accent was very mid-Atlantic: soft, round consonants and fierce vowels. That big, commanding voice of hers filled the room, cutting through the darkness.

"Awful," Shelton said to David and Donna. "That was just . . . I'd tell you to try it again but I doubt you'll do any better." She waited for David or Donna to speak. They didn't. They couldn't even look at each other. "Poor selection of material, as well. I saw nothing good. Nothing *useful*." She paused. "I'm sorry."

That was another thing about Shelton. You never felt as though she *enjoyed* being negative. She always seemed to genuinely want you to be great. As David and Donna climbed from the stage and collapsed into front-row seats, Shelton looked around. "Does anyone want to do anything? We still have some time. The stage is open." The seats in the theater were old, so their creaking served as a good indicator as to how restless the class was feeling. On this evening, the chairs were creaking like crazy: Everyone was ready to leave.

To my—and, I'm sure, everyone else's—astonishment, someone stood in the back row. It was the pirate from the previous week. Today he was wearing black pants, an ostentatiously studded belt, and a gleamingly pearlescent button-down shirt. He had a slightly hunch-backed posture, and when he walked his arms barely moved. He was also taking his sweet time getting to the stage. He went backstage and slowly picked around before returning with a foldout chair, which he snapped open and slammed down onstage, so that its back was facing the audience. He straddled the chair, legs spread wide, and pushed his long dark hair from his face. It suddenly seemed possible this guy was actually sort of great. No one who *wasn't* great could afford to conduct himself like this.

Shelton asked him, "And what are you doing for us, Thomas?"

"No, not Thomas. It's Tommy."

Bored already, Shelton scratched her nose. "What are you doing for us, Tommy?"

"The Shakespeare, Sonnet 116."

I heard someone mutter, "Oh no, not this again."

I was watching Shelton very closely now. We all were. "Proceed," she said.

"Let me not to the marriage of true minds," he began, "admit impediments." He bludgeoned his way through the rest, each line a mortal enemy. Where the sonnet demanded clear speech, he mumbled; when it asked for music, he went singsong. Everything he said was obviously the product of diligent mismemorization, totally divorced from the emotion the words were trying to communicate. He was terrible, reckless, and mesmerizing.

Once again we waited, frozen within a dreadful glacier of Sheltonian silence.

"What is it exactly," Shelton finally said, "that you're trying to do here?"

The guy drew his head back and flipped his hair over his shoulder. "Sonnet," he said.

"Yes," she said. "But what are you trying to *do*?"

His bearing tensed up. "Send the message," he said. "Express emotion of Shakespeare."

That accent, I thought. It sounded almost French, but not quite. Was there some Austrian buried in it?

"It's a sonnet," he continued. "You know, sonnet?"

"Oh, God," someone said next to me, her hand clamped over her mouth.

"Yes," Shelton said, which she followed with a quick, huffy laugh. "I know what a sonnet *is*. What I don't know is what you are trying to *do*."

The guy was silent. His face was getting red, rapidly.

Shelton noticed this and went into salvage mode. "Look," she said. "The chair is not helping you. It's distracting. Maybe you should do it . . . standing up."

His face was now a tomato with orifices. But he didn't budge. "I disagree with that," he said, now barely keeping control of himself. Everyone in that class was at least a little afraid of Shelton. No one ever got *mad* at her for expressing her opinion, certainly. But this guy wasn't afraid of her. It felt oddly liberating to watch someone confront her.

"I see, then." Shelton lifted herself from her chair and turned to the rest of us. "You're all free to go."

What I had just seen almost never happened in acting classes. The pirate was not only confrontational but *fearless,* a trait I wanted better acquaintance with. Of anyone in our class, this guy had the least cause to be so outspoken, so confident, yet he was. I was intrigued.

My mother, who was meeting me for dinner that evening, was waiting outside the studio. Just as I was describing to her the interesting French guy I'd seen in class, the sonneteer himself passed by us. "There he is," I said.

My mother enthusiastically marched over to him to say hi, just as any French person outside of France does when informed that a fellow native is within two kilometers. *"Excusez-moi? Mon fils me dit que vous êtes Français. C'est vrai?"*

The guy whirled around as though he'd been pickpocketed. *"Non, merci,"* he said quietly.

My mother didn't give up. *"D'où venez-vous?"* she asked pleasantly.

"I have to go," the guy said with a sick, half-secretive smile.

My mother and I watched as he slithered away into the night. "I thought he was French," I told her.

"That guy is not French," she said. "Whatever he is, I think he's been put through the wringer."

"Something big" was how my agent described it to me, and the more I learned the bigger it sounded. A film called *Wildflowers,* starring Daryl Hannah, Eric Roberts, and Clea DuVall, was going to be shooting in the Bay Area. I saw this as my chance to land something that would pluck me out of obscurity and plant me in Hollywood.

I ended up getting called back several times. Then my agent called. "Everything was right," she said, "but someone else fit the part better." When she saw how upset I was, my mother said, in so many words, "I told you so." When the person you're closest to is telling you to quit, it's not easy to go on. Her voice was still in my head. An acting career? A pipe dream. Agents? Evil with a Rolodex.

I was feeling defeated and almost didn't bother going to acting class that night. Any momentum I'd thought I'd gathered had vanished. Classes, it was becoming obvious, didn't guarantee anything.

The only thing that made me consider going to class that night was the prospect of watching the unpredictable pirate go bananas onstage again. During the previous week's class, in the middle of his scene, he had grabbed a glass full of water from a prop table and thrown it against the wall. Then he kept going with his scene as though nothing had happened. When Shelton asked why he had done this, he answered, "I was in zone." In fact, whenever Shelton questioned his creative choices, he answered as though he had as much right to expound on craft as she did.

That night would be the pirate's final performance with his current scene partner. They'd decided to do a scene from *A Streetcar Named Desire*. I had no doubt which scene they'd chosen.

Cut to: Pirate Guy in a white tank top, his wild hair in a ponytail, wandering around stage left, crying out, "Stella!" many more times than the script called for and occasionally breaking into exaggerated sobs. He wasn't even bothering to direct his agony toward his partner, the intended focus of the scene. He was just launching his performance out into space. Two girls in the first row were squeezing each other's hands in an effort to contain their laughter. The actor sitting next to me—an older guy who was normally subdued to a fault—actually began laughing so hard he had to bunch his sweater up around his mouth. The pirate's scene partner valiantly tried to bring him around with the smelling salts of actual lines from the script, but he kept yelling over her, "Stella! Stella!" until he went to his knees, covered his face with his hands, cried for a moment, and finished with a final and piercingly wrong *"Stella!"*

Most bad performances are met with silence. This was something else. There were murmurs. There were giggles. Everyone in that basement studio knew they had just witnessed one of the most beautifully, chaotically wrong performances they would ever see.

As for me, I felt resuscitated. I'd never been so happy to be in a classroom.

Jean Shelton did not wait to address the lunatic who lay prostrate before her. "Thomas, or Tommy—I'm sorry—I must ask you—again—what you are trying to accomplish?"

He was rising from the floor now. His face was flushed, his eyes intense little blurs of exhaustion. "I am performing the Tennessee Williams scene," he said. At this, his scene partner—an older woman—shook her head hopelessly.

"No, Tommy," Shelton said. "I don't think that's what you were doing." I sensed Shelton's brain trying to plan its attack in a distractingly target-rich environment. "First, you did nothing to demonstrate Stanley's *objective* in the scene." She stopped, shifted, reversed. "What *is* Stanley's objective in this scene?"

"Stanley is hysterical," he said.

"No, that's . . . not an objective. Stanley loves Stella. He's trying to *reach* Stella. And if he's trying to reach Stella, to speak to her, he is not going to shout at the stagehands or audience members. He's going to address *her*. But you hardly noticed Stella. As far as your performance was concerned, she wasn't even on the same stage."

That's when I realized what he'd been doing up there: He was looking for the camera. He wasn't thinking about Stanley. He was thinking about Brando. For him, there was no stage. There was only an appeal to a camera that didn't exist.

"You're wrong," he said to Shelton.

I don't think she heard him, because she kept going: "Also, Stanley is a very strong man. A strong character and a strong man. He's *pursuing* Stella. He's not screaming because he's in pain. Stella is right in front of you, and you're yelling in the opposite direction. And so I ask again: What are you doing?"

"I'm sorry," the pirate said. "May I correct you?"

"No!" Shelton cried out, pointing at him. "No, you may not!"

No one was laughing now. But I had a thought, a thought I can't fully explain, even today: *He should be my next scene partner. I have to do a scene with this guy.*

Maybe he'd cheer me up. Maybe I'd learn some of his fearlessness. What made him so confident? I was desperately curious to discover that. It wasn't his acting, obviously, which was extraordinarily bad. He was simply magically uninhibited; the only person in our class—or any class I'd ever taken, for that matter—whom I actually looked forward to watching perform. The rest of us were toying with chemistry sets and he was lighting the lab on fire.

After Shelton dismissed us, I made a beeline for the guy. He was getting his stuff together, putting on his jacket, the adrenaline still draining from his face. I knew he probably didn't feel like talking, so I got right to it: "You want to do a scene together?"

He looked at me, his eyes narrowed, his mouth partly open. I couldn't tell if he was annoyed or offended or pleased. "You and me?" he asked.

"Yeah."

"Why you ask me?" he asked, irritably.

The directness of this question caught me off guard.

"I just thought that since you don't have a partner anymore—"

He stopped me and reached into his jacket pocket and pulled out a business card for something called Street Fashions USA. "Well," he said, "pick a play and call me on this number. Only this number. We see. I think about it."

On the card below the Street Fashions logo: THOMAS P. WISEAU.

"Call me Tommy," he said, as I read the card. "Not Thomas."

His was an odd last name. It sounded sort of like *oiseau,* the French word for "bird." But French names don't begin with *W*.

"I'm Greg, by the way."

To this he said nothing. Then he walked away.

I called him a day later. Again he sounded irritated and asked me what play I'd picked out.

"I couldn't find one," I said. "Walnut Creek doesn't have too many places where you can buy plays."

"Ah," he said. "You live in suburban area. Come to city, San Francisco, and we pick one. I see you Thursday at three p.m. in front of Bank of America. Van Ness and the Market. Don't be late, okay?"

I didn't know what to expect, or if he'd even show up, so I brought my soccer ball along, thinking that, if things went haywire, I could at least redeem the day by playing some pickup soccer in Golden Gate Park.

Tommy turned up twenty minutes late, driving a shiny new white

1998 Mercedes-Benz C280. I hadn't been expecting that. What had I been expecting? A hearse. Maybe a decommissioned ice cream truck. I would have sooner expected him to land a crop-dusting biplane on Market Street than pull up alongside the Bank of America curb in an eye-searingly spotless white Benz. I popped the door and climbed inside.

"Nice car," I said, unnecessarily.

Tommy was staring at me through his sunglasses. "Don't talk about me, okay?"

"Don't talk about you?"

"In the class. Don't talk about me in the class."

"Okay." I had no idea what he was talking about. "What do you mean?"

"We don't talk about the car. What I drive, et cetera. Okay?"

"You mean now, or—?"

"We talk now. But in class we don't talk."

He took note of my soccer ball and his mouth did something quick and ghoulish, which was, I think, intended to resemble a smile. "So. You have ball." He pointed at me. "I see the scheme you have in your forehead."

Scheme? "I don't have a scheme," I said.

But he'd become serious again. "So. You bring play?"

I didn't say anything for a moment, not quite getting his meaning. Ball, scheme, play: it was a little confusing, especially with his accent and tense-adrift syntax.

"Play," he said again, more insistently. "For scene."

"Oh. No. I thought you said—"

"So we go get play and we plan scene together. Okay?"

"Okay," I said. What had I gotten myself into?

I'd never been that interested in stage acting. I knew a few household-name playwrights, but beyond that my experience with theater was pathetically minimal. Compared to Tommy, though, I was a PhD candidate specializing in contemporary American drama. At the bookstore, I suggested a couple of big-name playwrights who wrote good male parts for us to take a look at (Mamet, Simon), but Tommy said no. He suggested *The Glass Menagerie,* claiming Tennessee Williams was his favorite playwright, but I suspect that was because he knew Williams had written *A Streetcar Named Desire,* a movie he obviously loved. *The Glass Menagerie* had enough scenes in which the play's two male characters interacted without others present, but I wanted to see Tommy do something more modern. "Let's try something different," I said. "More contemporary." I handed Tommy some plays that had been written within the last decade.

I'd annoyed him, it seemed. He didn't accept the plays and removed his sunglasses. "Why do you have donut hairstyle?"

I looked back at him, confused. "What?"

"You have the donut hairstyle."

Whatever he meant, I didn't respond.

"Here," Tommy said, holding a play out to me. "I like this. We do this one."

It was an Australian play. I'd never heard of it before and I haven't heard of it since. It was about dudes hanging out and talking about women and music and life and occasionally threatening to beat each other up. Before I could say yes or no, Tommy was heading to the register with the store's only two copies.

Back in the car, Tommy seemed aloof and standoffish. "I have to eat now," he said, "because I get cranky little bit when I don't eat." He rolled his eyes. "I pay. Don't worry."

His tone was so brusque, and his spontaneous offer to pay so passive-aggressively presumptuous, that I just nodded sullenly. Why had I thought that having Tommy as my scene partner would be fun?

Tommy noticed my sullenness. "Hey. Greg."

He was tapping this Transformer-y robot thing he'd affixed to his dashboard. It looked a little bit like an armored crab—the cheap, Happy Meal–ish toy that a boy might stick to his bedroom windowsill.

"Be careful, Greg," Tommy said, as he bobbled his dashboard toy. "Be careful or monster will get you."

I think he was trying to break the ice, but typically you break the ice before venturing out into a frozen lake, not after you've gotten stuck in the middle of it.

How old was Tommy, anyway? He dressed like he was in his

twenties. Some of his mannerisms and affectations did, occasionally, seem boyish—for example, the robot crab he'd stuck to the dash of his $60,000 car—but there was something about his face and eyes that appeared wrung out. If I'd had to bet, I would have guessed that Tommy was fortysomething. At least.

Tommy wanted to eat at Pasta Pomodoro on Irving Street, which was in the general area of Golden Gate Park. We sat down and ordered our food. Tommy asked for pesto pasta, minestrone soup, a Caesar salad, and a glass of hot water. After noticing the waitress's surprised face, he said, "I'm demanding, I know. I eat like elephant."

Moments after the waitress left us, Tommy whipped out both copies of our chosen play and handed me mine. "All right," he said. "Now we do scene."

"Wait," I said. "Now?"

Tommy was unperturbed. "So what? Yes. We do it now."

I looked around. All the tables around us were full. "Shouldn't we eat first?"

"What? Are you not dedicated actor? Rehearsal is very important."

Tommy was already demonstrating a lot of promise in knowing how to embarrass the shit out of me. I opened up my copy of the play. With a sigh, I asked, "Where do you want to start?"

He was on the first page. "We start in the beginning."

Tommy wanted to be the character who spoke first, whose name was Jock. These were Jock's first lines: "The noisy friarbird. The featherhead. Like my English teacher." Tommy managed to nail his performance on "The," faltered on "noisy," and succumbed to utter bafflement on "friarbird." He asked what a friarbird was. I said I had no idea. We moved on to "featherhead." He wanted to know what that was, too. Again, I didn't know, but told him it was probably just a flavor word. Nothing to worry about. Let's move on. Amazingly, "English teacher" also tripped him up. Yes, Tommy had made something less than an ideal choice in going with this play.

My character's first line was this: "A poet." I said my line and waited for Tommy to read his.

He didn't.

"Greg," he said, "you have to raise your voice. Okay? It's too low at this time."

My voice was low, I wanted to say, because I was in a crowded restaurant. "I think it's okay," I said, quietly.

"Is *not* okay," he said. "Your voice is too low. It has to go up. I don't like monotone stuff."

I said the line again, to avoid further humiliation.

"Okay," he said. "Better. For now."

We went on a bit more, until Tommy came to the line "I've ploughed a whole paddock," which he read with all the force and vigor of a Senegalese immigrant on the first day of an ESL class. Again he looked up at me. "Why don't you correct me? You're not helping." He stared at the page. "What does this mean?"

It meant he'd picked the wrong play. When we came to one of the rare moments in which my character actually got to say something that was not a direct response to something his character said, Tommy again told me to raise my voice, like a teacher rapidly losing patience with an unpromising student.

We blundered through the whole play like that. The people sitting close to us at first pretended not to be listening, but were soon freely exchanging laughter and eye-rolls. None of which Tommy seemed to notice. I sort of admired his obliviousness.

It was almost five o'clock by the time we got back to Tommy's car. "So," he said, "I see you have this soccer ball."

"Yeah," I said. "I was thinking I'd go play later."

"Then let's go play the soccer."

I looked at his black slacks and long-sleeved shirt. "You're sure?" I asked. "You're not really dressed for soccer."

"Forget about this stuff. I want to play."

I'd been playing at Golden Gate Park's Polo Fields all summer and suggested we go there. A few minutes later we pulled up and parked beneath some large eucalyptus trees. There were no summer-league games going on at the moment so it wasn't too crowded. "My God," Tommy said, "the sun shines like *hell* today." He went back to the car to plaster sunscreen on himself. His pale face now looked even paler in the light. I noticed irritated red patches on the sides of his face and small bulges at his cheeks. His jaw was his best feature, as big and rugged as that of an old matinee idol. Everything else was . . . off, somehow. "This park is perfect place for vampire," Tommy said, looking around happily. "I think vampire from Alcatraz live here."

I had nothing to say about that.

"Okay," Tommy said, running ahead. "Let's play before I get heart attack!"

Tommy said not to take it easy on him, because he'd played plenty of soccer before. When we got to the Polo Fields I fed him a through pass. He bobbled the ball badly when it reached him.

"Where are you from, anyway?"

"New Orleans," he said.

Tommy kicked me the ball. I kicked it back to him. From the look of things, I doubted Tommy had ever dribbled a soccer ball before. He was trying, though. In time he managed to boot the ball back to me, just as a misty fog started to roll in. The temperature dropped savagely, as though to accommodate Tommy's undertaker presence. Tommy began making some peculiar "Woo woo woo!" noises. He was loosening up. When he managed to kick the ball into the goal, he said, "Touchdown!" At some point I realized that I, too, was having fun.

Tommy asked me what I thought of Jean Shelton.

"I like her," I said, sending the ball over to him. "She's tough but fair."

Tommy kicked it back. "We argue, as you know. I don't think she like me, but so what. I say how I feel. Feelings. That's all we have as human beings. You know I have to work so hard to get to her."

"What do you mean?"

"I study with her son first. Chris. You don't know him?"

I didn't know Jean Shelton had a son. "No," I said. "I don't."

"He's not so friendly guy. In one class we had big argument and he threw pencil at me."

Despite not knowing Shelton's son Chris, I had no trouble believing this.

"They play the politics," Tommy said. Then: "I saw you one time when I come to observe the Jean's class."

"Really? When was that?"

"A few months ago. You were sitting there like you own the world."

"Me?" Own the world? I lived with my parents. I didn't even own a *bicycle*.

"I wanted to do performance in front of you, but you left before I could ask."

This was bizarre. "Why?"

"I think, 'Oh, I want to impress this all-America kid. I can show him good performance.'"

We kicked the ball in silence for a little while.

"You been to Los Angeles?" he asked.

"A few times."

"In L.A., my God, everyone want to be big star! You go to gym and classes and all you see are actors, actors. Where do these people go? What happens if they don't make it? Keep in mind, everybody there waiting for their chance. All these pretty boy."

"You just have to do your best," I said.

"No, I'm sorry, young man. May I correct you? You have to do more than that. You have to *be* the best."

I'm not sure why, but Tommy's words ran through me like a lance. Maybe that's what I was doing wrong. Trying my best and not even thinking about *being* my best.

I told Tommy how close I'd come to landing a movie part the week before, and how disheartened I felt.

He stopped kicking the ball and walked over to me. "Then you should be proud of yourself! You need to think positive. Many people never get close to anything." He paused and removed his sunglasses. "You can be big actor."

In the time since I'd learned I wasn't going to be in *Wildflowers,* not one person had consoled me. Tommy was the first. So he had a kind side to him after all.

"Thanks," I said, touched by his sincerity. Tommy had no way of knowing how close I was to quitting acting. His little speech helped. It helped a lot.

As we were leaving, Tommy spied some pull-up bars and gymnastic rings at a workout area along the Polo Fields' edge. "Watch this," he said. He lifted himself into an iron cross position and held it for several seconds, before flipping himself backward while still maintaining his grip on the rings. He didn't touch the ground—or, more surprisingly yet, dislocate both shoulders. As a display of upper-body strength it was incredible, but he'd also managed his flip with real grace. Tommy dropped back to the ground, every vein in his neck and forehead engorged from the effort.

I asked, "Were you an Olympic gymnast or something?"

Tommy, struggling for breath, laughed. "You ask too many questions!" He grabbed one of the rings and held it out to me. "Why don't you try?"

"That's okay," I said.

"Come on! Just try. Don't be chicken."

"If I try to do what you just did, you'll have to take me to the hospital."

"No, not hospital." He walked over to me and gave my back a manly swat. "Don't be so dramatic. But you good sport overall."

When he dropped me off at the Powell BART station, he did this extremely complicated fist-bump-good-bye-bro move. "Be cool," he said. "We need to rehearse at least two or three times before the class. Very important. I'm serious actor."

"I know," I said. "'Bye, Tommy."

He drove away. I wasn't sure when I'd hear from him, but he called me the next morning, not bothering to introduce himself. "I'm sore," he said.

We rehearsed again a few days later, this time at Tommy's condo on Guerrero Street. He picked me up at Virgin Records on Market. It was pouring rain and he was late. When I got into the car he said, "We have groovy time playing with your soccer ball, but it's time now to rehearse and do real work."

We drove back to his place. Why Tommy didn't tell me his address and have me meet him there, I have no idea. He also didn't know how to use his windshield wipers. He drove leaning forward as close to his windshield as possible and made the sign of the cross after every church we passed. After nearly killing us several times, Tommy descended into his complex's parking garage, which had hardly any cars in it. Every time he did see one, though, no matter how far away it was, Tommy slammed on the brakes. He pulled into a space that had a *Bad*-era Michael Jackson poster on the storage door in front of it. Once parked, he reached into the backseat for the anti-car-theft device known as the Club. He hung his Club over the steering wheel but didn't lock it. I asked Tommy if he was going to lock the thing into place. He'd lost the key, it turned out, but the mere appearance of a Club, he explained, was enough to deter thieves.

Next to his parking spot was another car he owned, a beige, early-1980s Trans Am. All of its tires were flat and it was covered in roughly five coats of dust—in which someone (Tommy?) had used his finger to draw the Zodiac Killer's symbol. This unnerved me greatly until Tommy admitted he had no idea what that symbol meant. At least I now knew that Tommy was (probably) not going to murder me when we got to his condo.

The parking-garage elevator to his third-floor condo required a key. When Tommy pulled his key ring from his jacket pocket, the Mystery of the Missing Club Key more or less solved itself. Tommy's key ring had the diameter of an appetizer plate and was strung with so many keys that he suddenly looked like a medieval jailer. For several seconds, Tommy fumbled to find the elevator key. A few moments later, with a distant rumble, the elevator began to come down, clanking as ominously as I imagined an elevator in an old mental institution would.

"I must ask you again," Tommy said, as the elevator doors opened, "that you please don't talk about me. Where I live, for example."

"I'm not going to talk about you," I said. "Not even to my cat."

Tommy's condo felt like a foreign noir film—some dark, fascinating, catastrophe-breeding space. On every flat surface was a scatteration of papers and documents; along every wall were rows of boxes spilling over with videotapes and office equipment; in every corner were clothes-stuffed shopping bags emblazoned with a STREET FASHIONS USA logo, which I recognized from the card he'd given me a week before. In one corner of his condo was a blue unicorn statue with a gold horn. Near it, he'd parked a shopping cart filled with empty plastic bags. In the opposite corner was a life-size mannequin that had been posed . . . oddly, I guess you'd have to say; the thing sort of looked like it had been assaulted and left for dead. On the shelves were dozens of Dalmatian figurines and Disney toys. Every window was shrouded with red drapes, dyeing the little sunlight that managed to seep inside a hysterical, horror-film red. Tommy's hardwood floor was partly covered with zebra skins. From what I could see of the floor, a lot of it had been ruined. This condo had a long, complicated archaeological history of mess behind it.

Tommy showed me around, starting with the photos on the walls, many of which were of himself, including a few grand, framed neo-classical portraits he'd had done. I didn't have to be a French speaker to diagnose the syndrome afflicting a man who decides to commission an oil painting of himself: nouveau riche. He showed me his Skeletor death masks, his Pinocchio sculpture, his vases of crisply dead roses, his Julius Caesar bust with a sketch of Tommy directly next to it (uh-oh), his African and Aztec objets d'art, his impressive collection of memorabilia that somehow featured the American flag, his pyramid diorama, his small Statue of Liberty shrine, and a framed poem entitled "I Do Not Choose to Be a Common Man."

On one cluttered desk, Tommy kept a picture of himself standing in front of the Eiffel Tower. It looked as though it had been taken in the 1960s. When Tommy noticed me looking at it, he said, "I almost got arrested because I try to walk on the grass. French assholes."

One thing he didn't show me, but which I noticed when I passed by it, was his framed degree from Laney College, a junior college in Oakland, where he'd made the honor roll.

"What did you study at Laney?" I asked, turning to him.

"I study the psychology."

We came to his bookshelf, crammed with a peculiar collection of books: *How to Write a Letter. Wealth 101. Shower Power: Wet, Warm, and Wonderful Exercises for the Shower and Bath. The Pill Book: A Guide to the Most Prescribed Drugs in America. Foot Talk. 100 Ways to Reward Employees.* One shelf was filled with books about acting, the Stanislavski method, Brando, and James Dean. The year before I had read *Rebel*, Donald Spoto's James Dean biography, which Tommy owned. He also owned another Dean biography I hadn't read: Joe Hyams's *Little Boy Lost*.

"James Dean?" I said, picking up the Hyams book.

"You must be kidding me," Tommy said. "You don't know James Dean?"

I did, of course, but I allowed Tommy's misunderstanding of my question to hang there.

"Well," Tommy said. "He's the best. The best actor. You borrow this, you read about him, and it will all make sense."

Like a million other young male actors, I was fascinated by Dean. The aspect of Dean's life story that affected me most deeply was the lack of support shown to him by his father, who urged his son to pursue law. Spoto's book had made clear that a lot of Dean's legendary appeal was a result of his dying fast and young, with only three films under his belt. Still, Dean was compellingly raw in *East of Eden,* which remains one of my favorite film performances of all time. Maybe that was what I liked about Tommy, too. He *went for it,* however insanely.

I wanted to drink some water before we started rehearsing, so Tommy took me into his kitchen. All the cupboards were open and his sink was filled with a pile of dirty dishes and cloudy water. Hanging from the ceiling were two long sticky flytraps, both prodigiously covered in fruit flies. I no longer wanted to drink anything.

"How about some carrot juice?" Tommy asked.

I checked the date on the bottle he gave me. "This expired three months ago," I said.

"Well, excuse me," Tommy said. "The maid is on vacation." He put the carrot juice back into his fridge.

On his refrigerator door Tommy had an array of magnets he'd collected of iconic American tourist sites: Las Vegas, the Space Needle, the Grand Canyon, the Hollywood sign, Graceland. Just in case his patriotism was in any doubt, he'd arranged them around a larger magnet of the American flag. Magneted to the fridge door was an outdated headshot with THOMAS P. WISEAU written underneath it. Below that was a picture of Tommy with what looked like his natural hair—it was shorter, and chestnut brown—sitting in a storefront window at what appeared to be Christmastime, in a place that may have been New Orleans. In the photo, Tommy was looking off into the middle distance, past the camera. How clean and untroubled these young-Tommy eyes were, especially compared to the eyes of the man standing next to me, and their spook-house repository of secrets.

"When was this taken?" I asked him.

Tommy looked from the photo, to me, to the photo. "A few years ago. When I was little kid."

He looked at least thirty in this photo. "You look really young. Different."

"I'm not so old now, you know."

"So how old are you?"

He smiled and shook his head. "Okay, you rub it in now. Don't go to certain territories."

I leaned in for a closer look at the fridge-door Tommy as the following thought passed coldly through me: *Something really awful happened to the guy in this picture.*

In the living room we started preparing to prepare for our rehearsal. Tommy told me he used to take acting classes in Los Angeles with a teacher named Vincent Chase. I hadn't heard of Vincent Chase at the time, but I would later. A lot of people would. Mark Wahlberg studied with him and named Adrian Grenier's character in *Entourage* in his honor. Tommy referred to Chase as "the Vince." I asked Tommy what kind of stuff he'd done with the Vince. Within seconds he was pulling an old camcorder from a box and hooking it up to his television. "Watch," he said, and hit play. In the clip I saw Tom Sizemore critiquing the class along with Vince. A much younger-looking

Tommy was doing a scene with an actor I recognized. He and Tommy hadn't gotten very far into their scene when Vince began ripping both of their performances apart. "Hey," I said. "Hasn't that guy been on *Baywatch*?"

"Yeah," Tommy said. "We were supposed to be roommates, but he find different place. I think he do gigolo stuff for money."

The footage bore aging-videotape waveforms along the bottom of the screen, and both Tommy's and his scene partner's clothes had a Max Headroom, mid-1980s vibe to them. "When was this class?" I asked.

Tommy turned the video off. "I'm sorry," he said, "but we don't ask about that. Don't be smart guy, okay?"

I dropped it. "So how was class," I asked him, "when you weren't being shredded by the Vince?"

Tommy shrugged. "It was okay. He's good teacher. The Vince was tough, tough cookie. He kick your ass." This wasn't Tommy's only L.A. class. He told me he'd also taken a film class at Los Angeles Community College.

"So you lived in L.A. for a while?"

"No," he said. "Was like . . . commute. I would fly to L.A. on Thursday for class and fly back home the same night."

I'd never heard anything so ridiculous. How did he afford that?

"I know, so crazy," Tommy said. "But I have to take class. I want to be filmmaker. I make movie in class. I got A minus."

"You made a movie? What was it called?"

"*Robbery Doesn't Pay*," Tommy said proudly. "Tiny little thing. Shot on the super-eight."

He showed me a couple of frames of the tiny little thing, which consisted of a large, hairy-looking guy in a white T-shirt casing an L.A. neighborhood for a car to steal, all of it scored to Orgy's cover of "Blue Monday." Surprisingly, Tommy wasn't in the film.

"Enough for now," Tommy said. "Time to rehearse."

We ran through the scene a few times, after which I suggested we put the scripts away and go off book. Tommy was hesitant but agreed. To give him a minute to prepare, I asked to use his restroom. There I found a professional makeup mirror and a pair of rusty twenty-five-pound dumbbells on the floor next to the toilet. Above the toilet was a large framed poster of the Disney character Aladdin.

Going off book turned out to be a bad idea. Tommy couldn't remember anything, not even lines made up of nothing more than "Yes" or "No." When he couldn't remember his lines he waved his hands around, shouted, made up new lines, or did all those things at once. His mouth and mind had trouble establishing any lasting connection to each other; English was obviously not Tommy's first language, but I was beginning to wonder if it was even his third or fourth. When he wasn't being hysterical, he was critiquing my performance. "It has to be big," he kept saying. "It has to be *powerful*."

Of *course* this guy loves Brando and Dean, I thought. They're captivating actors because they know exactly *when* to yell, *when* to floor it. Tommy believed you had to floor it for the duration of every scene.

What on earth compelled this man to want to act? His money explained his condo, his Mercedes, his weekly acting-class commutes to Los Angeles, but nothing I'd seen or heard so far explained *him*. I was no longer rehearsing a scene; I was private investigating another human being.

"What's Street Fashions USA?" I asked him, in the middle of our scene, motioning toward one of the shopping bags in the corner.

Tommy looked over at the bag, suddenly uncomfortable. "I do marketing—you know, retail stuff." He stopped himself. "My God! You are such nosy person!"

I found it hard to believe that this guy could do marketing for *Fangoria* magazine, much less fashion. The Street Fashions USA locations listed on the bag were Haight Street, Beach Street, and Sutter Street. But the bags were cheaply printed; the Levi's logo didn't appear to have its standard, trademarked look.

"You don't seem like a retail guy to me," I said.

Tommy took this with a good-humored shrug. "You don't know me yet. I have many skills."

"So why acting?"

Tommy's hands retreated into his pockets and I sensed him fight some small, quick battle over how much to tell me. "Well, you see, since I was little kid, it's always been my big dream to be actor, for long time. I try Los Angeles, et cetera, but it didn't come out right. Then I have business here, so I stop the acting. But then, to make long story short, I had accident. I was driving and got hit by guy who runs the red light."

He'd said this so quietly, and soberly, that I didn't dare say anything.

"It was pretty bad," he went on. "Like wake-up call, you could say. I was in hospital for many weeks. After that, I decide to go back to my acting dream."

He picked up his playbook and we continued rehearsing. After a few read-throughs, Tommy asked if I wanted to grab dinner. I suggested a Chinese place called Hunan on Sansome Street. While waiting for our food, Tommy once again began to tell me that I could succeed as an actor if I wanted it enough. "You can be star, but you have to be more powerful. When you are aggressive in scene, this is worth one million dollars."

"What about you?" I asked, not trusting the thickness of what he was laying on me.

Tommy didn't answer that question. Instead he started playing with his chopsticks, which he'd learned to use, he said, when he was living in Hong Kong. But I brought him back to the question: "What about you, Tommy? Tell me."

Tommy set his chopsticks aside. "For me," he said, "I always wanted to have my own planet. Call it Tommy's Planet. Build a giant building there, you see, like . . . Empire Tower. Some casino thing. My planet will be bigger than everything."

I found myself unexpectedly charmed by this burst of subdued bravado. It wasn't obnoxious. It was sort of endearing. I felt like I'd just asked a child what he wanted to be when he grew up. And a child had answered me, honestly, with no adult filter telling him what was and wasn't possible.

"Your own planet," I said. I wanted to laugh but I couldn't. In fact, I had goose bumps. This man sitting in front of me had no detectable talent, did everything wrong, wasn't comfortable saying how old he was or where he was from, and seemed to take an hour to learn what most people picked up in five seconds. Still, for that moment I believed him. I believed he could have his own planet.

"Yeah," he said, looking up. "I see this big thing and big light and big events with stores and hotel and movie. All these things all together. It will be spectacular." He reached for his glass of hot water but hesitated before lifting it to his mouth. Tommy peered at me from beneath his large protruding brow. "And you can live in my planet, if you decide. Maybe I let you stay for little while."

What did I think of living on Tommy's planet? I wasn't sure. What I was sure of was that Tommy had something I'd never seen in anyone else: a blind and unhinged and totally unfounded ambition. He was so out of touch, so lacking in self-awareness, yet also weirdly captivating. That night there was this *aura* around Tommy—an aura of the possible. Stick with him, I thought, and something *would* happen, even if I had no idea what that something might be. Maybe that was it: Tommy made me listen to the right voices in my head. This big, childish vision of his—what was it if not every actor's secret dream?

My own planet was increasingly icy and lonely and minor. And while I did not rule out the possibility that Tommy's Planet was a civilization-ending comet headed my way, what if it wasn't?

"Here," Tommy said. "I have present for you." He handed me a red-white-and-blue pen, the casing of which bore the Street Fashions USA logo. He gave it to me as though it were a sacred scepter, as though I'd passed some test. When I looked more closely at the pen, I saw something else: a tiny globe with the words TOMMY'S PLANET printed across it.

five

"People Are Very Strange These Days"

You don't yell at a sleepwalker. He may fall and break his neck.
—Joe Gillis, *Sunset Boulevard*

Sandy walked over to Kyle, Tommy, and me with an alarmed look on his face. "Tommy," he said, "what the hell's going on? I just learned we haven't been rolling film on Don."

Tommy was looking down, his eyes hidden by his white Gilligan sun hat. He said nothing.

Sandy sighed. "Tommy, make a decision. If you want Greg in this picture, do the decent thing and let the other kid go."

Tommy crossed his arms but, again, said nothing.

"Is it a talent thing?" Sandy asked, still assuming that Tommy worked off a comprehensible decision-making matrix. "Are you doing this to watch both of them on tape and see who you like better? Is this some sort of . . . postcasting tryout?"

Tommy: no response.

Sandy was getting desperate now. "Jesus, Tommy. *Pick* one."

Tommy grew visibly uncomfortable when Sandy raised his voice. He was all for creating drama, typically, but only drama that he could control. "I want this guy out," Tommy said, looking up at Sandy. "We stick with Greg at this time. And I want what's-her-name, blondie girl—Michelle—she's gone, too." Tommy had been rehearsing with Brianna for weeks, but, like Don, who was really Dan, he still didn't know her name.

Sandy stared at Tommy in disbelief. "Tommy, we don't *have* another Michelle—and we've already shot those alley scenes inside with Brianna."

"Don't worry," Tommy said. "We get another one."

The cast and crew, though they couldn't hear Tommy and Sandy, were all carefully monitoring their conversation. Tommy pulled me aside, lowered his voice even more, and said, "Stay quiet. We don't want legal issue." With that, he headed straight for Don and Brianna, who were standing at the other side of the lot. Don started shaking his head. "What is this about, Tommy?" he asked.

"Don't worry," Tommy said, stopping. "We pay you. Come back tomorrow and I give you check."

Don: "Greg's not even an actor."

Tommy: "This is what producers want." Then he looked at Brianna and, with a lazy hand flip, said, "You have to leave, also. I'm sorry but the producers don't want you in the movie at this time. Come back tomorrow and we pay you check."

As Tommy walked back toward the rest of us, Kyle said, "Tommy, I hope you're aware that Greg doesn't have a contract. And he can't film until he has one."

Tommy glanced over at Kyle. "Please mind your own business, smart guy. This is not your issue. You want to be actor, act like one."

Kyle bit his tongue, put his hands up, and went off, I think, to go scream a bit before filming his and my next few scenes on the Rooftop set, which still wasn't completely built. After a few takes, a frustrated Tommy announced that we'd resume filming the next morning. When Tommy left the set that night he insisted on bringing his HD camera home with him. When I asked why, Tommy said, "Thieves."

By the time I delivered Tommy to the set the next day, the crew had completed construction of the Rooftop; the lighting was all set up and the dolly tracks were laid. Breakfast had already been eaten, several games of chess had been played atop the bed of Sandy's pickup truck, and multiple cigarette breaks had been savored. Tommy, as always, had demanded that everyone—cast, crew, *everyone*—arrive on set at 8:00 a.m. He graced the set with his presence a little after noon, just as half the cast and crew were beginning lunch. The one person who figured out Tommy's modus operandi early on was Amy, the makeup artist, who after the second day of production started showing up three hours late and was never once busted for it.

Tommy was sporting his white Gilligan hat, red-lensed Oakleys, a black tank top, and sand-colored cargo pants. He was, I knew from the car ride over, a man with a mission today. Tommy was carrying several dozen eight-by-ten printouts, which he began papering all over the set. These printouts read: ACTORS DO NOT INTERACT WITH CREW. The words had been rendered in three different colors, four different fonts, and five different type sizes. Then Tommy began to set up little postcard piles in high-traffic areas around the set. These read: THE ROOM: THE PLAY, THE MOVIE, THE DRAMA, IT'S COMING! Finally, Tommy handed out business cards to every member of the cast and crew. Some said: TOMMY WISEAU: THE ACTOR. Others said: TOMMY WISEAU: THE DIRECTOR. Others said: TOMMY WISEAU: THE PRODUCER. And one said: "He Can Do Your Project (or Be Part of It) Well, with Passion and Dedication." The last was generally accepted among *The Room*'s cast and crew as the most extraordinary document anyone had ever seen.

While everyone marveled at Tommy's chutzpah, the man himself sat down and started doing curls with rusted dumbbells. In the last few months he'd gotten extremely and upsettingly ripped, and now looked like a man who'd spent several months starving to death on a desert island with a Soloflex as his only company.

I took a look at the finished Rooftop set, which seemed funny surrounded by parked cars. Almost everyone involved with *The Room* had asked Tommy why he was building a fake rooftop in the middle of a studio's parking lot rather than filming on a real rooftop or, I don't know, using the actual studio space whose parking lot he was filming in. Tommy brushed all these questions away with the mistaken postulation that "We do no different than big studios."

Filming *The Room*'s Rooftop scenes in the parking lot of Birns & Sawyer created many problems, the most persistent being light. Due to Tommy's lateness, he almost always missed out on filming in mellow morning light. From noon to 5:00 p.m., when Tommy liked to film, you get a wide range of light conditions, most of which are hostile to camera lenses. This should explain why, in the finished film, the Rooftop scenes all look like they're taking place in different climates and countries, depending on the angle and the shot. Shooting outside made every Rooftop scene a protracted battle against fading and changing light, necessitating the constant, busy draping of the Rooftop with blockers, curtains, and gauzy white screens during the day, and, after sunset, illuminating the Rooftop with a battery of supernovally intense lights, making it look like a little fluorescent igloo.

The makeup chair was Tommy's favorite place to learn his lines and he always insisted I stay near him when he was running them. Between sips of Red Bull, Tommy recited the first line of the first scene he wanted to shoot that day: "Oh, hi, Mark." He did the line with different spins and emphases (*"Oh,* hi, Mark," "Oh, *hi,* Mark," "Oh, hi, *Mark,"* *"OhhiMark"*) until he was sure he had it. Amy, the makeup artist, was working on Tommy throughout this process, dabbing at his face while he gestured. Tommy, satisfied with his "Oh, hi, Mark" delivery, moved on to a moment later in the scene, which involved Johnny and Denny. He read the line woodenly: "You can love someone deep inside your heart. There's nothing wrong with it." Then he turned to me and asked, "How is my voice today? I know I do something wrong. I'm losing my mind. Can you correct me?"

"You're doing fine," I assured him.

Sandy wandered over to find out what Tommy wanted to shoot first. "We are shooting roof scene with Johnny and Mark," Tommy said. "Don't worry. We ready in five minutes." Sandy lumbered off, certain that Tommy's "five minutes" meant more like an hour and a half.

The Room's costume designer, Safowa, had ducked out for a moment to run some wardrobe errands because Tommy was so late. Of course, the moment Tommy learned that Safowa was no longer around, he decided he was ready to get dressed for his scene. He began to panic. "We need her now, not tomorrow!" he said. "I don't hire her not to be here! I'm not doing her job."

Amy told Tommy that Safowa would be back any second, but

Tommy, unsatisfied, headed directly to wardrobe and dressed himself. He probably could not have picked a worse outfit had he been blindfolded: an ill-fitting navy blue sport coat over his favorite black tank top and sand-colored cargo pants, the pockets of which were stuffed with lotion bottles, antiwrinkling gel, purple scrunchies, hair clips, and cash. He looked like an aging metrosexual commando.

Safowa returned from her errand, took one look at Tommy, and nearly fainted. I believe the word she used to describe his outfit was "unfilmable."

Tommy, of course, refused to change. "I keep my stuff, sweetie. You are late. Please don't do this again."

"Tommy," Safowa said, "you can't just pick things off the rack at random and start shooting." Sensing she wasn't going to win this argument, she turned to grab her camera. "I need to get a Polaroid of your outfit for continuity."

"Continuity," Tommy said, stopping her, "is in your forehead."

"Would you at least empty your pockets?" Safowa asked. "Can we agree to that?"

"I cannot," Tommy said. Safowa briefly looked like she was about to punch him. Tommy, noticing this, put his hand on her shoulder. "You are very sweet, and I push you little bit. But don't hate me yet." From Safowa's expression it was clear that Tommy's request was several seconds too late.

The scene Tommy wanted to shoot was my first with him that didn't involve other cast members. We started with the master shots of the conversation Johnny and Mark have after Johnny spontaneously storms onto the Rooftop, denying that he's hit his future wife, Lisa. The ensuing conversation concerns women, mostly, and the possibility that they are evil. When Johnny tells Mark that Lisa is "loyal" to him—remember, Mark is banging Lisa pretty regularly by this point in the film—Mark says, "Yeah, man. You never know. People are very strange these days," which is one of the most majestically odd lines in the whole film. Mark then tells Johnny a story about a woman friend of his who enjoyed the company of "a dozen guys." Unfortunately, one of these surly gentlemen discovered his lover's promiscuity. "He beat her up so bad," Mark tells Johnny, "she ended up in a hospital." To which Johnny responds: "What a story, Mark!"

For reasons neither I nor anyone else could gather, every time I got to the part in Mark's story about the woman being beaten up, Tommy would laugh warmly before delivering his line. It was unsettling. It was disturbing. Take after take, Tommy/Johnny would react to the story of this imaginary woman's hospitalization with fond and accepting laughter.

After a few takes Sandy took Tommy aside and, as though speaking to a child, told him that this beaten-up-woman business was not funny, not at all; it was, in fact, a very *sad* line; and maybe Tommy should shoot for a response that was more, shall we say, emotionally involved. Sandy went so far as to demonstrate for Tommy what Johnny's "concerned body language" should look like. It was as though Tommy had never bothered to contemplate what the line he wrote actually meant.

Tommy laughed again during the next take. Sandy stepped away from his monitor, looked at the ground, and said, "Okay. Not funny, Tommy! No laugh there! Remember, be concerned!" Sandy's eyes were bleak with false enthusiasm and his voice sounded like a cable getting ready to snap. We'd been shooting this idiotic conversation for more than an hour.

Tommy and I did the exchange again. This time Tommy didn't laugh. Instead, he said his line—"What a story, Mark"—with absolutely no emotion at all. This effect was, improbably, even weirder than the takes he had laughed in. Sandy gave up and we moved on.

Then it was time to do the coverage shots of our individual close-ups. In an attempt to loosen Tommy up a bit, I changed the line that had been provoking his laughter. Instead of "He beat her up so bad, she ended up in a hospital," I ad-libbed, "He beat her up so bad, she ended up in a hospital *on Guerrero Street*."

Of course, there is no hospital on Guerrero Street, but Tommy's San Francisco condo was located there. I knew full well that anything having to do with Tommy's personal life was a matter of national security, but the reference was so obscure that I couldn't imagine him being worried about it. No one involved in *The Room* even knew that

Tommy had lived in San Francisco, let alone that he had a condo there. This was going to be a ridiculous scene no matter what, and I guess I was trying to remind Tommy to approach it more playfully. Attempting to mine Tommy's scenes for authentic or plausible emotion was never going to work. You couldn't make these scenes realistic, I figured, so why not have fun?

Tommy laughed again, more ghoulishly than before.

When the cameras stopped, Tommy dragooned me into a quiet place, away from the crew. "Are you insane completely?" he said. His eyes were all dancing panic. "You must be crazy in the head! Now we can't erase this information from thirty-five-millimeter film!"

I tried to calm him down. "Tommy, it's a street name. Nobody knows what I was referring to."

Tommy gave me a hard, cold look. "I'm not happy about your statement." He was even less happy when the only usable audio from all of the coverage happened to be in the take where I ad-libbed the Guerrero Street line, which was why it wound up in *The Room* at all.

We filmed the first part of Tommy's and my scene—Johnny making his dramatic entrance onto the Rooftop—last. To shoot him doing this, the crew had to rearrange the Rooftop walls and push into place the tiny, tin-roofed outhouse that was doubling as the Rooftop's access door.

Since the outhouse was so small, there was no room inside to create the illusion of continued movement. This meant that anyone being filmed exiting it had to stand perfectly still while waiting until action was called. Coming out of that thing, you stumbled into your scene.

In the original draft of the *Room* script, the stage direction reads: "JOHNNY OPENS THE DOOR TO THE ROOF ACCESS. MARK IS SITTING THERE." Tommy had decided this wasn't dramatic or emotional enough, especially now that he'd rewritten his script to include scenes in which Lisa claims to others that Johnny has abused her. To establish that Johnny is incapable of abuse, Tommy concocted a new opening for this scene, in which Johnny steps onto the Rooftop saying, "It's not true! I did not hit her! It's bullshit! I did not." After which comes this: "Oh, hi, Mark." There are seventeen words in this sequence. Eleven of them are nonrecurring; only one carries the burden of a second syllable. In other words, these are not terribly difficult lines to learn.

Sandy had blocked the scene so that Tommy would emerge from the outhouse; hit his mark on the second "I did not"; look up; nail his eyeline; say, "Oh, hi, Mark"; and walk off camera to where we, the audience, imagine Mark to be sitting. Most school plays contain scenes that pose bigger technical acting challenges.

Tommy couldn't remember his lines. He couldn't hit his mark. He couldn't *say* "Mark." He couldn't walk. He couldn't find his eyeline. He would emerge from the outhouse mumbling, lost, and disoriented. He looked directly into the camera. He swore. He exploded at a crew member for farting: "Please don't do this ridiculous stuff. It's disgusting like hell." Sandy stood there so openmouthed that it looked as if he were waiting for someone to lob something nutritive at him.

Finally Tommy commanded me to sit off camera, hoping that my becoming his living eye line would help him. It didn't. Everything became infectiously not-funny funny. People were turning away from the set, their faces constipated with laughter they dared not release. Tommy didn't notice any of this. He was locked into a scene and a moment he couldn't bring to life. It was as horrifyingly transfixing as watching a baby crawl across the 405 freeway. We were all waiting for a miracle.

It took Tommy thirty minutes to feel comfortable enough to walk down the outhouse's two steps without staring at his feet. It took another thirty minutes for him to take those two steps while also remembering his lines. With time, and effort, he got the walking-talking aspect of the performance down, but doing all this while hitting his mark *and* looking at me remained a grand fantasy. Sandy kept saying, "Now you need to look *up* when you say hi to Mark." Tommy would nod. Yes. Indeed. Exactly what he needed to do. He would try, and try again.

Tommy/Johnny: "I did not."

Sandy: "Look up!"

Tommy/Johnny: "Oh, hi, Mark."

Sandy: *"Up! Up!"*

Sandy stopped everything and took Tommy aside. He tried to reason with him, as though Tommy's understanding and not Tommy's ability were the real problem. "You have to *look* at Mark when you say the line, okay? Because right now you're looking down."

"Okay," Tommy said.

He'd rehearsed this moment for half the day and this was the result. Soon the cameraman was laughing so hard that his camera started to shake during takes.

Sandy decided to watch some VHS playbacks, to see if there was anything—anything at all—usable. I was still sitting off camera, feeling as though I'd been dosed with something potent. Tommy came over to me, looking worried. "How am I doing?" he asked. "Give me the feedback. Something."

It was a genuine request. I felt sorry for him at that moment. I knew how hard he was trying. I also knew that being a dramatic actor was the most important thing to Tommy. Everything he'd done in life was to get to this point. How could I help him? I had no idea.

"You're doing great," I said.

But the obvious peril Tommy was in—that the whole production was now in—had broken through his vanity. For once Tommy wanted something more than chummy assurance. "How," Tommy asked again, more insistently, "am I doing? Don't pull my legs!"

I looked around, thinking, *Props,* because props always helped Tommy; they took his mind off trying to act. I saw a nearby water bottle and grabbed it. "Here," I said, handing the bottle to Tommy. "Use this. You know what you're supposed to do, right? So do it. What do you always tell me? Show some emotion."

Tommy smiled in pure, holy relief. "Why didn't you tell me *emotion*? My God! That's easy part! Now you see why I need you here? These other people don't care." He immediately started peeling off the water bottle's sticker, because nothing scared Tommy more than having to pay someone for permission to use a logo. Tommy is probably the world's single most copyright-obsessed human being who does not also have a law degree.

Sandy joined us on the side of the Rooftop set. He looked for a long time at Tommy's water bottle before speaking. "What's this?"

"Water bottle," Tommy said.

Sandy took in a lungful of deep, calming breath. "Yes," he said. "I know. What are we doing with it?"

"I need to throw something, dammit. During scene."

Sandy turned away, removed his glasses, sat down, and rubbed his eyes.

Tommy headed back to the outhouse, his water bottle in hand and his script hidden in his breast pocket. I sat down. Sandy stood by the monitor. "Action!" The door flew open and there was Tommy holding his water bottle and stepping out of the outhouse and hitting his head on the doorjamb so hard that it took twenty minutes to ice the bump and conceal it with makeup. I heard one of the cameramen say, desperately, "How are we ever going to get this? It's impossible. We'll be here *forever*."

Then, just for comic relief, Don and Brianna arrived on set to pick up their checks. Tommy, sitting in the makeup chair while Amy iced his forehead down, ignored them at first. Brianna talked to Juliette as Don ginned up the courage to approach Tommy. Their brief, chilly exchange ended with Tommy signing two $1,500 checks. Don, I could tell, was a little relieved not to be doing *The Room*. Really, he was surprisingly decent about the whole thing, even telling me that someday we'd be able to laugh about this. Tommy had deigned to acknowledge Don, but he wouldn't, for whatever reason, talk to or even look at Brianna.

I gave Brianna her check. "Look at him," she said, holding it as though about to rip it in half. Tommy was still sitting in makeup, pressing an ice pack to his forehead. "He won't even acknowledge me. He's such a pussy."

Tommy noticed me idling too long with Brianna and called me over. "Greg! I need you here!" He wanted to continue running his lines. It was hopeless. He still couldn't remember them—and now, to make things worse, it was possible he had a concussion.

Sandy and I huddled together and came up with a handy formula for Tommy to remember. When I returned to Tommy I said this: "Okay, so here's what you do: 'I did not,' mad, mad, mad, throw the water bottle, stop, notice me, look up." Tommy asked that I repeat the formula. Several times. "Show me once more," Tommy said. By now his bruise had been buried beneath a beige snowdrift of concealer. He was, finally, ready. He took a breath, returned to the outhouse, and did the scene. At long last we got the shot. It took three hours and thirty-two takes, but we got the shot.

If you can, I implore you to watch this scene. It's seven seconds long. Three hours. Thirty-two takes. And it was only the second day of filming.

The next day, Tommy came to the set with some ambitious ideas for camera angles. He wanted to begin by filming the scene in which Johnny and Denny talk on the Rooftop and have the camera do some fast "spinning" motions, or maybe do some bird's-eye shots from a crane. His other demands: "Where is football? Art director? We need football! Greg? I need script! I'm missing page forty-nine. Lighting department? We need more lights! The more lights the better." To make things even more exciting, Tommy decided he wanted to film his and Philip's scene while tossing a football back and forth, which is a more complicated thing to stage than it sounds.

Tommy, in short, was driving the crew bananas. Raphael was particularly flabbergasted and began taking long walks around the set, tapping his left foot, and sometimes calling out, "Can we do a scene, please?" Tommy, meanwhile, fretted over minute details with Sandy, such as which direction a thrown football would rotate. These Tommy v. Sandy discussions occasionally became a little surreal. During Tommy's scene with Philip, Sandy suggested they get a fan to create the illusion of a windy rooftop. Tommy said that wasn't necessary, because it wasn't too hot out. Sandy said, "I'm not trying to cool you down. I'm trying to make the scene feel real." Tommy laughed and said, "Are you tripping me? A fan? That's a good one."

During the scene, Denny confesses to Johnny that he thinks he might be in love with Johnny's future wife, Lisa. Johnny says this is okay, because if everyone in the world loved each other, the world would be a better place. Raphael, who had never seen a full script, watched with a look of disbelief as Tommy recited these lines. Sandy's hand was plastered to his forehead, as though he were trying to keep the weirdness from penetrating his mind.

While Tommy was shooting the Johnny/Denny Rooftop scene, the art department was busy dismantling the indoor alley set where Denny's confrontation with Chris-R had been filmed. They planned to begin assembly on Johnny and Lisa's living room set as soon as they were finished. When Tommy discovered what the art department was doing, he went crazy. It turned out Tommy wasn't finished with the alley set; there was another scene he wanted to shoot on it.

Sandy couldn't believe this. Most productions film on a given set until they've completed that set's allotted scenes. When you change sets, you send a clear signal that you're moving on. The scene Tommy still wanted to shoot in the alley was probably the least important one in the entire script. It opens with Johnny and Mike running into each other in the alley, after which Mike explains to Johnny how he broke into Johnny's apartment to have sex, forgot his underwear, and was yelled at by Johnny's future mother-in-law. Johnny's response: "That's life."

The head of the art department was a woman named Merce. She eventually agreed to rebuild the alley but only once Tommy promised to pay her for doing the same job twice. It took twenty-two hours to dismantle the alley set and another twenty hours to put it back up. Once finished, Merce gave Tommy her receipts. One item leaped out at him: "Two hundred dollars for nails?"

"Yes, Tommy," she said, evenly. "That's what they cost."

Tommy handed her back the receipts. "I've done construction before, my dear. I've built steel building with my two hands. You must be kidding me." Merce wound up having to eat most of the nail expenditure.

As the alley set was being reassembled, many of the cast and crew begged Sandy to talk Tommy out of shooting the scene. Leading the call was Scott Holmes, who played Mike. Scott was saddled with having to say many of the scene's most preposterous lines ("I've got to go see

Michelle in a little bit to make out with her") and collapse in pain at the end of the scene for no reason. The original script says only that "Mike has a sudden fall" into some trash cans and "hurts his leg," but the script was curiously silent as to what provokes this sudden fall. Now Tommy wanted to make the scene about (what else?) football. Mark injures Mike by roughly and unexpectedly handing him the ball. This causes Mike to collapse and Johnny to suggest a visit to the hospital. How you get from an unanticipated football hand-off to potential hospitalization, I have no idea.

Scott and I more or less settled on how I was going to injure him with the football, but by the time we were ready to shoot the scene, Tommy was gone. He'd rushed off to work out, since he decided he'd be wearing his tank top in the scene. He returned thirty minutes later, slightly out of breath, and smelling not unlike an onion that had been stored inside a man's shoe.

We shot the scene. Everything in *The Room* is bad, but there's often an integrity about it. This alley scene has a different character. It feels like a bunch of clueless film students got together with some jerk-off improv group and decided to make 5 percent of a movie together.

Tommy watched the footage of the scene with his headphones on. He was staring so intently at the monitor that some of us became certain that Tommy saw this scene, at last, as the pointless disaster it undeniably was. Sandy tried to comfort Tommy. "It's okay," he said, tapping him on the shoulder. "Forget this scene. Nothing happens in it anyway. Save your money. Let's move on and film the living room stuff."

Tommy looked back at Sandy in shock. "No," he said, smiling. "This is good, fun scene. We have good chemistry. And look at this." He directed Sandy's attention to the monitor. "You see that? I look strong, like little eighteen-years-old kid." That's when I realized why the scene meant so much to him: In that monitor, at least, Tommy was young and had a fun life and many, many friends.

six

Too Young to Die

You're the brother I never had. I'm the brother you never had.
—Tom Ripley, *The Talented Mr. Ripley*

Making my way to the stage in the lower basement of Jean Shelton's theater was always a little disquieting. The lights were blinding, and I was always aware of Shelton's small, penetrating eyes on me. So you can probably imagine the degree to which my anxiety was intensified when I was about to go onstage with Tommy for the first time.

Three exchanges into Tommy's and my scene, I blew a line. To fill in the resulting silence—Tommy had absolutely no hope of remembering his lines if his scene partner screwed up—I instigated a fake onstage fight, trying, I guess, to out-Tommy Tommy. I fake-kicked Tommy: he fake-collapsed and writhed in fake pain. "Okay, you two," Shelton said. "We can calm down now." We got up and tried to continue with the scene, but Tommy was so "completely shocked," as he would later say, by my theatrics that he spent the rest of our time onstage making up new, uniquely useless lines.

The class loved it. Shelton didn't. When we were done, she yelled at us both, which was every bit the bowel-loosening experience I'd feared it would be.

When we sat down, Tommy whispered to me, "You are completely off the wall." Which is when I had to accept the shocking truth: *I* had embarrassed *Tommy*. For the rest of the night Tommy barely looked at me. When class let out, he demanded I buy him "apology chocolates" from the nearest See's merchant. "Get me the mint," he said.

Still, what I appreciated about Tommy early on was how willing he was to go, no questions asked, on whatever strange crusade I was thinking about. I'd finished reading the James Dean biography I'd borrowed from Tommy and had become newly fascinated by Dean's sad, crooked journey into legend. I had the idea to take a pilgrimage south and find the exact spot of Dean's fatal car accident near the tiny town of Cholame, California. Most people would have found this a morbid, long, boring road trip, but the moment I brought it up with Tommy, he said, "Sure. Why not? Sounds like adventure."

We took his car. I drove. Tommy reclined his seat, covered his face and neck with a T-shirt, and promptly fell asleep. I pushed Tommy's car to 110 miles per hour and still the man did not stir; when Tommy was out, he was *out*. (Years later I saw him fall asleep in the middle of a conversation. Once I even saw him fall asleep while *eating*.) We arrived at the fateful spot on Highway 46 around sundown—the time when Dean had been killed. The moment I put Tommy's Benz in park, he sat up. Another talent of Tommy's was being able to sleep for exactly as long as a car trip took. In this respect, and this respect alone, Tommy's brain was digital.

We got out of the car and stood on the side of the road; I described for Tommy how the Dean crash went down. I showed him the roadside monument that had been built in Dean's honor, which greatly impressed him. There was also a Dean-centric restaurant close by called the Jack Ranch Café. Maybe, I said, we should check it out.

Outside the café was a sign: BEWARE OF RATTLESNAKES. Inside, it looked like an Old West diner with a fifties theme: complete with a jukebox, vintage bubble gum machine, antiquated Pepsi ads, life-size cardboard stand-ups of Dean from *Rebel Without a Cause*, and a big wooden wagon positioned in the middle of the dining room. Tommy and I took in all the Dean pictures and memorabilia, including an original copy of the local newspaper's account of Dean's death. In almost every photo, Dean was doing that famous squinty wince-pout that a lot of young male actors go through a phase of trying to approximate. Tommy kept making small, impressed sounds as he leaned in close to read the photos' captions. I'd never seen Tommy so rapt before, so respectful, so silent. Even when we sat down, Tommy continued to look around.

"You have resemblance to him," Tommy said suddenly, "but your face is in. His is more out."

"What?" I said, wondering where he was going with this.

"My God, you are behind the schedule. Listen to me, young man. I'm sorry, but you need more than resemblance. Dean has this signature thing."

"Yeah," I said. "It's called being James Dean." Tommy didn't respond to this. "So tell me: What do you like so much about James Dean?"

Tommy's hands moved around excitedly. "Look. He's very, you know, moment to moment. He's emotion. *Real* emotion. Not plastic. From the heart. Words are secondary. The way he speak. Style. And that's what you need. Don't be jealous. You can do it." He was back in Elder Thespian mode, bullshitting about the craft. It was funny nevertheless. "Greg," he went on, "I keep telling you: You need to watch the James Dean. *Watch* him. Very close, you watch him, and you'll learn. Also, before I forget: I want my James Dean book back, for your information."

We headed back to San Francisco. Having just spent so much time thinking about Dean, and cars, and dying, this time I didn't speed. Tommy, as though reading my mind, asked that I take it easy around any curves. Then he added: "I have my own James Dean story, you know." A long time ago, he said, when he was "just a kid" in France, he'd been in a car accident. It happened during a "joy ride" with a friend who did "tricky stuff." With Tommy and this friend were two girls they'd picked up. Tommy's friend was showing off for the girls by taking turns on a perilously twisty road far too fast. Eventually he missed one of these turns. The car flipped over four times, punched through the guardrail, and plunged into a lake upside down. The girls were screaming as the car filled up with water and began to sink. Tommy kept shouting at them to shut up as he tried to get the door open. He couldn't. Tommy told me that he saw "a big light," and his entire life flashed before his eyes. The only thought in his mind, as the water reached his chin, was: *God, please help us. I'm too young to die.* Then the water stopped rising. Tommy was able to force the doors open. All four escaped and swam to the shore. Tommy described coughing up water on the shoreline and watching as the car's headlights disappeared into the dark water below. "It was like *Titanic,*" he said. "I couldn't believe I survive."

It was the first time Tommy had ever opened up to me. While I doubted some of his story's particulars (to say the least), it was obviously a life-changing incident for him, and he believed his version of events. "After the accident," he said, "I was sick for two weeks. I have bad dreams for long time. I never have been so scared in my life." He told me that not even his second big car accident, which also had almost killed him, had been as terrifying.

I remained silent for a little while, thinking of a way to tell Tommy how glad I was he'd told me this story, but then I looked over at him and he was asleep.

I watched the mileage signs drift by and thought about what Tommy had shared. I hadn't known him long, but in that short time I'd learned to detect when he was telling the truth. Something, I think, changed between us when he told me that story. Tommy had removed one small piece of his armor and placed it trustingly before me.

Before I met Tommy, I would not have day-tripped to the spot where James Dean died. There would have been too many critical voices in my head telling me how dumb and pointless such a trip would be. Tommy, though, made me realize I could drive to James Dean's crash site for the simple reason that I felt like doing it. He made me realize that doing such things was the whole point of being young. This was not an attitude that came easily to me, but I could say or do anything around Tommy and he wouldn't judge me. How could he? He was the weirdest person I'd ever met—but lovably weird. Around Tommy I could be who I wanted to be—and to me that felt like freedom.

When we got closer to San Francisco, I cranked up some music to keep myself awake. The only CDs Tommy had in the car were Van Halen and Richard Marx, so Van Halen it was. When the song

"Dreams" came on, Tommy woke up and sang along for a couple of choruses, getting 90 percent of the words wrong. He sang with such deranged feeling, though, that I knew he would have been the toast of any karaoke bar worth its salt.

When the song was over, Tommy noticed how late it was. Which was when I realized that I'd missed our exit and gotten us lost. "You see," Tommy said. "You act like crazy man first in class and now on highway. It's midnight and you are lost like hell. But that's okay. Don't need to have panicky situation. No restrictions. Be yourself."

I took the next exit I saw and only succeeded in getting us more lost. Tommy, meanwhile, pulled out his cell phone and called someone. I heard a woman's voice on the other end. Their conversation was nothing but small talk, but who makes small talk after midnight? When Tommy told the woman he'd spent the day in Santa Barbara, I couldn't decide if he was lying or simply confused. When Tommy hung up, I asked him to whom he'd been speaking.

He looked over at me. "None of your information," he said.

"Come on," I said. "Was that your girlfriend?" It hadn't been a young voice on the phone. It sounded thin and trembly, more like an older woman.

Tommy laughed out loud. "No, not girlfriend."

"Who, then? Your aunt?"

"Chloe is her name. Maybe she is my girlfriend, maybe not. You might meet her, but not at this time."

By now we were lost enough to need a search party. Tommy pointed out a desolate truck stop and demanded we pull over and get directions. What he really wanted was a chance to buy himself several boxes of Cracker Jack. Tommy, I realized, didn't care if we were lost. It wasn't his bedtime for many hours yet and driving around rural California was a lot more interesting than being cooped up in his condo. Thanks to a road map inside the truck stop, I was able to figure out where we were.

Back in the car, Tommy animatedly pulled the prize out of every one of his Cracker Jack boxes, but the only one he liked was a little toy figurine he seemed to think was Pinocchio. I forged on back home.

As we were driving, something caught Tommy's attention outside the window. He pointed. "You see that? My God. Monster!"

"Yeah," I said. "That was a deer."

"Deer, my foot. That thing will kill you. You don't know why or how. Speaking of killer, when I sleep, I have dream that you try to kill me."

"How is it that you begin to get *less* tired at one in the morning?"

"Can I teach you something? Don't say the word *tired,* or you will become more tired. Also, please be careful how you drive. I don't want to die. I have many dreams in my life. I want to make a lot of movies, like Hitchcock. Maybe live two hundred more years, too."

At the time, any one of those things sounded roughly as plausible as the other.

"And what about you, young man? What is your dream, other than finding map? Is it that you want to be James Dean? Class is over next week—you know that, don't you? School is over, as they say."

Tommy was right. Even worse, I hadn't made any postclass plans. All I knew was that I didn't want to take more acting classes anytime soon. So what *did* I want to do? I told Tommy the first thing that popped into my head: "I want to go to L.A."

"Really," Tommy said, impressed now, sitting up. "Okay. So why don't you stay in my place?"

"Your place?"

"In L.A. I have apartment there."

"You have an apartment *in* L.A.?"

"Yeah. I charge you two hundred dollars a month, and you can use it if you want."

I have always believed that all dots connect eventually, that all experiences serve a distinct purpose. When I didn't get the role in *Wildflowers* I tried, unconvincingly, to tell myself that there was good reason. That something positive would eventually come from it. Then I became scene partners with Tommy, and he brought up his hitherto unmentioned L.A. apartment. It was the opportunity I'd been waiting for.

"When is the apartment available?" I said, trying to seem only vaguely interested.

Tommy shrugged and smiled, seeing right through me. "Don't play the politics, young man. So look, I have to go to L.A. next week after class. You can check out apartment. We go to L.A. together and you can decide. It's up to you. I don't force you."

I trusted Tommy. He was secretive and moody but also giving and supportive. From watching Tommy in Jean Shelton's class, I got the sense that he'd been judged his whole life. When it came to friendship, at least, I suspected that almost no one had given Tommy a chance. I was willing to take that leap of faith. What I wasn't admitting to myself—what I probably *couldn't* admit to myself back then—was that I met Tommy in the midst of the most aggressively, desperately lonesome months of my life. I needed a friend as much as he did. Maybe even more.

My mother wasn't going to like the sound of me checking out an apartment in L.A. The worst thing I could imagine was Tommy and my mother discussing my future together. I couldn't give her a chance to talk me out of this or forbid it. If I was going to pursue my dream, I had to take this chance. It was the only way.

"L.A., after class?" I said to Tommy, as though I hadn't just torn my mind to shreds thinking the matter over.

"Yeah," Tommy said. "Next week. We go. If you want."

"Okay," I said. "That sounds good."

Tommy's and my final scene in Jean Shelton's class was a pillow fight. This was a Shelton-devised exercise to keep Tommy and me from stepping on each other's lines. After I said my line I would gently hit Tommy with my pillow. After Tommy said his line, he would hit me with his pillow three times. Shelton started laughing the first time Tommy did this, which only made him whack me more furiously. That was how our last class ended.

I told a few people about my upcoming trip to Los Angeles with Tommy, including an old unicycle-riding hippie friend of mine who worked for Lucasfilm as an editor. My hippie friend did not like Tommy. He'd sat in on one of Jean Shelton's classes once and thought Tommy was almost certainly an addict of some kind; the word he used to describe him was "ravaged." Based on what I'd seen, at least, the most dangerous thing Tommy put in his body was piping-hot water. My friend also thought it was incredibly odd that Tommy would offer me his mysteriously vacant L.A. apartment at such a cheap price without wanting anything from me in return. "There's a catch to this," he told me. "Please be careful." None of these were unreasonable observations, and had I not spent a good amount of time around Tommy, I probably would have thought the whole situation was insane, too.

I called Tommy the night before we were supposed to head to L.A. to see what time he wanted to leave. Instead of hearing his usual outgoing message, I heard this: "Hi, Babyface. I'm not around until ten p.m., but I call you later." *Babyface* derived from something Tommy had said on the fly in class a few weeks ago, when comparing my face to his during a rant about what "type" we were acting-wise: "I have potato face. Your face is delicate, like a baby face." He'd never used it as a nickname, though. I hoped this would be the first and last time.

I'd told my mother I was going to Los Angeles with Tommy. She'd managed to hold her tongue until the morning of our departure. "You're crazy to be doing this," she said, over and over. I countered that she had to trust me, just this once, and let me find my way. She heard me out but wasn't convinced. "It's just . . . *crazy,*" she said. "You realize this, *mon cher,* yes? That you're crazy? I hope this trip is not your end."

My *end?* My end, I wanted to tell her, my *real* end, would be never trying anything, not taking any risks, and working a job I had zero passion for. I reassured her that I'd be back in less than thirty-six hours. I hadn't decided if I was moving to L.A. or not. I'd call her every hour if she wanted me to.

She drove me to the Walnut Creek BART station, where Tommy was picking me up. He was, of course, late, and as the time piled up, one swollen gray minute atop the other, my mother sat there and detailed the many ways in which my one day in Los Angeles was going to wreck my life forever. I have never been so relieved to see Tommy as when his Benz finally floated into that parking lot.

My mother followed me to Tommy's car like a shadow. I started to say something to her, but she looked at me with such intensity that I knew I couldn't stop her. I owed her the courtesy of letting her speak to Tommy directly.

Tommy obviously wasn't expecting my mother to be waiting with me, and he powered down his window with the queasy, smiling nervousness of an inveterate speeder welcoming the arrival of a California State Trooper. He kept looking at me, but I couldn't save him. He was going to have to endure this.

My mother didn't bother reintroducing herself. "Are you going to L.A., Tommy?" she asked him. When my mother said "Tommy," it sounded like *Tome-EE,* with a rise at the end so sharp you could jump a bike off it.

"Yes," Tommy said. "I am. We are. We are going." He was, unpromisingly, stuttering from sheer nervousness.

My mother nodded. "Perhaps you could wait to go until next week, so I can join you?"

"No, I'm sorry. I have to go now. I have meeting there. People waiting for me."

She didn't even bother pretending to believe him. "Tommy, I'm a little bit concerned, because I'm looking at your eyes and they are completely red. It's obvious you haven't slept."

"Well, I don't know what to say about that."

"You're going to drive like this?"

"I'm okay." He put his arms up, smiling. He knew better than to tell my mother that I drove his car.

My mother stared at him with prosecutorial eyes. "Tommy, how old are you?"

"I'm twenty-eight."

She didn't believe this, either. No one on planet Earth would have believed this. "Is that so, Tommy? Maybe, then, you could tell me why you want to help my son?"

"I think he's cool guy."

"Well, that's very interesting. Because I'm very concerned, Tommy. Where are you going to stay in L.A.?"

"I have my place. It's fine. We go for one day."

"Is it safe, Tommy? I just don't feel good about this."

"Mom," I said. "Mom, come *on*."

My mother looked at me. She breathed very deeply, as though letting go of something. Which was, I guess, me. Then she looked back at Tommy. "Be careful, Tommy. Please."

"I will."

"Tommy, don't hurt my son."

I put my hand over my eyes. The worst thing Tommy could do in response to this request, I thought, would be to chuckle creepily.

"I would not," Tommy said, chuckling creepily.

"And one more thing, Tommy. One more thing. No sex, Tommy, okay? Are we clear?"

"Mom!"

"Well, we all do."

My mother looked at him coldly for a moment. Then she took a step toward him. "What was that, Tommy?"

Tommy shrugged, beginning to panic. "You know. We all do."

"I'm afraid I don't know what this means, but I think you understand me now." Translation: *If you touch my son, I will kill you.*

She walked away without saying good-bye. It took me a long, painful moment to accept that my mother had just asked another man not to have sex with me.

I got into Tommy's car, emotionally concussed. Once my mother was gone he whirled on me: "What the heck was that? She's crazy. Your mother is off the wall! Crazy. My God! 'No sex.' What a story!"

My mother was right about one thing: Tommy really hadn't slept all night. He started nodding off at the wheel as he drove away, so he pulled over and we switched seats. Tommy put a white T-shirt over his head and neck, tilted the seat back as far as it could go, and was bombed out and snoring by the time we hit the highway. It was August 31, 1998. I had known Tommy Wiseau less than a month.

Tommy finally woke up at the moment we hit the Sunset Boulevard exit on the 405. "How do you always do that?" I asked him.

"Do what?"

"Know exactly when to wake up."

"Vampire trick," Tommy said.

Sometimes it really did seem as though Tommy wanted to be a vampire. Maybe being a vampire formed for Tommy a bridge between being objectively unattractive and subjectively attractive. The last thing Tommy Wiseau wanted to be was average. He had that in common with most people, of course, but Tommy took it several steps further. He took everything several steps further.

As we drove down Sunset Boulevard, Tommy described to me the vampire movie he wanted to make. It had, I must admit, a killer title: *The Vampire from Alcatraz: King of Vampires.*

Before we headed to Tommy's apartment, though, he announced that he was hungry. I knew exactly where to go. James Dean's favorite restaurant in Hollywood was an Italian place called the Villa Capri, where, according to legend, Sir Alec Guinness had warned Dean a week before his death that if he insisted on driving his speedy new Porsche Spyder, he'd be dead in a week. At Villa Capri Dean had become close with a young waiter named Mario Marino. In the acknowledgments of his James Dean biography, Joe Hyams thanks Marino, who now owned his own restaurant in Hollywood called Marino. I relayed all this information to Tommy and said, "Let's go have dinner and meet a guy who knew James Dean."

"Babyface's ideas," Tommy said approvingly, "are crazy. They never stop."

I was unexpectedly nervous inside the restaurant. Was I really going to get to meet a man who knew—had spoken intimately to—James Dean? Halfway into our meal, I couldn't hold back my curiosity any longer. I walked up to the hostess and asked her if Mario Marino was in tonight. He wasn't. I returned to our table sorely disappointed.

"My God," Tommy said. "You are obsessed. This is obsession! You will meet him. Don't worry."

"Thanks, Tommy."

"You know," Tommy said, forking away at his pesto, "I shot my super-eight movie near here."

"The one you showed me? Starring Bigfoot?"

"Not Bigfoot. You must be kidding. *Robbery Doesn't Pay*. I show you, remember?"

"Of course. How could I forget?"

"So we shoot few blocks from here. In Westwood. I live there, too. My roommate had, like, a huge snake. I was so scared of it I had to move out. I thought maybe it will kill me. Then I get my own place on the Crescent Heights, which you will see tonight." Tommy stopped eating for a moment. "I don't know, maybe it's not good for you. Maybe you don't like it. We see."

"Okay," I said, getting a little anxious. These were a lot of caveats.

Tommy noticed my unease. "Don't worry," he said. "I think you will like the place. It's not castle, though."

"Okay." That didn't make me feel much better.

Tommy looked at me. "I used to live in such small apartment with my family, you know, when I was little kid." His voice lowered, as though drawing back into his memory to reclaim something truthful. "I even have to share bed sometimes with my entire family. When my little cousin fall asleep, sometimes he twirl my hair with his finger." He quickly warded that memory away. "But let me tell you," Tommy said, "coming to L.A. is not easy, my friend. But, you know, you take your time, you grow up. You are just sixteen now—"

"Actually," I said, "I'm twenty." I'd told Tommy my age several times. For some reason Tommy always lowered it—much like, I assumed, he lowered his.

"Oh," Tommy said, pausing. "Well, whatever. But you are just kid now and you become independent. So you have my support. You know, when I start my business, I make twenty-five cents an hour."

"What business? Street Fashions?"

Tommy looked around. "Don't say so loud! Yes. Twenty-five cents an hour."

He had to be lying. Who other than third-world laborers made twenty-five cents an hour?

Suddenly Kirk Douglas walked into the restaurant. Spartacus himself! I pointed Douglas out to Tommy, but Tommy thought I was indicating one of Marino's heavyset waiters. When I finally got Tommy to look directly at Douglas, Tommy returned to his food and said, "Big star. Who cares?" Tommy wasn't interested in giving the power of stardom to somebody else.

"So," he said. "I tell you another secret, maybe. You know how I start my business? Nah, maybe that story wait. Maybe you not ready for it. But the fact is I have many jobs in my life—so many you can write book about them all."

"Yeah? Like what?"

"In many other places. France, Louisiana, et cetera. I'm pretty good in the business but not so good with the love. Girls can be very tricky, but that's life. You know the expression: ten seconds pleasure, ten years hatred."

I suspected that Tommy had probably had a normal life at one point. Then, I presumed, some kind of personal calamity—nervous breakdown, midlife crisis, heartbreak, addiction, *something*—caused him to grow his hair long and go into hibernation, only to come out broken and different. I was catching Tommy as he emerged from that reclusion, and the thing powering his emergence was his reignited desire to become an actor.

I was curious to learn as much about Tommy as I could. It felt like I was seeing a case study of what happens to someone whose dreams had been stifled. I was reaching out to Tommy, and he was reaching out to me, but for entirely different reasons. Both of us were stuck; neither of us knew what to do next. If either of us bailed on the other now, I thought, we'd both sink.

Mario Marino entered the restaurant. The waitress walked over to point him out to me. Could we meet him? I asked. Sure, she said, and went to fetch him. I told Tommy we were about to meet the man who knew James Dean, and suddenly there Mario was, standing beside our table, looking incredibly youthful and vigorously black-haired for being almost seventy years old. *"Buona sera,"* he said.

I shook Mario's hand and told him I had read about him in Joe Hyams's James Dean biography.

"James Dean!" Mario less said than exploded, in the Italian way.

You half expected there to be confetti floating around the ends of his sentences. "Yes, yes! Very nice young man. He loved pasta! A lot of pasta."

I asked what Dean was like, his favorite dishes, whether the Villa Capri was still open, everything. In retrospect, it was a little embarrassing. But Mario answered patiently. He had perfected the restaurateur's gift of pretending you were adored and welcome even if you were being a total dork. At which point Tommy got involved.

"What do you really think of James Dean overall?" Tommy asked Mario.

"Oh, a very nice boy. Very nice."

"He's not overrated a little bit? You know what I'm saying. Come on. Give us something. What crazy things he do? Don't be phony. You can be honest. I won't say anything."

"No, no," Mario said, eyeing Tommy suspiciously. His voice deepened and firmed up. "*Very* nice. *Very* nice guy." And with that Mario gracefully excused himself.

We were back in Tommy's car now, and he pulled out a piece of paper. "This," he said, "is code to parking garage. I don't know if it change from last year." *Last* year? When was the last time Tommy was here? He then informed me that he'd told the building manager he was showing the apartment to his "little cousin," so if I saw her, I had to pretend to be Tommy's cousin. We were driving down Fountain, headed toward Crescent Heights. Tommy told me to take a left. No, wait. A right. Then a left. Soon enough we were lost. Tommy could not find his own apartment.

We found the place, eventually. It was right down the street from the Laemmle Sunset 5, where, years later, *The Room* would play regularly. We neared the apartment complex and I saw the palm trees and the swept sidewalks and the handsome security gate and caught myself thinking: *This is actually a good start.* Only then did I realize how dire my expectations had grown over the course of this very long day.

Tommy said he would recite to me the security code he'd written down earlier. While he recited the numbers, I was supposed to type them in. The security code was this: 1-2-3-4. I asked Tommy why he bothered writing that down. Tommy responded that he wrote it down because he could never remember it.

"This is a really cool place," I said when we got out of the car. "And you're a block from Sunset. Why don't you use it more often?"

Tommy shrugged. "I have very busy schedule in San Francisco. I come here when I have some business." I could tell he was enjoying my surprise at how nice the building was. The apartment was on the third floor, but we had to check Tommy's mailbox before going up. When he opened the tiny metal door, two or three envelopes popped out as if spring-loaded. The rest of his mail had been crammed into the slot so tightly, it didn't look like anything less than a crowbar would be able to extricate it all. When Tommy saw the look on my face he just laughed. "It's not easy to manage life in two different cities," he said.

On the elevator ride up to the third floor Tommy told me, "I pay for the place already, so it's fine for you. Rent is nine hundred dollars a month, but I pay ahead so I don't have to worry about it. I pay six months, four months in advance. No stress that way. I don't like the stress."

The elevator doors opened and I was hit by crisp, summery air. The corridor overlooked the complex's turquoise swimming pool, surrounded by deck chairs and glass-topped tables. Tucked between several dramatically lit palm trees was a Jacuzzi. I could hear its soft nighttime burbles.

At the apartment door Tommy handed me his armful of mail while he cycled through the keys on his one key ring to rule them all. On his fourth try, the right key slid home, and we stepped inside. One bedroom. Balcony. The kitchen was large for one person, as was the living area. But for the dust, everything seemed clean and operable. Pinned to the entryway bulletin board was a single card: Sports Connection, a West Hollywood gym. Tommy strode ahead of me to turn on the air conditioner.

Little by little, though, I noticed a few odd things. For instance, knee-high stacks of old *Hollywood Reporter*s were spread around the living room, their covers advertising five-year-old production deals and cancellation notices for television shows I had forgotten existed. Tommy had that famous Jim Morrison "American Poet" poster unevenly taped, all by itself, on the left-hand wall. It also took me a few moments to notice the apartment's striking lack of furniture, unless the *Hollywood Reporter*s *were* the furniture. There was a bed in the bedroom, and a glass desk in the living room, but no kitchen table, no couch, and no chairs. A boxy and ancient antennaed television set sat on two Roman-style pillars. There weren't any plates or glasses in the cupboards or any silverware in the drawers. In the bathroom I found hundreds if not thousands of tiny black spatter stains—almost certainly the result of numerous black-hair-dyeing sessions. If it weren't for the dye stains, it would have been hard to believe that anyone, much less Tommy, had *ever* lived there. The apartment had so little personality that it could have been the complex's model apartment, or some love nest kept by transient adulterers. Or maybe it looked like exactly what it was: the rarely visited apartment of a strange and lonely man.

"So what do you think?" Tommy asked me.

I was already plotting out my life here. "I think it's nice. I'll take it, if that's still okay with you."

"You don't have to rush. Take your time. See if you are comfortable." Tommy busied himself with his mail for a bit. It was getting late now and I was exhausted from driving all day. I set up camp using a rolled-out sheet on the living room floor and a few *Hollywood Reporter*s as pillows. Tommy was still carefully opening, reading, and throwing away his mountain of mail. I was almost asleep when I heard Tommy step around me and close his bedroom door. The shower spat to life a moment later and he began belting out *Aladdin*'s "A Whole New World." I listened to the thrum of the air conditioner, the whooshing of passing traffic outside, and thought about how easily I could get used to this space. It felt right. I could live here. And it was so central. But I still didn't know how Tommy managed to afford "life in two different cities," as he put it. What did he really do?

I was moving past the last drowsy checkpoint before sleep when Tommy's bedroom door opened. I didn't open my eyes at first, but I could sense Tommy watching me from his doorjamb. I squinted my eyes open. Tommy was in a tank top and sweatpants. His toothbrush was in his mouth; his hair was wet. "Hey," he said. "Yo. Are you comfortable? Do you need anything? Sleeping process?"

I blinked at him. "What?"

"Are you fine?"

"Yeah," I said. "I was falling asleep." I put my arm over my eyes to block the light. Tommy lingered there a moment longer. At last he started to close the bedroom door but stopped before it clicked shut. Then I heard the bedsprings accepting Tommy's weight and the dry, papery sound of sheets being pulled, pillows rearranged. Churning, restless silence followed that. A strange silence. As I began drifting back into sleep, I thought I heard Tommy say in a high singsong pitch, "Somebody's chicken." *Somebody's chicken?*

I'd just pretend I never heard it. It was probably just Tommy being Tommy, right? It didn't matter. Moments later, I could hear Tommy snoring.

seven

"Where's My Fucking Money?"

Shut up, I'm rich!
—Norma Desmond, *Sunset Boulevard*

The first time Tommy gave Sandy a check, Sandy was certain it would bounce. Sandy was so sure of this that he made a wooden-nickel joke with the teller at Tommy's bank. The teller, though, told Sandy not to worry. "What do you mean?" Sandy asked. "This account?" the teller said. "It's a bottomless pit." Sandy was dumbfounded. How much money would move a teller to inappropriately confess something like that? Whoever Tommy was, Sandy now decided, he was obviously backed by someone or something big.

This was very much the impression Tommy wanted everyone to have. As he said to me one morning on the way to the set, "We are shooting now for two weeks. You know what that means? People in Hollywood know we are fully loaded."

As usual, I let Tommy hear himself. Which was all he wanted to do anyway.

"Have you ever seen one million dollars in cash?" Tommy suddenly asked me.

"I have not," I said.

"Well, I have, young man. And it looks really nice—like this." He did a gesture with his hands, outlining an imaginary pile of money. "Very big pile. Looks very nice."

If I asked him the question he wanted me to ask—"How was it that you were able to see a million dollars in cash, Tommy?"—I knew he was going to back off, get defensive, or make a joke. So I didn't say anything. I just sat there in the car with Tommy and his imaginary pile of money.

"Last night I have vision. I think we need to do Chris-R scene again, but on roof. It will be spectacular. He is such good character. Like Al Capone. My idea is that when we fight him, the gun will fall off the roof, like in gangster movie."

As *The Room*'s line producer, I felt obliged to ask, "You want to shoot the Chris-R scene *again*?"

"I don't like the dailies. They just don't cut it. We need something bigger, more spectacular."

For Tommy, "bigger" and "more spectacular" meant green screen. The green screen was like a portal into Tommy's imagination and having it as an option gave him a scarily limitless range of possibilities. A few days before, Tommy had pulled Raphael aside and told him his latest big idea.

"I want my car," Tommy began, "to fly off the roof and into the sky." By now, Raphael was prepared for literally anything when Tommy discussed his ideas. Even so, I could tell this particular vision had really, deeply stunned him.

"Why," Raphael said, "do you want to do this, exactly?"

"It's just possible side plot. Maybe Johnny is vampire."

Raphael stood there, looking up at the sky. He began to nod. The next time I saw Raphael he was laughing uncontrollably while he relayed Tommy's flying Mercedes-Benz vampire vision to one of the cameramen.

Now, in the car on the way to the set, Tommy said, "You see how creative I am? Somebody's good director."

I said nothing. I couldn't get over how much effort reshooting the Chris-R scene on the Rooftop set would entail.

"You see," Tommy said, "you never give me credit. No one ever give me credit. Well, I give *myself* credit."

The biggest problem with reshooting the Chris-R scene was that Tommy no longer had half the characters the scene called for. Dan Janjigian was long gone. Brianna, who was included in the version of the scene shot in the alley, had been fired.

Tommy gathered together Philip, Carolyn Minnott, and Juliette—all of whom would figure prominently in the scene's new Rooftop version—to explain why it was being reshot. He described how much more dramatic it would be. He described the gun falling off the side of the roof. He mentioned Al Capone. He also added an additional and pretty significant detail, which was that Chris-R would actually be firing his gun in the air during the scene.

But before Tommy could start reshooting, we still needed to confirm Chris-R's involvement. Neither I nor anyone on set could imagine that Dan would be willing to come back and reprise his role, given the general wackiness of his experience with Tommy. I told Tommy as much, but he didn't see a problem: "Get this guy here now! No excuses!" I explained that Dan probably couldn't report for acting duty today (or ever) and that it was ridiculous to expect anyone to come in with only a few hours' notice. "Well," Tommy said huffily, "then I guess he not professional actor."

So I called Dan. He didn't answer. "Call him again now!" Tommy said.

A few minutes later, I found a quiet spot on the set and called again. This time, Dan picked up right away. "Tommy hasn't blown up Birns & Sawyer yet?" he asked.

"No," I said, "but he's working on it. What are you up to?"

"With my girlfriend. Doing a little shopping at Ralph's."

Tommy, standing at the other side of the lot, saw me talking on the phone and started yelling: "Greg, tell him we need him here now! We don't have time for the bs'ing!" I covered the receiver to shield Dan from hearing Tommy and went for a little walk around the block.

"Yeah," I said, "so get this. You ready?"

"Uh-oh."

"Tommy wants to reshoot the drug-deal thing you were in. He wants to do it on the Rooftop set. Also, he wants to do it now."

Silence.

"As in right now. Immediately."

"Good one," Dan said, but he knew I wasn't kidding.

"Yeah, so . . . you ready to become Chris-R again?"

"Why on the Rooftop?" Dan asked.

"I don't know. He said something about it being more dramatic? He wants you back on set ASAP. That's pretty much all he said."

Dan was quiet. Later he told me that he thought about how relieved he'd been when his *Room* gig ended—but then, weirdly, how much he'd kind of enjoyed being an actor. Maybe doing it again would be fun. He also wondered if there might be more scenes in the movie for him if he really managed to wow Tommy. Like everyone else in the cast, Dan had no idea what the script was about; all he'd been given was his scene. For all he knew, the whole film was crawling with charismatic drug dealers.

"I can't believe I'm saying this," Dan said, "but all right. I'll come by tomorrow around one. Actually, wait. How about you let me know when you're headed over. I know Tommy. No matter what time we settle on, he'll be four hours late."

"Good call," I said. "You're a wise man."

Dan laughed. "Am I?"

I passed the good news on to Tommy. His response: "He should come now!"

"Tommy, he's grocery shopping with his girlfriend."

Tommy shook his head sadly. "Not everybody has dedication. We prepare now anyway. First we do test of me running onto roof, then we prepare with gun. Et cetera, et cetera. When gun falls off roof, I want big struggle. We may do crazy stuff, so be prepared. Then I review footage."

We obviously weren't shooting anything today. The actor most central to the scene Tommy wanted to shoot wasn't even present. Even so, he decreed that no crew or cast member could leave the set. He wanted a full day's worth of rehearsal for a scene we'd already rehearsed and shot. This was, at best, an extravagant use of everyone's time. When the complaints started coming in, Tommy had this to say: "Rehearsal is very important. You need preparation. You can't just do scene in five minutes!"

• • •

The next day, Dan emerged from wardrobe already in character. If anything, he had taken his Chris-R game up a notch.

Even though we'd moved out of the alley set, Tommy still wanted Denny to open the scene dribbling his basketball. The Rooftop, I probably don't need to point out, had no basketball hoop. Sandy tried to talk Tommy out of this, but Tommy saw no logical issue with Denny practicing his dribbling on a condo rooftop. "He plays basketball," Tommy said. "Let Denny do what he want! You can play basketball without hoop. I do it all the time. It's fun!"

Philip and Dan now joined Tommy on the Rooftop set. His initial direction was impressively without substance: "Okay, we begin with Chris-R talking to Denny. Denny try to trick him little bit. Chris-R, your voice go up. Denny, you get scared."

Between rehearsals, Dan again began stalking around the Rooftop's pavement edge, swearing to stay angry and in character. Philip watched him, looking more and more worried, having already been mauled once by Dan. "I think you're in for a good time," I said to him.

"Yeah," Philip said. "A blast."

Sandy and Tommy stood by one of the monitors. Tommy was wearing big gray headphones with pastry-size ear cushions, his long black hair spilling over his shoulders. After the eighth or ninth time through the scene, Dan turned to Tommy and said, "Why do I keep saying the same line over and over again? 'Where's my fucking money?' Can't I mix it up or something? Vary it a little?"

"We will not change lines," Tommy said, his eyes not leaving his monitor. "You want to be actor, act like one." Tommy's response only made Dan angrier, and for the next couple of run-throughs it looked as though Philip were about to melt in terror as Dan pressed him for his fucking money. Although the effect Tommy's response had on Dan was unintended, the moment nonetheless stands as one of the only successful things I ever saw Tommy do as a director.

So yes: As unlikely as it may sound, the scene between Chris-R and Denny actually *did* get better on the Rooftop, no thanks to Tommy's wizardly direction. (He kept telling Dan to "imitate" Denny during the confrontation scene. It took everyone a while to realize that Tommy wanted Dan to *intimidate* Denny.) Tommy hit his first real snag when it came to the moment he cherished most: Chris-R firing a warning shot in the air to frighten Denny. Tommy seemed to believe that if he wanted the gun to fire, it should. But prop guns need blanks. Tommy began to talk about sending the art department out for blanks immediately, but Sandy wasn't comfortable with this.

"Tommy," he said. "The last thing we need right now is—"

"I stop you right there," Tommy said, stopping him right there. "This is Hollywood. Everything is possible. If Hitchcock hear you talk like this, he would fire you on the spot."

"You," Sandy said, laughing, "are not Hitchcock, my friend."

"That is your business," Tommy said. "I am not Hitchcock. I'm myself."

"What?" Sandy said, confounded.

The debate ended when Bill Meurer got word of what Tommy wanted to do. Through Peter Anway we learned that Mr. Meurer would "not tolerate" a gun going off on the premises of his retail business. Tommy was disappointed but said nothing. Hearing from Meurer was, in Tommy's mind, like hearing from God. Besides, his other beloved idea for the scene—the gun somehow flying off the roof when Mark and Johnny disarm Chris-R—was still in play.

Until it wasn't. Sandy pointed out that there was no good way to dramatize the gun flying off the roof without a lot of extra camera-and-blocking work. Raphael's resistance was more boldly stated: "If you knocked the gun out of that guy's hand," he said, pointing at Dan, "he would tear both of you to pieces."

"That's true," Dan said. "I would. And if you don't believe it, let's try rehearsing it your way, Tommy."

We came to the moment in which Johnny and Mark launch themselves out of the tin-roofed outhouse to disarm Chris-R and rescue Denny. Due to the outhouse's solitary-confinement dimensions, Tommy and I had to run out of it separately. Tommy was adamant that we both have "intense" expressions on our faces when we emerged. This was, for Tommy, a pure action-hero moment. As soon as we finished shooting our first run-through of the scene, Tommy wanted to watch the results on playback. He was terribly impressed with his intensity and deeply disappointed in mine. Tommy emerged from the outhouse looking like he'd just discovered Chris-R eating Denny's intestines; I looked like I'd discovered two strangers playing jacks. I couldn't take it seriously. I finally did my best approximation of Tommy's wide-eyed, O-mouthed expression and burst into laughter the second Sandy called "Cut!" It was good enough for Tommy. We moved on.

Now all we had to do was film our attempt to disarm Chris-R, which had turned out so badly the first time through, on the alley set. Our runs on the Rooftop, sadly, were just as pathetic. Dan actually stopped in the middle of one take and wheeled around on Tommy and said, "If you're going to grab my arm, really fucking grab it! You're jumping on me like a pussy!" With that, he headed off to shout some more expletives.

"My God," Tommy said, watching Dan go. "He's like *monster*."

As hard as it may be to believe, it took us two weeks to film this whole sequence, including the part of the scene that involved Carolyn and Juliette. This is about the same amount of time it took Steven Spielberg to shoot the D-day landing sequence in *Saving Private Ryan*. But even though Dan's scenes were finished in a few days, Tommy forbade him to ever leave the set. "Tommy," Dan said, "if I'm not doing any more filming, there's no reason for me to be here."

"But we may need you," Tommy said. "There's still more scenes in the script for your character. Maybe we use them, maybe not."

"Really?" Dan said, warily.

"Chris-R is big character," Tommy said.

"Can I see the script, then? That would be helpful for me."

"I'm sorry but you cannot. It's confidential at this time."

When Dan asked me if it was true that Chris-R had more scenes in the film, I was straight with him: There weren't any in the script I'd seen, but then again, Tommy had recently been planning for a subplot involving Johnny's flying vampire car. If Dan stuck around, it was entirely possible that the film could turn into *The Room: The Story of Chris-R's Gun*.

When Dan realized that Tommy had no plans to use him again, and that his time was being wasted, he presented Tommy with an eighty-dollar receipt for a new pair of Skechers boots he'd purchased. "What is this?" Tommy asked.

"You stepped on my boots so many times during our scene, they got all scuffed. I had to replace them. I'd like to be reimbursed."

"I am not the Santa Claus," Tommy said, turning away.

Dan grabbed Tommy by the arm and kept him there. He reminded Tommy that he'd been promised a full wardrobe during filming, but no one had given him boots. He'd thus worn his own, which were damaged. Replacing them was Tommy's responsibility. Dan explained all this to Tommy calmly, but there was an unbreakable steel rod in his voice.

Tommy, I think, gulped before saying that he'd have to ask his producers for permission.

"Tommy," Dan said, not letting go of his arm, "I do speeches for five thousand dollars a day. I run a business—a professional one. If you're really an honest businessman, as you claim to be, and you're really true to your word, as you claim to be, you wouldn't be fighting me on this. Right now, you're being unprofessional."

"We are very professional," Tommy said quietly.

Dan let Tommy go. "Good. Then be a man and pay for my boots."

Tommy ran his hand through his hair and looked around. "I need check!"

Tommy balked at replacing Dan's eighty-dollar Skechers. I later learned that Tommy's decision to reshoot the Chris-R scene—a scene, I should note, that had no impact on the film's plot—cost the production over $80,000.

That is how it went, every day: Tommy behaving like a gregarious spender one moment and a brutal miser the next. It wasn't new behavior; he'd been like this since I'd known him. Once, back in San Francisco, I was in a Big Five store with Tommy; he was shopping for workout gloves. A pair of Rollerblades caught his eye, though, and after trying them on, he spent an hour Rollerblading around the store, saying, "So beautiful. I *love* it!" He ended up grabbing four pairs of Rollerblades to take home with him. When he went to pay, Tommy asked the cashier what kind of discount he could get. The cashier said it was a set-price store. "Oh, come on, be good sport!" Tommy said. "Give me discount. How about five-dollar discount? Student ID or something?" The cashier laughed. "My God!" Tommy said. "She is so difficult! Somebody doesn't understand American way!" He pulled this stuff constantly, even in restaurants: "How about we pay for one drink, and you give us two. Come on, be good salesman!" Tommy, I guess, utterly rejected the idea that the entire point of Western civilization is not having to haggle like a peasant every time money changes hands.

Strangely, though, Tommy never haggled at Birns & Sawyer, maybe because he desperately wanted to be accepted as their golden boy. Whenever Peter Anway suggested that Tommy needed to buy something, Tommy usually did. "We are first-class production," he'd say, right before slapping a WISEAU-FILMS sticker on his new purchase. For the record, I don't fault Bill Meurer and Peter Anway for taking Tommy's money. They were running a business, and when someone turns up on your showroom floor determined to spend, the businessman's duty is to accommodate him. Still, I imagine it came as something of a shock to Anway when he found himself listed in *The Room*'s credits as one of Tommy's five assistants.

Three executive producers were listed in *The Room*'s credits. One (Chloe Lietzke, whose nighttime conversation with Tommy I'd overheard during our James Dean road trip) was a much older woman who lived in Oakland, was confined to a wheelchair, and had never been involved in film production before, during, or after *The Room*. Another (Drew Caffrey, with whom Tommy became close soon after moving to San Francisco) had been deceased for years at the time of the film's production. Along with being the executive producer, Caffrey was credited as another one of Tommy's assistants and the San Francisco casting director, making him the busiest dead person since Tupac Shakur.

The only real executive producer was, of course, Tommy Wiseau himself. In other words, *The Room* had no producers, which Tommy knew that I knew. That didn't stop him from lying about it to me. Whenever any issue came up that Tommy wanted to deflect, he attributed his needs to what "the producers" wanted. This was also a way of creating the illusion that Tommy had confidently navigated Hollywood's upper echelons. And it worked. Initially, at least, no one involved in the production doubted the existence of these producers. Considering how much money Tommy was throwing around, how could they have?

But eventually, members of the cast and crew began asking, "What the hell is this really all about? Where is Tommy from? Where is he getting all this money?" I told them I didn't know. After knowing Tommy for fifteen years, I *still* don't know how he originally acquired his money. What I do know is this: Whenever Raphael or Sandy discussed with Tommy ways to be more cost-efficient, Tommy responded, "We don't worry about money. We worry about movie." Anyone with that attitude is not operating out of a normal economic framework.

The question then becomes: What types of businesses are capable of generating a cash flow that allows one to spend $500,000 on a never-screened HD film? Tommy poured money into promoting the ultimate flop, despite making no profit, for years. He spent tens of thousands of dollars on merchandise. He spent $5,000 per month, for five years, keeping up a Highland Avenue billboard advertising the film. He spent thousands of dollars a month paying one theater in Los Angeles to screen *The Room,* earning a return on his investment somewhere between $100 and $200 per month—if that. If you want to make large amounts of money disappear, this is certainly one way to do it; but at a certain point, don't even money-laundering schemes diversify?

So it didn't surprise me when I heard whispers on the set about the source of Tommy's money. But here's the thing. The last person I would ever entrust to oversee any part of any criminal enterprise would be Tommy Wiseau. In fact, were I involved in illegal activity, I would think twice before launching a criminal enterprise in a country where Tommy Wiseau was even resident. And after all, if you were the legal face of a presumably international money-laundering scheme, what on earth would impel you to try to get the world's attention by becoming a movie star—and why would your less public colleagues allow you to do so?

When I told friends about Tommy early on—his secrecy, his wealth, his cheapness, and his frivolousness—they always warned me to be careful. I recall one friend saying, "Just wait. One of these days there'll be a knock on your door and it'll be an FBI agent." But after knowing Tommy for a decade and a half, I've never gotten a call or a knock. There were never any suspicious (or, really, any) people around him.

Money is what allowed Tommy to not only produce and release *The Room,* but also to extensively advertise it and keep it alive in the dark time between its disastrous initial release and eventual cult success. The origins of all of this money are still unknown. Money, you could say, is the elephant in *The Room*.

eight

May All Your Dreams Come True

The funny thing is, I'm not pretending to be someone else, and you are.
—Tom Ripley, *The Talented Mr. Ripley*

I was driving through central California with the windows of my Lumina open to the rural, manure-laden air. It had been eighteen days since I'd first seen Tommy's apartment. Earlier that Thursday afternoon, on a whim, I decided to move to L.A. What was I waiting for? I'd dreamed of this moment since I was twelve. Now I was actually doing it.

Before leaving Tommy's apartment a little over two weeks before, I'd grabbed a stack of his ancient *Hollywood Reporter*s and brought them with me to San Francisco. Back home in my bedroom, I paged through them, one by one, figuring out which agencies I wanted to approach. In one of the more recent issues I read an interview with a famous young actor represented by the Iris Burton Agency. I did a little research and learned Iris had started out with a small boutique agency that had since become the stuff of legend in the business. (According to that legend, Iris became the first—and, I'm guessing, remains the only—agent able to secure a contract for a *fetus*.) Iris had a particular gift for representing young actors who succeeded in bucking the typical young-actor trend of being washed up at twenty. River Phoenix, Drew Barrymore, Jerry O'Connell, the Olsen twins, Hilary Duff, Joaquin Phoenix, Kirsten Dunst, Josh Hartnett—these were just some of Iris's clients. A casting director in San Francisco told me that Iris was someone who could "get Steven Spielberg on the phone." I sent Iris, along with a bunch of other agents, my headshot and résumé. For my contact info I used my new apartment's phone number, which didn't yet have a phone hooked up, though I planned to rectify that immediately. That phone number is still working, incidentally. It now serves as the *Room* hotline. Feel free to call it if you'd like to hear Tommy personally invite you to a screening: (323) 654-6192.

After seven hours, I made it to Sunset Boulevard, feeling a bit automotively emasculated among a sudden blitz of Porsches and Ferraris. I didn't care. I was damned proud of my Lumina, which hadn't broken down once on this drive. I came to Los Angeles to do a big movie. Something with a huge impact, like *Interview with a Terminator*. I was here now, and I could make it happen. And it was all thanks to Tommy, wasn't it? I wondered what he was doing up in San Francisco. Probably vamping out in his lair, getting ready to sell some pirated Levi's. And good for him! I had nothing but appreciation for the man at this moment.

Around 2:00 a.m. I parked at Tommy's complex and hauled my luggage (a duffel bag filled mostly with socks) up to the third floor. There was the door. My home. I was at the end of my first night in Los Angeles and about to crash in my new apartment. I got to the door, pulled out the key, stuck it in. It wouldn't open. I tried again. I tried for ten minutes. Nothing budged. This was, quite obviously, the wrong key. Tommy gave me the wrong fucking key.

The apartment manager's office was, of course, closed. I didn't have a cell, so my first order of business was to get to a pay phone. I found a Chevron gas station on Sunset and called Tommy collect. He didn't answer, so I waited in the gas station for a few minutes and fulminated. In the short time I had known Tommy, I had learned this much: He had established an entirely new category of personal disorganization. *You know better,* I thought. *You should have gotten the key from him when you first saw the apartment. You idiot!*

I called Tommy again, very much hoping that my first night in Los Angeles would not be spent in my Lumina. This time, he answered. After accepting the charges, he said, "I'm listening!"

"Tommy?"

"Oh, hey! How is Babyface?"

"The keys don't work. The manager's office is closed. Do you have a spare somewhere?"

"What?"

"The *keys* don't *work*. I don't know what I'm going to do."

"Oh, come on! Try again. It works!" He sounded jovial. Playful, even.

Why did I bother calling him? Even if Tommy's organizational skills weren't so hopeless, what could he do from San Francisco at this hour? Teleport? I didn't want to get mad at Tommy, because he'd been so cool and supportive, but the only way to keep from getting mad at him was to end our conversation immediately. "It's late," I said. "Don't worry. I'll figure something out. Maybe a hotel."

"No, no," he said. "Don't stay in hotel. You have your own place now!"

"Thanks, Tommy. I still can't get the door open."

"I'm here if you need anything."

What I needed was for the key to work. My next move was to drive east down Sunset Boulevard, looking for a side street to pull over and go to sleep. Sunset Boulevard at 3:00 a.m. is not the most welcoming place, and I soon realized I was liable to be robbed or worse if I slept in my car. And the farther east down Sunset I went, the rougher, darker, and stabbier it got.

Out of this unpleasant darkness the blinky lights of the Saharan Motel emerged. The place had an Egyptian theme. More interesting yet was the part of its sign that read: $59.99 OR HOURLY RATES. I was a sheltered twenty-year-old from Northern California, but even I knew from which segment of society the Saharan likely lured most of its customers. I pulled in, only to be greeted by a gentleman of Middle Eastern descent who ran out of his check-in hut screaming at the top of his lungs, *"Turn your car! Move your fucking car!"* The man yelled at me some more when I got out and walked over to him. "I need a room," I said. Happily, there was one vacancy left. After procuring my key from the still-screaming man, I walked to my room past several dead palm trees and an empty swimming pool. I could smell rotting Indian food and, yep, people were actually getting it on in the rooms. Not in a nice, loving way, either. As I was opening my door, a trashed middle-aged man with two wobbly-legged prostitutes young enough to be his daughters emerged from the room next to mine. "Hello," I said. They laughed the cruel laughter of the damned. My first night in Los Angeles and I'm in a hooker motel. Thank you, Tommy.

I couldn't sleep. I reclined in all my clothes on top of the still-made bed, which smelled like the perspiration of hundreds, wondering what on earth I was going to do in the morning. Someone started knocking through the bars on my street-side window. "Hey, man!" a voice said. "Hey! Do you have some beer? Can you help me out?" His voice was creepy and desperate and so close it was as though he were standing at the foot of my bed. Eventually, I was able to close my eyes.

I have lived in Los Angeles for more than a decade and never seen it smoggier than the first morning I awoke as an official resident of the city. I drove through this wicked blue-gray haze back to Tommy's apartment building, the manager of which, Stacey, seemed resistant to the idea that I should be living there. Stacey was younger and kind of cute, with glasses that made her look like the secret identity Wonder Woman never had. I finally convinced Stacey to give me the key, though we wound up debating the correct pronunciation of Tommy's last name. *Why-zo? Wee-saw?* It was clear that she didn't believe Tommy and I were cousins. I didn't blame her. Nor did I want to contemplate what else she thought.

I unpacked my socks, napped for a while, then went back to my car for my big-ticket move-in item: a colossal fax-machine phone my father had lying around. It was about the size of a European economy car, but I found just the place for it. Beneath Tommy's crummy television were two small white Doric-style pillars (you can see these pillars, and that television, at several points in *The Room*), so I decided to swap out Tommy's television with my fax machine. I stuck the phone cord into the jack and had begun to do something else when, out of nowhere, the phone rang. I hadn't recorded an outgoing message yet, so I waited for the allotted six rings to pass. Then a voice said: "I'm calling for Greg Sestero. I received your headshot and résumé and would like to set up a meeting for next week." Given where I'd spent the previous night, this seemed like an unusually auspicious turn of events.

Five minutes later, another call. Same gist ("This message is for Greg Sestero; we're interested in meeting you regarding representation"), different agent.

When, ten minutes later, I got another call from *another* agent, I started to laugh with awe. Then I learned who exactly was calling: "Hey, Greg. This is Chris from the Iris Burton Agency. I got your package. I want to set up a meeting for next week." I probably replayed that message twenty times before I convinced myself it wasn't some sort of joke. Iris Burton's agency really had called me. This was my Harvard acceptance letter.

I called everyone back and set up meetings. I scheduled the Iris Burton meeting for later in the week, which I hoped would allow me to gain some educational experience before I had to face her.

My first meeting was in a bland corporate office on Melrose with a blandly friendly agent. Everything about it felt generic. "I'd love to see some of the stuff you've done," she said. I mentioned I'd studied with Jean Shelton. The woman had no idea who Jean Shelton was. Clearly trying to salvage our sad, forgettable meeting, she abruptly ended with "Can you get your demo reel to me?"

That was not going to happen. I had never even seen the episode of *Nash Bridges* that I was on, and I didn't have my *Patch Adams* footage, either. Not that it would help; I was only a glorified extra.

In the next meeting, I might have given the agent the impression that my role in *Patch Adams,* and my relationship with the film's director, Tom Shadyac, were slightly more significant than they were. She then started telling me that she'd recently seen Shadyac and teased him about having all of these hit movies—*Ace Ventura, The Nutty Professor, Liar Liar*. He was on such a roll, she told him, that he should open his own movie studio! Ha-ha, et cetera. She promised that she'd mention me to Shadyac the next time she saw him.

"Oh," I said lightly, "don't even mention it." What I meant was: *Dammit, please don't mention it!*

"We'd really like to see some of your work," she said as we parted. Once again I left completely demoralized. It was becoming clear that I'd need tape before anyone would consider representing me.

Next I met with a younger male agent who was dressed like a mannequin. He didn't talk to me so much as lob insults disguised as professional concern: "You've got a lot of work to do. A lot of work ahead of you. You need tape, experience, and a new look. Get all those things, and we can talk."

"Okay," I said, standing up.

Then he said this: "I've got some meetings with friends tonight, but after, do you want to play tennis?"

I knew a euphemism when I heard one. "Actually," I said, "I can't."

He nodded, frowned, reached into his desk. "Let me give you my card." He looked at me as he handed it over. "If you ever want to play."

Iris Burton was my final meeting. None of the fancy clothes I'd worn to previous meetings seemed to be working, so I put on my normal casual attire: a short-sleeve button-down and cargo shorts. For Iris Burton, I wanted to be as genuine as I knew how to be, and at this point in my life, that meant, God help me, wearing shorts.

I was a little confused when I first approached Iris's address. It wasn't an office building but a house in a Beverly Hills neighborhood, the exterior of which was dominated by rose gardens. In the driveway was a new black Mercedes as well as a motorcycle. I was approaching the place warily when I saw Joaquin Phoenix coming out of the guesthouse. We walked down the long driveway toward each other. I tried to pretend it was no big deal running into him. "Hey," he said, quick and relaxed. "Hey," I said back, just as quickly but manifestly less relaxed.

Inside the guesthouse was Chris, the man who'd left a message on my phone, and who was Iris Burton's executive assistant. He wore a Caesar cut and expensive clothes and stood a couple of inches taller than me—and I'm not short. I liked Chris instantly. There was no Hollywoodish vibe to him at all. He wasn't trying to intimidate, impress, belittle, or seduce me. I came in and he smiled, shook my hand, and told me to sit down. He talked, I listened; I talked, he listened.

"We're always trying to find people who fit the agency," he said.

I told him I'd come from San Francisco and related some of my close calls, or the calls I was discussing as though they'd been close—for instance, that I'd read for *The Virgin Suicides.*

"Really?" he said. "What part? Because we have two clients on that—Kirsten and Josh."

"I was up for Trip Fontaine."

"Josh's role," he said.

"I guess so," I said. "Yeah."

Chris smiled. "Let's see those headshots of yours," he said, mercifully. I had brought in all the contact sheets from my most recent headshot session, which we spread out on Chris's desk. "These are great, actually," he said, and started telling me about the kinds of calls he'd feel good sending me out on. I could tell this was different. I sensed he was thinking about what he could do for me.

Then the Dreaded Question came: "Do you have some tape we can see?"

I just stared. I felt defeated. I wanted to say, "Come on, Chris! After everything we've been through!" *Tape* was like this roadblock that had no room around it. As I sat there attempting to come up with something exculpatory to say, Chris looked back at my contact sheets and said, once again mercifully, "How about we send you out and see what happens."

"Okay," I said. *Thank you,* I thought. Just hearing that made me want to hug Chris, but I managed to contain myself. Such a simple gesture on his part, but it meant so much.

Chris got on the phone with someone; he didn't dial. "Can you come check something out for a second?" Moments later I heard the sound of high heels coming from deeper inside the house and then Iris Burton herself was standing in the doorway. This was a woman who'd played a heathen dancer in *The Ten Commandments,* who could tell stories about Cecil B. DeMille, and I must say she was a scrotum-tighteningly intimidating figure.

"How are you, kid?" she said. Me: deer. Her: headlights. Before I could say anything, she walked toward me. "How did you find me, anyway?"

An old issue of the Hollywood Reporter, I had no intention of saying. So I told her, "I heard about you when I worked on *Patch Adams*."

She wasn't even listening. She turned to Chris and said, "He's beautiful. Miramax would love him."

"Miramax?" I said.

Her eyes were on me again now. "Are you meeting with anybody else?"

"A couple people."

She laughed. "Why? Why would you meet with anybody else? Who are you kidding? Come *on,* kid. Do you know who I am?" This was all playful, I think, except for the parts that weren't.

Chris jumped in with waving, calming hands. "Okay, Iris. That's enough." I could tell that Chris was her assistant because he was the only person who could handle her. They had a routine—and moreover, they liked it.

Iris walked back into the house without saying good-bye. Chris watched her go and turned to me and said, "We'd love to have you." A few minutes later I signed a contract of representation. What had just happened was impossible. As I walked away from Iris's house, I kept wondering if I was going to wake up in the Saharan Motel.

Chris and Iris got me my first audition a little over a week later. The part was Max Evans, the lead role in the Warner Bros. show *Roswell*. Tommy, who was almost as excited as I to hear that I got such a big audition, asked if he could help me with my lines. I said I'd let him know when they came in. Finally, they did, and I left him a message to ring me back. I missed Tommy's return call. When I played his message, I heard this: "Why do you have so many rings on the phone? It should only ring *three* times before message. Change this shit, dammit. I hate this stupid beeping. No one likes the Mickey Mouse stuff."

When I got Tommy on the line he lectured me some more about my six rings. I tried to explain that three rings, in a lot of cases, didn't let you get to the phone in time, and then you had to stand and apologize to someone while your stupid message played. Tommy was adamant that three rings were more "professional."

"Why the hell do you even care?" I asked him.

"Let's run the lines," Tommy said. "Come on, fax me the script. We do it together."

I'd always gotten a kick out of running lines with Tommy. Tommy's approach to acting helped soothe my nerves and took my mind off the possibility of failure. Above all, he reminded me how important it was to have fun while performing. The only problem was that Tommy wanted to run my lines as his own.

"Tommy," I said. "It's *my* audition."

"I like this Max character," he said, and started reading Max's lines in such a horrendously unconvincing way that all I could do was laugh. Max Evans is an alien. In this scene he was talking to a girl he was falling in love with about being an alien. Maybe Tommy should have been auditioning for *Roswell*. The part had practically been written for him!

I didn't get Max Evans but ended up getting a callback for the other lead role, and the casting director said some nice things, including this: "You're still a baby, remember. We'll be seeing you again." Tommy as acting coach was one for one.

Iris and Chris wanted a few different selections of headshots to send out, so I headed for the nearest Kinko's. I'd gotten my hands on an Iris Burton Agency logo and made sure that it was featured prominently on all my headshot prints: she was, of course, my big (and only) selling point. The guy behind the desk at Kinko's—SETH, his nametag read—noticed this and said, "How long have you been with Iris Burton?"

I told him only a week or two. Seth, an aspiring actor himself, promptly gave me some advice. I'd always heard actors normally maintain a solid distance between one another, but Seth was apparently uninterested in that little dance. He said, "What you should do is send out your headshots to all the casting directors. With that logo, you're going to get attention."

Seth went in back and returned with all the relevant casting directors' addresses in handy label form. He called these "the casting director label edition thing." Los Angeles!

"So," he said, "send your headshot to everybody. Just send it out. In this town you've got to rely on yourself; you've got to be your own agent. You've got a good agent, yeah, but you want to be doing a lot of the busywork."

"Thank you," I said, a little overwhelmed and taken aback by his kindness.

Seth shrugged. "That's what I would do if I had Iris Burton behind me."

I bought the Kinko's Casting Director Label Edition Thing—it came with four hundred labels—and got to work. By the end of the weekend I'd sent out around three hundred envelopes with Iris Burton's name on them. What I didn't know was that Chris was out of town for the week, which meant that Iris would be answering her own phone if any of these casting directors reacted to the self-promotional carpet-bombing I'd just given Hollywood. Of course, these casting directors would think that Iris had sent my headshots out, that she had some hot young heartthrob hunk of talent on her hands who was going to be the next River Phoenix. And right away Iris's phone started ringing. They'd taken the bait. Before too long she called me.

"Honey, it's Iris," she said. "You *really* need to tell me what's going on. We've been getting calls about you every fucking minute. It's Greg Sestero, Greg Sestero, *Greg Sestero*! Did you send your picture out to everyone—including the people that scrub the toilets? You're getting calls from *everyone* in town."

Oh, fuck. Oh, *fuck*.

"Listen to me, honey. Don't. Be. So. Ambitious. It's unseemly."

"I'm sorry, Iris."

"Well, the VP of casting at Disney, Warner Bros., and ABC all want a meeting. I'm telling the others, 'He's adorable! But you can't meet him unless you have work for him.' So go on and meet these ones, honey, but that's it. You've got to stop these mailings. They're driving me fucking nuts." In spite of this fiasco, Iris started getting me one audition after another, which is much more to her credit than mine.

For my first few auditions, I superstitiously wore my Iris Burton Meeting Outfit, which is to say shorts and a short-sleeve shirt. This included an audition for a submarine flick with Matthew McConaughey.

The casting director took one look at me and said, "Oh, how *cute*. He wore his *shorts*." I took this in stride, having decided to live or die by the shorts.

One day I picked up a message from Chris: "You need to call me ASAP, buddy. We need to talk. I have an audition for something called *Retro Puppet Master*, which didn't come from us. There's also something else. Call me, Greg. Please. 'Bye."

All of it sounded weirdly ominous, especially that "buddy." *Retro Puppet Master*, though, sounded exceptionally strange. Actually, it sounded like something I was capable of getting. When I came in to see Chris, the first thing he said was, "So I got an irate phone call from the casting director of *Patch Adams*."

At this I may have gulped. I instantly knew what had happened. I was in *Patch Adams*, but not in a role the L.A. casting director had filled. My role was that of a "featured extra"—and that didn't belong on any résumé. That casting director had seen *Patch Adams* on my résumé and probably thought: *I cast all the primary parts in that film. Who the hell is Greg Sestero?* I was absolutely in the wrong. "And what," I asked Chris, "did the casting director of *Patch Adams* say?"

"She said she cast the movie and you weren't in it. So, word to the wise, you might want to leave that one off your résumé from now on."

Oh, God, I thought. *Iris and Chris are dumping me. This is a dumpable offense.*

Chris must have noticed my disintegrating spirits. "Look, Greg. Forget her. Just don't—if you ever go in for her—just don't put that on your résumé."

"Okay," I said, exhaling.

"Whatever you're doing, it's working. We're getting calls—and it's a good thing I'm back this week, believe me. Iris's hair was about to catch fire. These *Puppet Master* people are going to be in touch with sides. I'll let you know." The way Chris said "*Puppet Master* people" made it perfectly clear what he thought about their particular production's value. I didn't care.

When I got home there were six messages on my answering machine, all from Tommy. The first: "Hey, yo! How's audition? Big encounter? Know what I mean? Ha, ha, ha!" The second included Tommy's lilting rendition of "Hold On to the Nights." The third was him saying, "Don't be scared. Enjoy yourself. Life is beautiful, la, la, la. By the way, this girl Jennifer call me. You don't know her. She wants something." His messages kept getting weirder and weirder. But I couldn't really complain. So many actors who've just arrived in L.A. wind up doing all sorts of unpleasant jobs to stay afloat: Brad Pitt dressed up as a chicken for El Pollo Loco, Johnny Depp worked as an over-the-phone pen salesman. Surviving Tommy's message-a-thons was obviously the price I had to pay to live in his apartment.

Finally I returned Tommy's calls. He answered, as always, "I'm listening."

"Tommy, what's up?"

"So," he said, "I'm watching your show *The Bridges*." I quickly realized he meant *Nash Bridges,* and the episode he was watching was the one in which I'd appeared. "It's just okay, you know. They do arresting with these guys, sissy guy, with the handcuff. You know what I mean?"

"Not really."

"Sexuality! You don't know this stuff? Maybe you learn in five years from today. You put on the handcuffs and crazy stuff happen. I rest my case."

I wanted and needed to steer the conversation in another direction pronto. "So . . . yeah. Um, what's up?"

Tommy was still absorbed in the show. "Oh," he said, "this guy has some issues, my God."

"Tommy!" I said.

"Okay, I get the picture. So what's the—what was the name of the school you auditioned before the Jean Shelton class?"

"A.C.T."

"You know what I'm thinking? Maybe I take some classes there. Maybe I go to this A.C.T. Why not! I try Shakespeare and the voice class. I need to lose this stupid accent."

I knew, suddenly, that Tommy was somehow feeling challenged by me. All this time he'd been living in San Francisco, doing his business, believing that taking acting classes was the best way to keep his dream alive. But now that I was in L.A. and auditioning for real projects, he realized that his dream was on the most pitiful form of life support. "Sure, Tommy," I said. "You should do that." But I was thinking that Tommy and A.C.T. would be the worst possible match. A.C.T.'s instructors were top-notch and brutally honest.

"By the way," Tommy said. "I get fat a little bit. What should I do? Don't worry, I'm not your competition."

I wanted to laugh, but he sounded serious. Almost dejected. "Get a stair stepper. Do it for forty-five minutes a day."

"Where to get stair stepper?"

"You can get one at Big Five or something."

He started talking about something else, and I knew this little chat could go on for hours if I let it. "Hey, Tommy," I said, "I think I'm gonna go grab a bite and learn my lines. I'll talk to you later, okay?"

"Wait, wait, wait." He never wanted to let me get off the phone, not even now, when nothing was being said. "Five more minutes, okay?"

I could always sense Tommy's loneliness and he was so lonely now he was practically radioactive. "Okay," I said.

"I found new restaurant in the Mission Street. Such good crepes, my God."

"Yeah. I'll try it next time I'm there. But I have to go."

"Wait, just a minute. Have you tried that mama-papa deal down the Crescent Heights? Such good potatoes."

"Tommy, I've got to learn my lines."

"You get all these auditions. Wow! I'm so proud of you. Somebody have good luck, huh? Somebody has nice apartment!"

"Yeah, we'll talk later." I hung up, went down the street, grabbed a bite, and returned home. I was gone a little over an hour, yet I had a message from Tommy waiting for me when I got back. All I heard at first was something rhythmic and repetitive happening in the background, beneath Tommy's huffing and puffing. "I'm sweating like *hell*," he said. In the time it took me to eat, he'd gone out and bought himself a stair stepper.

•　　•　　•

I'd never seen any of the *Puppet Master* films, but I felt instantly at-tracted to André Toulon, their titular character. For one thing, Toulon was European, and I'd always felt as European as I did American. For another thing, *Retro Puppet Master* was a prequel that showed Toulon as a young Parisian puppeteer before he went mad with power and became the Puppet Master. Like any good *Star Wars* nerd, I thought, *Do it like you're doing Anakin Skywalker*. An Anakin Skywalker who talks to puppets.

Less heartening was the audition script, which was four pages of me speaking to newly arisen puppets, whom Toulon has brought to life with a secret potion. In this audition I was also expected to theatrically bestow upon Toulon's puppets their names as living beings: Dr. Death, Six Shooter, Cyclops, Blade, Tunneler! It was all monologue, basically, and easily the strangest thing I'd ever gone out for. Even *less* hearten-ing, though, was that the audition called for a British accent, which I couldn't do. But I could do a French accent. The character actually *was* French, and I assumed they'd asked for a British accent because it was usually easier to find a young actor able to do one. A good French ac-cent, I felt confident, would be my ace in the hole.

The audition was at 1645 Vine Street, where Ed Wood made a few of his movies. I stood across from the casting people in the building's penthouse, a view of Capitol Records and the Hollywood sign visible behind them. I could tell they'd already seen a lot of people that day; I've since learned that James Franco was one of them. They looked bored, disheartened, and as drained as the empty Diet Coke bottles spread before them. The head casting guy decided to jab me right away. I'd sent in four separate headshots, all stapled together, all show-ing different looks, which I've since learned is a no-no. One is always enough. "I'm surprised," he said, lifting up my stapled headshots, "that you didn't send us your baby photos."

I said nothing. I had nothing. I smiled, or tried to. But I felt the wind rushing out of the room rather quickly.

Then he said, "Iris Burton. You better impress me."

This was in response to Iris's reputation. One of her famous quotes was, "I don't eat steak. I eat filet mignon." These guys were definitely hamburger men casting a hamburger movie, and moreover they all knew it.

"We were shocked when we got a submission from Iris," the one woman among them said, obviously trying to lighten the mood.

But they didn't get a submission from Iris. The culprit behind that submission was standing before them.

"So," the first, dickish guy said, "we need you to do an accent with this. A British accent. Can you do an accent?"

"Actually," I said, "I'd like to try it with a French accent."

They all looked at each other. "Okay," the dickish guy said, the disdain in his voice making it clear he wasn't expecting much. "Go for it."

They'd placed facsimiles of all the puppets on the floor, so I sat down and started playing with them, saying my lines with a French accent. I was used to playing with *Star Wars* figures, so that's what I pretended I was doing. I was five years old, I was Anakin Skywalker, I was a nice French boy who'd grow up to be evil.

When I finished, they all looked like they'd just seen the puppets come alive. They'd been trying to cast this part for weeks. They'd seen hundreds of people. "Kid," the guy who hated me five minutes ago said, "do you have a passport?"

They offered to pay me SAG scale, which was $2,500 a week. We were filming at Castel Films Studios in Bucharest, Romania. It was, as the saying goes, a dream come true: *I was flying to Bucharest, to star in a movie.* The *Puppet Master* people called Iris, because now they could call Iris, and loved the fact they were calling Iris. They were working with Iris! Or so the casting director, with whom I eventually became friends, said to me. He also told me that when they informed Iris I got the part, she said, in shock, "He can actually act?" Iris herself summoned me to her rose-covered Beverly Hills mansion.

"Kid," she said, "congratulations." (I found myself dearly anticipating the day I would no longer be "kid" to anyone.) "This is a chance. This is a good chance. Do what you can with it. I tried to get you more money. They're not going to give you more money."

"It's fine," I said. "I'm not interested in money."

She smiled. "You're not allowed to say that ever again." She reached into her desk and pulled out a thick knit hat. "It's cold as hell in Romania. You'll want to wear this. Also: Don't fuck your leading lady until the shoot is over and remember to take your vitamins." She patted me on the cheek and sent me out.

Thanksgiving was coming, and I had to get home to see my family. From San Francisco, I'd be flying to Bucharest. When Tommy found out I was coming back to town, he told me he wanted to meet up. I hadn't seen him in almost four months; I hadn't told him anything about my film. We met at Virgin Records in San Francisco, per his request. I was excited about the film and wanted to share the good news with him. On top of that, I felt immensely grateful to Tommy, without whom none of this would have happened. Had I never met Tommy, I probably would have still been stuck living with my parents. For some reason, when I was heading out to meet him, I grabbed my football.

I think I may have winced when I saw Tommy. He looked dejected, gunned down, burned out, insomnia-plagued. He looked so much worse than the last time I'd seen him—which was saying something. His hair was crusty and his eyes were droopy and his skin looked pasty and thin. He was wearing sweatpants and flip-flops and an old white T-shirt that looked like it had been washed within an inch of its life. He gave me an awkwardly complicated bro-fist greeting, but he wouldn't look at me directly. Every glance was furtive, shot from the corner of his eye. Otherwise he stared at the ground.

I suggested we go to Golden Gate Park to play football. Tommy admitted that he'd never played catch, let alone thrown a football, before. He claimed to like football, though, much better than soccer. As he shot-putted the ball toward me, his inexperience showed. I asked him how he managed to spend all these years in San Francisco, home of the five-time Super Bowl champion 49ers, and not once throw a football. "Tommy," I said, "Joe Montana would be disappointed in you."

To this Tommy replied, "The Joe Montana is prick." Tommy had no idea who Joe Montana was. It was like he lived in Galilee and had never heard of Jesus.

After playing for a while, Tommy announced that we had to go fix his cell phone. We were driving to the cell phone place when I finally told him about the movie. "Oh my God," he said, and pulled the car over. "I need candy!" He lunged for a See's box in his backseat and started to tear into it.

I watched him gobble the first couple of chocolates as though they were sedatives. He calmed down, eventually, and I think he actually managed to convince himself that he *was* happy for me. "We go celebrate," he said, turning the car around and leaving his broken cell phone for another, less exultant day. "We go see feature movie."

As we sat through *Meet Joe Black,* I could feel pain and confusion radiating from Tommy in the darkness of the theater. Maybe he felt he was losing me to something. Worse, he was losing me to something he wanted to lose himself in. Tommy was wondering why nothing had happened for him—and why it was happening for me. He didn't want me to outgrow him. He wanted to feel like he was still needed. I didn't know what to say or how to comfort him. After the movie, he dropped me off at Virgin Records and we said good-bye quickly.

A few days later I flew to Bucharest. We finished production on Christmas Eve, and I went back to my hotel. I remember sitting there, on the edge of my bed, taking in the moment and welcoming the tears filling up my eyes. I replayed the last few months, the last few years. Tomorrow it would be Christmas, and I was going to be alone. That was okay, because I felt like I had been given such an amazing gift.

I fell asleep, only to be woken up by someone forcefully knocking on my door and a Romanian voice saying, "Telegram!" A telegram? I opened it:

> *Merry Christmas. You are a special person.*
> *May all your dreams come true.*
> *TW*

I still don't know how Tommy found me.

nine

"You Are Tearing Me Apart, Lisa!"

The whole place seemed to have been stricken with a
kind of creeping paralysis—out of beat with the rest of the world,
crumbling apart in slow motion.
—Joe Gillis, *Sunset Boulevard*

On the day we were set to shoot the scene in which Johnny and Lisa have a wrenching heart-to-heart about their relationship's long-term feasibility—a scene famous for the line "You are tearing me apart, Lisa!"—Tommy was watching Safowa do a wardrobe check on the other actors who'd be filming that day: Robyn Paris, who played Michelle, and Juliette Danielle, who played Lisa. As usual, Tommy was micromanaging the situation while skillfully failing to manage much of anything.

Safowa had decided to dress Lisa in a sleeveless, backless, charmless, powerfully unfortunate red blouse. This blouse did Juliette's body no favors. On top of that, the camera, as they say, adds ten pounds—which became more like twenty pounds when illuminated by *The Room*'s unflattering lighting. When working with a character like Lisa, it's the job of the costume designer and the director to come up with clothing that makes the actor look *better* than she does in everyday life. In this respect, no one was failed by *The Room* more terribly than Juliette, who was shot and costumed and directed in such a way as to make her a magnitude less attractive, likable, and charming than she was and is. The first time I met Juliette, I thought, *This is an incredibly sweet person who's going through a tough, tough time.* It was an accurate impression.

She'd recently moved to Los Angeles from Texas and was essentially supporting her entire family; she had put her regular day job on hold to do *The Room*. Juliette believed that *The Room*—for which she was paid a pittance—was her one shot at making some real money down the line.

The best thing about Juliette was her on-set attitude, which was unfailingly kind and enthusiastic. A lot of times, after shooting, Juliette would go to a nearby karaoke bar and sing with anyone who wanted to join her. The guys on the crew loved Juliette.

Once Safowa got this awful blouse onto Juliette, Tommy began circling her. He stopped, though, when he came to Juliette's back. There's no other way to say this: Juliette had a few pimples concentrated on one small part of her upper back, which the blouse unforgivingly exposed. Now, there were several ways for Tommy to have handled this. He could have called the makeup person over and asked her, quietly, to make sure Juliette's blemishes got covered up before filming. He could have had Safowa put her into a different outfit. What he did was to say, loudly enough for everyone to hear, "Excuse me, I'm sorry. We can't have *this* on the camera." He waved the makeup artist over. "You see all this stuff here? Take this shit out. We can't have this." Juliette knew exactly what Tommy was talking about and started to cry quietly, while the makeup artist sprang into action. "This is American movie," Tommy said, over Juliette's desperate sniffling. "It needs to be sexy. She needs to be beautiful." With that, Tommy went off to do his seagull thing elsewhere on set—making a lot of irritating noise while simultaneously shitting on everyone.

Juliette was slow to recover from Tommy's cruel treatment. "I'm okay," she said, shaking her head, wiping her tears, her voice brittle and angry. "It's okay. I'm *fine*." It was obvious she was already at her breaking point. She'd definitely been feeling uneasy around Tommy. Everyone had been. But Tommy treated Juliette more like a daughter than a colleague, and this made their relationship especially uncomfortable given their roles in the film. If, for instance, Tommy caught the scent of cigarettes on Juliette's breath, he'd say, "Do not smoke the cigarettes!" If she giggled before a take, he'd tell her to knock off "that squeaky stuff" and grow up. At times it really did feel like the most dysfunctional incestuous relationship this side of *Jerry Springer*.

Tommy's fears about age are embodied in *The Room*'s characters: Why would Johnny, an obviously middle-aged man, have a twenty-one-year-old future wife, a twenty-four-year-old best friend, and a bunch of other friends only a few years out of college? With the exception of Lisa's mother, no one in the cast is close to Tommy's age. According to Tommy's script, Lisa is between twenty-one and twenty-five and has been with Johnny for either five or seven years. How old, then, was Lisa when she and Johnny got together? A writer less fixated on youth as the ideal state of human existence might have considered that question.

I've often been asked why Tommy cast Juliette as Lisa, a character intended to be so heart-slayingly seductive that virtually every male character in the movie loses his mind over her. Maybe no character in the history of film is called "beautiful" more often than Lisa is. From the very beginning of *The Room*'s conceptualization, Tommy said he wanted Lisa to be "the biggest thing" in the movie—other than him, of course. "She has to be absolutely beautiful," he'd say over and over. "Young. Super-duper sexy. I want her to be as beautiful as Angelika Jolie." Paging through the Victoria's Secret catalog, he'd say, after every page, "That's the perfect Lisa!" The kind of sexiness Tommy wanted Lisa to exhibit is something that's *existential,* and Juliette was too young, too insecure, and too inexperienced to inhabit such a persona.

So Juliette was put into a terrible, unfair situation, and all things considered, I think she handled it well. She's not given nearly enough credit for that. Juliette was set up to fail, and most people in her position would have quit. But Juliette never quit. When Tommy threw a water bottle at the original Michelle, the whole cast walked out. Juliette, though, was disconsolate; she wept. She cared about the movie more than anyone. In the end, Juliette was cast as Lisa because she was the only actress capable of surviving the meat-grinding torture of Tommy's casting process. For Juliette, serial humiliation became just another obstacle to smash through.

When I came aboard the USS *Room,* Juliette had already been cast—

as Michelle, not as Lisa. The original actress Tommy had settled upon for Lisa was not ideal. Her teeth were discolored from what I assumed had been years of heavy smoking, and she was Latina, with a heavy accent, thus not quite fitting Tommy's vision of an all-American girl. She wasn't unattractive, but viewed through the cruel lens of movie-star expectation, she was even less Jolie-like than Juliette. This woman had signed a preliminary contract, though no payment had been discussed. Eventually, after weeks of auditioning and long, unpaid rehearsals, ur-Lisa wanted to know when she'd start filming. One day she showed up at Birns & Sawyer and demanded some money and a firmer contractual commitment, which somehow offended Tommy.

After Tommy brushed off the ur-Lisa, there was a knock at the door. In walked Juliette, who looked at Tommy and me and said, very coolly, "I'd like to start auditioning for Lisa." This was actually a very Lisa-like move for Juliette to pull. As soon as she left, Tommy looked at me with a grin. "Can you imagine? She's very manipulative. Her competition is vicious!"

Later that day, Tommy sent the ur-Lisa a fax with a world-record number of misspellings, terminating her contract.

This didn't mean that Juliette had an automatic in. Tommy began yet another round of casting calls for Lisa. Some very attractive young women wound up coming in to audition. The first one to show up, Alexis, actually *did* look like a young Angelina Jolie. Her audition went well. After it was done she asked me, "So who's playing Johnny? Has he been cast yet?" I knew if I told her, she'd walk, instantly. But she seemed talented, and cool enough that I didn't want to waste her time. So I pointed over at Tommy and said, "He's playing Johnny."

Alexis looked at Tommy with narrowed, suspicious eyes, as though running through her mind a number of scenarios involving fame and what she was willing to do to have it. "Oh," she said. "Oh!" Then she turned back to me. "Yeah, so I don't think I'm going to be able to work this into my schedule. It was really nice meeting you, though."

The next few auditions were just as rough. It didn't help that Tommy had placed a bed in the audition room—the same bed he later used in Johnny and Lisa's apartment. Almost every woman who came in needed to be reassured that *The Room*, whatever it was, wasn't a porno.

Meanwhile, Tommy's idea of directing an actress during auditions was to push her in front of a camera and emotionally terrorize her. "Your sister just became lesbian!" he'd say, and wait for the "acting" to kick in. If that didn't work, he'd yell: "Your mother just die!" Every actress with confidence or a strong sense of self bailed. The few able to withstand Tommy's attitude fled at the first mention that they'd have to lock lips with him.

Juliette, though, was willing to kiss Tommy, even though you're barely supposed to kiss in rehearsals. With no contract signed and no camera running, she and Tommy would stand there in rehearsal and make out. For minutes. Whenever I told Tommy, "You don't need to go that far," he'd say, "I need to see if they can perform. If they can't perform, I'm sorry, they have to leave. Out. And don't be jealous, young man." (After *The Room* was released, my mother commented that to pay $6 million to make out with a girl was "pretty pathetic.")

Once Tommy cast Juliette as Lisa, we had to find someone for *The Room*'s other important young woman character: Michelle. After Tommy sacked Brianna, the original Michelle, the production staggered on for some weeks before Tommy realized he needed to think about recasting her. "I need a young, beautiful girl," Tommy urged. "Not some old prune." Well past the point at which finding another Michelle had become an emergency, I yanked a bunch of headshots out of a pile on the floor of Tommy's apartment and started making calls. A few hours later, at 10:00 p.m., Tommy was surveying a lineup of eighteen non-prunes in the Birns & Sawyer parking lot. There was no time to book an audition room, so they all had to perform to the camera in front of one another in the parking lot. In terms of filmmaking, this was the very definition of amateur hour, and they all knew it. It was so bad that I apologized to every actress the moment she finished her audition. My apologies weren't good enough for some actresses near the back of the dwindling casting line. When Tommy had unkind things to say about one actress's audition, the last three women in line looked at one another in disgust and walked off the lot. This left us with four actresses, the first three of whom couldn't survive Tommy telling them their sisters had just become lesbians. The last woman up, Robyn Paris, was a newly married graduate of Duke University who'd been doing commercial work in Los Angeles. The first thing I noticed about her was her unbelievably genuine smile. She didn't ask any questions before doing her scene; she just walked up to the camera and did it. She was easily the best person we saw—and she didn't even have to be told that her mother was dead.

"Wow!" Tommy said. "Beautiful! Very nice. So we may give you part."

Robyn's amazing smile got even bigger, but I could tell she was thrown. This wasn't how directors talked to actors during auditions. For all sorts of practical and emotional reasons, most directors remain very Sphinxy and poker-faced with actors during auditions. "Okay," she said.

"We will let you know. We need you to perform the kissing stuff. Are you giving? Can you make it here tomorrow?"

"Sure," Robyn said, still smiling, but far more cautiously now. I don't think she fully understood him.

"Then maybe we see you tomorrow."

Talking to an auditioning actor in this way, promising and unpromising, givething and takething away, is basically a form of abuse. But Robyn left in what seemed to be good spirits. The second she was off the set, Tommy told me to hire her. I gave it a half hour, called her, and told her when to show up the next day.

The crew was knocked out by Robyn. Sandy compared her to Julia Roberts, which wasn't an insane comparison to make. Both had smiles that hit you like sunlight off a mirror, and Robyn actually knew which end was up on a movie set. Having ascertained from her audition experience that *The Room*'s wardrobe budget would be limited, she brought in her own clothes. She'd also done her own makeup. Within twenty minutes of arriving on set, she was rehearsing, learning the crew people's names, and generally charming everyone in sight.

As the production went on, Robyn would come to me and ask, politely, why she wasn't being paid according to how much time she was spending on set. I tried to explain, equally politely, that *The Room* was on something called Tommy Time. Jokes like that only made Robyn more skeptical. "If I'm here for six hours," she'd say, "is it a six-hour rate or does it qualify as overtime?" I had no good answer to such reasonable questions and couldn't press Tommy to provide one. Eventually, like everyone, Robyn gave in. It was a job; she was getting tape and experience.

For all of Tommy's issues with women, it should be said that he does try throughout *The Room* to provide his female characters with emotions and activities he regards as realistic. Unfortunately, these womanly emotions and activities usually involve sitting around, shopping, drinking wine, gossiping, getting banged, or some combination thereof. Tommy's female characters have no inner dimension at all; they're idealized, but halfheartedly. From Tommy's artistic perspective, a woman is someone who's supposed to be on the couch when a man gets home, someone who's supposed to know to order her man a pizza when he has a bad day, someone who's been trained to regard a dozen roses as a gift of universe-exploding significance.

The scene immediately preceding Johnny and Lisa's heart-to-heart was filmed the day after Robyn had been hired and the day of Juliette's back acne catastrophe. All of Tommy's ideas about women are at play: the women have apparently just returned home from shopping ("Did you get a new dress?" Johnny asks when he enters the scene), they're being manipulative (Lisa tells Michelle that Johnny hits her but—good news!—she's also "found somebody else"), and they're guzzling merlot. Tommy was watching Sandy instruct Robyn and Juliette on the living room set. I could tell that Sandy was having a good time. He was calling Juliette "Jules" and flirting shamelessly with Robyn. (I noticed that whenever Robyn was around, Sandy would begin talking about things like "the monstrous project I just did at Universal.") For a few moments it felt like an actual film scene was coming together.

It wasn't. The scene Robyn and Juliette wound up shooting is riddled with continuity errors. Throughout the scene, for instance, Lisa puts her wineglass down in one shot but is still holding it in another.

Even worse is the alarming thing that starts happening to Juliette's neck when she becomes animated toward the end of the scene: the cords in her neck begin popping out against her skin as though the alien from *Alien* were trying to fight its way out of her jugular. Her unfortunate blouse didn't help, putting her throat machinery on full display. I suspect this neck poppage was a result of the contorted way she was forced to sit; I leave any more granular explanation to an anatomist.

Other than Lisa's awful red blouse and apparently exploding neck and the dozen or so continuity errors, Robyn and Juliette's scene came off without a hitch. Now it was Tommy's turn to enter the scene. Because I was one of the only people involved in the production who'd seen the entire *Room* script, I knew this scene—in which Johnny melts down in front of Lisa—had at least one incandescent mistake in it. This mistake concerned Johnny's biggest line in the film: "You are tearing me apart, Lisa!" That's not what the original script said, though. The line in the original script read: "You are *taking* me apart, Lisa!" Tommy stole—or, rather, tried and failed to steal—the "tearing me apart" line from *Rebel Without a Cause,* spoken by James Dean's character, Jim Stark, who is drunk and lashing out at his parents. Naturally, Tommy loved this scene. The power and sheer balls-out emotional savagery of it. It's a moment where viewers don't really know whether they're watching a movie or an entire generation coalesce. Occasionally I wonder if *The Room* was not conceived and written just so Tommy could have this elemental, unbridled moment of performance. Which makes it even weirder that Tommy *still* managed to fuck up the line in his script. No one involved in *The Room* had caught this gaffe, because no one but I had any idea how much James Dean meant to Tommy. (Meanwhile Tommy's version of the line has a hundred times more hits on YouTube than James Dean's version, which quite frankly makes me feel like *I'm* being torn apart.)

In the scene's opening, Johnny sits on a chair across from Lisa. The first thing Sandy noticed when Tommy sat down was that a table in the background was distractingly empty. "We can't just shoot a blank table," Sandy said. It wasn't the first time it had come up that Johnny and Lisa's condo had all the charm of my room at the Saharan Motel.

(How did Tommy come to furnish his film's imaginary condo? By walking into a thrift furniture store in L.A. and purchasing the entire mock-up apartment in its display windows. This means that Johnny and Lisa's condo was modeled on a space purposefully designed to be uninhabited.) Early in the production Sandy offered Tommy the use of his own house to film the interiors, so as to avoid moments like these; he even brought in pictures for Tommy to consider. "Look," Sandy said. "It would be so much easier. We don't have to have all these props, or all these people around. Everything could be done much more quickly. We'd be in and out in a couple of days." Tommy refused, later telling me, "If Sandy takes over, he has control. I know what he does. He wants more money. Plus, I'm sorry, his house is Mickey Mouse."

Sandy was still staring at the blank table behind Tommy and Juliette. "Where," he wanted to know, "is the art department?" The art department, which was comprised of Merce and a revolving door of stagehands, volunteered that the budget didn't really allow for comprehensive, realistic decoration, and moreover, no one had told her to fill the tables with knickknackery. Tommy took command of the situation and sent the art department down Highland Avenue to a framing shop. A little later they returned with sample frames, all glorified with stock photos of spoons. Tommy, over Sandy's and the art department's objections, told them to use the framed spoons, for the simple reason that he wanted to get on with filming. I don't think the most gifted prognosticator could have predicted the fateful impact of this impatience-born split-second decision, much less the volleys of plastic spoons that *Room* audience members would later throw whenever these sad little stock-photo spoons appear on-screen. To the photographer tasked with the tedious job of snapping those spoon pictures, take heart: Your work has not been wasted.

Now that the framed spoons were in place, Tommy got back to the demanding if familiar task of not remembering any of his lines. Shooting the first part of Johnny and Lisa's conversation took longer than it should have, but given that it wasn't a huge Acting Moment for Tommy, he was able to relax and, with effort, eventually grind out his lines. When Tommy was faced with the pressure of nailing the argumentative, *taking*-me-apart moment of Johnny and Lisa's conversation, however, he came unglued. Johnny's declaration of "I cannot go on without you" was where the problems began. Tommy would move as far into the dialogue as "I cannot go on" and get confused and call out, "Line!"

Sandy would then dutifully feed him the rest: "Without you."

"I cannot go . . . Line!"

"On. Without you."

"I cannot . . . Line!"

"Tommy, for God's sake. 'I cannot go on without you.'"

"Okay. Thank you."

"Action!"

"I cannot go on . . . Line!"

The crew's mutinous mockery of Tommy began. Raphael, our director of photography, had by now retreated to the special tent he'd set up at the edge of the set. This allowed him to pretend to watch Tommy's performance on the monitor while he giggled so hard the tent sometimes shook.

"Line!" "Line!" "Line!" Over and over again. It became hard to accept. Unlike the scene in which Tommy emerged from the outhouse, he *wasn't doing anything* in this scene. It wasn't like he had to walk and talk at the same time; he was just standing there, looking at Juliette. Tommy eventually made it to the line "You're lying! I never hit you!" which wound up sounding like "You're a lion! I never heat you!"; this despite Sandy's repeated requests for a better, cleaner take. Not that it mattered. Virtually none of Tommy's captured audio performance was usable, given the sound crew's inexperience and the fact that they had to keep stopping and starting during Tommy's takes to load more film.

I was reclining nearby on the floor, next to Amy, the makeup artist. Tommy came over and squatted next to us. "I don't need you to talk to her," he said, as though Amy didn't exist. "I need you to watch the screen and help me."

"I can help you from here."

"No, you can't. Come with me to monitor."

We went over to Raphael's Giggle Tent. Sandy was there with him.

"How this come out?" Tommy asked Raphael.

"Great," he said.

I followed with "Perfect. Keep going." What else, at this point, could anyone tell him?

"Oh, you just say that," Tommy said, and left me, Raphael, and Sandy alone in the Giggle Tent.

"Where is he from, anyway?" Raphael asked me. "Where does he say he's from?"

"New Orleans," I said.

Close-up time. Time, in other words, for Tommy to say "You're *taking* me apart, Lisa!" with the camera right in his face. When Tommy made his first go at the shot, a few people on set recognized the attempted reference to *Rebel*, but no one had the heart to tell him he was mangling the line. "My arm's gone!" crew people started calling out. "Stop taking me apart!" Tommy became agitated and angry in the manner of someone with an itch he'd lost all hope of scratching. I'd mentioned to Safowa that Tommy had gotten the line wrong. She took me aside and said, "You should really tell him, Greg. Really. You should."

She was right. So I took Tommy aside, looked at him squarely, and told him he had the line wrong. It was *tearing* and not *taking*.

"Oh," Tommy said. I was surprised by how calmly he absorbed this news. It turned out that was just camouflage, because the first thing Tommy did was turn around and yell at the slate person for picking up his jacket off the floor. He followed that up by telling the camerapeople what a terrible job they were doing. "I see your camerawork," Tommy scoffed, "and you need to do a better job." One of the cameramen's assistants, who was charged with doing the lens, spent the rest of his tenure on *The Room* saying, "Just trying to do a better job!" whenever Tommy gave anyone camera-related direction.

Tommy returned to the heady task of saying "You are *tearing* me apart, Lisa!" He was still having trouble. Sandy had given up hope and Juliette was laughing in Tommy's face. Tommy was so consumed with getting the line right that he didn't seem to notice. "Keep rolling, dammit!" he told the cameraman, take after blown take. Then, suddenly,

Tommy got it, he said it, his arms thrusting up like terrible mallets: "You are *tearing* me apart, Lisa!"

Sandy, who was sitting on an apple crate, had not been expecting this. "Cut!" he said, springing up. *"Cut!"*

Tommy was veiny with exertion. He stood there, breathing, pointlessly triumphant. For a moment, it looked like his head might actually explode.

James Dean wept.

ten

Do You Have the Guts to Take Me?

Well, whatever you do, however terrible and however hurtful,
it all makes sense, doesn't it? In your head.
—Tom Ripley, *The Talented Mr. Ripley*

Upon my return from Romania to L.A., I discovered that someone had spent considerable time in my apartment while I was gone. All the cupboards in the kitchen were open. Dirty dishes were piled in the sink. Someone had dragged in a small rollout bed and left it in the living room. There were numerous long black hairs in the tub. Most troubling, an envelope containing my check for *Retro Puppet Master* was sitting on my desk; it had been opened.

I'd spoken with Tommy briefly a few weeks ago, from France, where I'd met up with an old girlfriend after *Retro* wrapped. During that conversation he hadn't mentioned anything about being in Los Angeles, much less being in the apartment. (He did, however, ask me if I was "doing sex" with the girl I was seeing.)

After I came to grips with the fact that Tommy had been here and opened my mail, I discovered another strange thing: Nowhere in my monthly Bank of America statements was there any indication that Tommy had been cashing my $200 rent checks, which I'd been sending him for months. I got him on the phone immediately.

"I'm listening!"

"Tommy," I said, "did you come to L.A. while I was gone?"

"I have meeting there. And I don't want to upset you but . . . you are messy person. You have no plants, no nothing. No life."

Messy? I hadn't moved anything into or changed anything about Tommy's place, having no idea how long I'd be living there. "Did you," I asked him, "open my mail?"

"On accident. I open your check on accident."

"On accident?"

"I'm sorry. My God, you're so sensitive!" I could tell this seemed fun to him. "Check is big secret, I guess! By the way, welcome home to the USA to you."

This was the first time I hung up on Tommy. I understand that he was curious to learn how much I got paid for *Retro Puppet Master*—he was probably also dying to know who my agent was—but *opening my mail?* And then not even trying to hide the fact that he had? That was worrisome. And why on earth was he even in L.A.? I was quite certain by now that any "meetings" he had were imaginary.

I could spend all day puzzling over Tommy's machinations, but I had better things to do, such as call Iris and Chris and figure out what was next. When I called Iris she told me she'd seen *Patch Adams* and that I had, in fact, made the final cut. "Maybe," she said, "you'll get nominated for best supporting actor." After that little zinger, she said something much more helpful: "Get ready. I'm going to open doors for you. It's up to you to do something with it."

True to her word, Iris began getting me meatier auditions. Working in Romania had given me a taste of what it was like to make a movie; I hoped it would be the start of something more. With that expectation came a lot of scary internal pressure. I was shocked to realize how much more pleasant it was to feel like an underdog.

My first month back in L.A. was January: pilot season, often the busiest time for young actors. As the auditions piled up, I recognized how easy I'd had it until now. Even if you're lucky enough to land a great agent, as I had, getting called in was hard, getting called back was *really* hard, and getting cast was even harder than that. Then came the hardest part of all: being in something that people actually *saw*. I tried not to get discouraged. Some days I felt certain I was close to breaking through; other days I felt like I was one of literally millions of people throwing themselves up against the same cold, indifferent wall.

In the middle of all this, Tommy was leaving me at least two messages a day. His messages had always been pretty out there, but now they became somehow *aggressively* out there: "Hey, yo. I just saw this movie *The Firm*. You run exactly like the Tom Cruise, for your information." Or: "'Hey, lady! Shut up!' What movie is this from? I challenge you." Or: "I eat oranges in bed now. Feels so good. You should try it sometime with your French girl. Call me!"

My message machine was so ancient that it didn't allow me to skip ahead through the Tommy-a-thons. I had to endure all his weird messages before finding out if I'd gotten any responses to my auditions. It was driving me crazy.

I was happy to learn that the *Retro Puppet Master* production team had cut together a ninety-second reel of some of my scenes from the film, which I could use as a demo; they'd even gone so far as to score the demo to classical music. It was much more elaborate than I'd expected and they gave me many more copies than I needed. I was extremely grateful. Because the footage had a period feel, however, Iris and I edited it to conclude with some of my headshots to show different looks. She didn't want me to be typecast as a period-piece puffy-shirt guy with a French accent.

Tommy's messages became more insistent: "It's urgent, Greg. *Urgent*. Call me." I knew perfectly well it wasn't urgent. But I was living in Tommy's apartment and felt I owed him a call.

"Hey, yo," he said. "Since you are now the expert, how do you become member of the SAAAG?"

This was his urgent business? "You mean SAG?"

"Yeah! You know: S-A-G?"

I'd always found it amusing when Tommy tried to be condescending, but right now I wasn't in the mood. "I know SAG, Tommy."

"Yeah, I know your IQ is 190. So, come on, expert, tell me how do you get the SAG card?"

I sighed. "You need to have either three vouchers as an extra, a certain amount of hours, or be a principal in a commercial."

"Principal commercial? Why don't you help me? Be specific!"

"Tommy, it's pretty clear. I just *said* it. You need to be a principal in a commercial—like a speaking role or something."

I could tell he was writing all this down and felt my heart crack a little. When he was done writing, Tommy said, "Okay, then. Thank you. So how is big star? How is the *Puppet Master* coming?"

"It's cool. I did some voice-over stuff for postproduction today. And they cut a little reel for me."

"Reel?" Tommy said. "Like the demo reel?"

"Yeah."

"I want to see right away," he said excitedly. "Mail to me, I pay for it."

Tommy seemed more psyched about my demo reel than I was. So I sent him a copy.

A few days later he called again to say, "I'm watching your reel now. I watch it twelve times so far."

I was, I admit, somewhat concerned for him. I was equally concerned for *me*. I tried to laugh this excessiveness off. "Tommy, it's a padded beginner's reel."

"No, no. Don't put yourself down. It's very good. I love beginning part, with all the candles. Very powerful!"

There was a scene in *Retro* where I walk up a flight of stairs lined with white candles. It was far and away the cheesiest moment in the reel. That Tommy was so affected by it made me even more worried about its inclusion. Tommy had some criticisms, though: "Why you tilting on the staircase? Why you have this stupid French accent? That doesn't sell in America, you know. Forget this stupid French. Also your hair is donut again. But overall you did excellent job. The pictures at the end are great. Who take your pictures? Which photographer? Or is it big secret?"

As I was hanging up, I heard, on Tommy's end of the line, the sound of the music used at the beginning of my reel start up again. I had a worrying mental picture of Tommy sitting up all night watching it.

A few weeks later Tommy surprised me with an announcement that he was coming to L.A. the next day for yet another "important meeting." He also said he had something big to show me. I had no idea what to expect. When he arrived, I was having a phone meeting with Michael Landon Jr. We were talking about the possibility of my playing him in an ABC movie based on his life. I'd already been in once to read for the part and had a good feeling after hearing Michael's comments. Our phone meeting was also going well. Then Tommy arrived.

He stood mugging in the doorway while I tried to conduct my phone business. When I didn't pay any attention to his grand arrival, Tommy started to preen and say, "Somebody is cranky today!" He ignored my shoo-away hand signals and went on to say, loudly, that, while parking, he bashed into the car in front of him and he didn't know what to do. I could tell that Michael Landon Jr. was wondering who the lunatic was talking in the background on my end of the line. I quickly hand-signaled *silence* to Tommy and went into the bedroom and closed the door.

When I opened the door, Tommy was beside himself with giddiness. "Look at me," he said, gesturing down at his baggy waterbed-salesman suit. "I feel like businessman big shark today."

"How was your meeting?" I asked him, concentrating on not being agitated.

Tommy held up a binder of papers. "I have exciting news," he said, handing them over to me. "I have joined the SAG!"

I looked at these papers and concluded that, indeed, Tommy was now a dues-paid SAG member. "Congratulations," I said, stunned.

Tommy began striking a conquering-hero pose. "You know what? I say, 'If this guy can do it, I do it, too.' You challenge me. Remember, I'm not your competition. Don't be jealous."

I knew how important this was to Tommy. For him getting into SAG was as significant as landing a part in a Clint Eastwood film. It meant he was respectable and no longer spinning his wheels. I didn't have the heart to tell him that, in the grand scheme of things, becoming a member of SAG was the easy part, so instead I said, "How'd you do it, anyway?"

"I wasn't going to show you," Tommy said, walking over to the television, "but why not?" He had with him a VHS tape, which he pushed into his ancient VCR. I had to wipe the dust from the television screen just to see the picture.

The tape began and there was Tommy, in colorful quasi-Shakespearean garb, standing on a staircase and holding a candelabra filled with lit candles while classical music played in the background. His opening line: "To be or not to be, that is the question." It was a commercial for Street Fashions that he'd written, filmed, and produced himself. Almost every visual and thematic aspect of this commercial had been swiped from my demo reel. I was speechless. Tommy had bought himself SAG membership!

The commercial was hilarious in all sorts of ways, beginning with his citation of "To be or not to be," which Tommy regarded as one of Shakespeare's insta-profundities, not realizing that the line is about whether or not to commit suicide. *Kill yourself or not at Street Fashions!*

When it ended I wondered if Tommy's commercial had sent the SAG people deep into their application's fine-print jungle, searching for something, *anything,* to prevent this Shakespearean denim peddler from joining their ranks. Then Tommy rewound the tape and played it again.

When the commercial ended for the second time, I cast about for the right words. But I didn't have to worry: Tommy rewound the thing and played it again. When it was over, he looked at me, smiling, wanting to know what I thought.

While I knew what I *thought*, I still had no idea what to *say*. I had to give him credit for one thing, though: He did exactly as I'd suggested. He'd earned his SAG membership. "That was really . . . well done," I said. "Great job."

Then we watched it again!

"So," Tommy said, after the fourth play-through. "Do you like candles?"

"Yeah," I said. "Very creative."

"But is it great? How is my voice? What age do you think? Be specific. How it compare to yours?" He said all this so innocently. Did Tommy even know what he was doing?

"It's great," I said, my voice soft and cold. I had to get out of that apartment. I was worried we'd have to watch his commercial twelve more times. I suggested we get away from the VCR and go somewhere, anywhere else. Tommy, after changing clothes, suggested we celebrate his SAG triumph by heading up to the Observatory at Griffith Park. He'd always wanted to see the place where the knife fight from *Rebel Without a Cause* was filmed.

I got lost on the way to the Observatory. "Babyface," Tommy said, shaking his head, "never change." Part of the reason I got lost was that I was constantly checking my cell phone to see if my agent had called with any good news, which Tommy noticed. "Greg," he said. "These people don't care about you. All these advisors you have. They will not do shit for you. You give them too much credit." Then Tommy said: "So who is your agent anyhow? Do they need new people?"

"I don't know," I said. "I doubt they'd do shit for you, either."

Tommy laughed, and I laughed, and at that moment it actually felt fun hanging out with him again.

Once we reached the Observatory, Tommy went to work in staging a Tommy-and-Greg reenactment of *Rebel*'s knife fight in the exact place where it had been shot in 1955. He even found a guy to take our picture. After one snap the guy tried to give Tommy his camera back, but Tommy wanted more pictures. "I need more. Now, tell me: Does it look like real fight?" He started giving the poor man all this complicated *direction*.

Tommy finally let his conscripted cameraman get back to his hike. We stood there at the base of the Observatory, looking out over the microchip grids of Greater Los Angeles. "You know what?" Tommy said. "Maybe I move to Los Angeles."

These were the words I'd been fearing the most. Was that his hint that I needed to move out? Had my start in Los Angeles roused Tommy's competitive side? Had Tommy allowed me to stay in his L.A. apartment in the hope I could pave the way to his becoming an actor? Was I just his L.A. crash-test dummy? A.C.T., SAG, his demo reel: I was starting to see a clear pattern.

If he moved to L.A., I had to move out. I obviously couldn't live with Tommy, but my savings weren't enough to pay for a decent apartment on my own. I'd have to get more than a part-time job. But being an unemployed actor *was* a job—a full-time job at that.

Tommy didn't mention moving to L.A. again, and later that day he went back to San Francisco.

I didn't end up playing Michael Landon Jr. The casting director in charge of the Landon movie did, however, bring me back in to read for something called *Lord of the Rings,* where I learned I was too tall to play something called a Hobbit. (Needless to say, I wasn't a big fantasy fiction reader as a kid.)

I made the mistake of writing down the number of auditions I'd been on since returning from Romania. Fifty. Of those fifty auditions, I got called back in for around twelve or thirteen; I was told this was a pretty good percentage. In other words, I was doing great at being an unemployed actor. I was desperately trying not to look desperate when I went in to read, which didn't help when most of the parts I was reading for were *Dawson's Creek* rip-offs, which I was wrong for. Iris and Chris were telling me to hang in there, that she was getting a good response, but she didn't seem to be returning my calls as quickly as she used to. Pilot season was about results—and callbacks weren't results. "I want to hear about the collisions," Iris would say, "and not the near misses."

To improve my odds, I signed on with a manager whom some of Iris's clients, including one of her biggest, worked with. Getting a manager doesn't mean losing an agent. A manager takes a more hands-on approach. A manager coaches you, gives you stern career advice, and sometimes even drives you to auditions, especially if you're a young actor with a crappy car. From what I'd heard, my new manager was renowned for being a terrific audition coach. Thus I was a little disappointed when her initial advice amounted to some superstitious gunk about arranging my desk in a certain way while learning my lines. To her credit, though, she almost immediately got me an audition for *Scream 3,* a part in a workshop version of *Hamlet* at the NoHo Arts Center, and a screen test for a sports movie in Palo Alto.

Over the next few months, Tommy was always updating me on his activities, which sounded to me like he was preparing a full-on actor's assault of Los Angeles. He was taking voice classes at A.C.T., doing a scene-study thing with Jean Shelton, learning Shakespeare at some place I'd never heard of, and getting headshots taken by at least four different photographers. Whenever we talked now he'd say he had to go; he wanted to keep his line open in case anyone called about his "available" acting services. He'd say this, mind you, when *he* called *me*.

One day I found in my mail a huge dump of Tommy headshots—at least fifty different versions. They were all professionally done, obviously expensive, and rather scary. He must have dropped thousands of dollars on these headshots. Soon enough he called, wanting my opinion. My own grim prospects had begun to erode my spirit, and I found myself saying things to him on the phone I wasn't sure I even believed. "Acting's not just about taking classes," I said. "It's about luck, first and foremost. Then it's about marketing yourself, fitting the parts, and having contacts. It's just a business."

Tommy resisted all this. "I don't want to hear about the luck! What about my headshots?"

I held one up and looked at it. In the shot, Tommy was unsmiling, duck lipped, and wearing an unbuttoned shirt. His hair was pinned in back, making him look like an old woman with no makeup and a bad dye job. "Okay. I'm looking at one right now. Can I be honest?"

"Of course! I want you to be honest."

"You're showing a . . . repellent side of yourself in these photos. This isn't the Tommy I know. You look scary when you're trying to look all suave or something." I picked up another one that resembled Dracula doing a fashion shoot for Jean Paul Gaultier's less talented cousin. The only casting directors who'd be willing to call Tommy in on the basis of this headshot were the ones curious about what it was like to be murdered. I asked Tommy, "Have you ever thought of smiling in any of these photos?"

"Are you kidding me? I need to be dramatic!"

"Tommy, you have a really funny, likable quality. You hide it pretty well sometimes but you're, like, *obliterating* it in these headshots."

Tommy didn't want to hear any of this. "Okay," he said, "you give your five cents. Now my turn. So look: I'm different than you are. You have certain charm, great feature, you know, than me. But I can be very powerful. I am unique. Maybe I'm *too* unique." Tommy had gotten pretty worked up, putting all this out there. "And now let me tell you something else, boy. People don't want to give me chance. You have to understand this. So you know what? I do myself, you watch. I send my headshot to this big agency, these fuckers, the CAA. And I ask them, I write letter to them. We see if they respond."

"You sent a letter to CAA?"

"Of course I sent it! What do you think? You think I afraid of these people?"

I started to laugh.

"Yeah," Tommy said, "you can laugh the rest of your life."

Oh, Tommy. "What did this letter say?"

Tommy started to read it to me. The most disastrously salient extract from Tommy's letter to CAA was probably this: "Do you have the guts to take me?"

I wasn't laughing anymore. "Tommy, to get repped by CAA, you need to have a lot of credits. You also need a referral."

"I challenge them! Fuck referral. From who? You? Tom Cruise? I'm competition for big star. Referral nothing!" Tommy was sputtering now. "They don't have the guts to take me. All these prima ballerinas do is take on big star, the people that already famous. So I challenge them! Take me and try to make me big star! We see if they have the guts to do that. Hollywood try to squash me, so I squash them back."

"Tommy," I said, "none of this is going to make you better. You have your long black hair. You're kind of quirky and crazy, right? *Embrace* it."

Tommy didn't want to hear this. Couldn't hear this. Tommy's chief talent was his ability to be both cunning and oblivious at the same time. When he went into that mode, he could make me laugh harder than anyone.

I then made the mistake of mentioning to Tommy that in a couple of days I'd be in the Bay Area for that screen test in Palo Alto. He flipped at this news and told me I had to attend some monumental gathering with him in San Francisco. "You must arrive at my condo no later than eight a.m. You cannot be late. You will be shocked. If you say you don't show up, I will hang up in five seconds."

Hanging up if I didn't immediately agree to something was one of Tommy's favorite persuasion gambits. "Tommy, I have a screen test the day before. I'll be way too tired to get up that early."

"I don't want to hear excuse. It is extremely important."

Tommy hadn't been this excited about anything since he'd bought his way into SAG. I'll admit I was curious. I flew to San Francisco, did my screen test, and, the following morning, made it to his Guerrero Street condo at five minutes to eight. Tommy was waiting for me in the front of his condo and had decked himself out in running gear—the same outfit he'd later wear in *The Room,* right down to the fingerless workout gloves. He seemed in a state of hypercaffeinated agitation. "Come on," he said. "We miss if we don't hurry!"

"Where are we going?"

"Come on!"

Tommy rushed ahead down Market, toward the Embarcadero. I was wearing sandals and couldn't keep up. Tommy was almost skipping as he walked. He was also spinning around, doing his hooting thing, his cheep-cheep chicken noise, and throwing out a few ecstatic whoops. Where on earth were we going?

When we arrived at the Embarcadero, I saw a teeming mass of people clogging the intersection. At first I assumed it was a protest of some sort. Everyone was yelling and cheering, and Tommy, of course, joined them. Then I saw the starting line. This wasn't a protest at all but the famous Bay to Breakers seven-mile run across San Francisco. Tommy, who'd signed me up for it the day before, now squired me to the registration table. I got my number—a sticky piece of paper you were supposed to affix to your chest or midsection—and looked at it for a moment. Tommy clapped me on the back. I used that moment of camaraderie to remind him that I was wearing sandals. "I don't care about your flippers," Tommy said. "No excuse. The first ten thousand to finish make it into newspaper. So now we see how good you are." Suddenly I was standing at the starting point. This was really happening.

I glanced around. A nearby woman runner was wearing a wedding dress with a WILL YOU MARRY ME? sign on her back. Several runners, both men and women, hadn't bothered to wear anything at all.

"Prepare yourself physically and mentally for this crazy stuff," Tommy said. "I see you at Golden Gate Park. Good luck!"

The signal shot fired and everyone took off, Tommy included. I went to find a bathroom as several naked runners hurled past me. Tommy looked back and yelled, "I'm not waiting for you!" I'd pretty much already figured that out. Tommy took Bay to Breakers very seriously, having run it several times before.

For my first Bay to Breakers, I walked. In sandals. It was actually a very pleasant stroll. I even made a pit stop at a race-side house party. Tommy was waiting for me at the finish line. He greeted me with: "You know I beat your ass, I'm sorry to tell you. I made top ten thousand. I will be in newspaper tomorrow. You will not."

We followed the Breakers crowd to the Polo Fields in Golden Gate Park, where the race's sponsors had set up a massive catering operation. As Tommy ate his plate of barbecued chicken and rice he continued to hector me about losing. I didn't mind, mainly because he hadn't mentioned anything yet about moving to L.A. Provided that topic didn't come up again, Tommy could recite an epic poem about his victory for all I cared. When we were leaving, he asked if I wanted to come see him perform that night in Jean Shelton's class. But I was heading back to L.A. in a few hours: I had my audition for *Scream 3* the following afternoon.

Tommy was not happy to hear this. "Don't play big-shot Hollywood with me," he said. "Just because you have audition doesn't mean you own the world. Friend is more important. Are you real cousin or fake cousin?" Tommy said I should postpone my audition. I explained to him that wasn't really the way auditions worked.

"Why don't I record you on camera and we send audition? I have resources for this. There is no problem."

"Tommy," I said, sighing.

"What, you think I'm not good enough to record you now? Why you give these people so much power?"

"I have to go back to L.A. It's important."

Tommy looked at me darkly. "Whatever," he said, turning away. "That's fine. If I'm not important in your life, it's okay on me." Before we parted ways he accused me of owing him several hundred dollars. At first, I thought he was joking. He wasn't. He left me standing on Guerrero Street as confused as ever. I'd just run—well, walked—a seven-mile race with him with zero preparation or forewarning. It was almost as if the more accommodating I was with Tommy, the stranger and needier he became.

I was so weirded out that when I got back to Los Angeles I sat down and wrote Tommy a thank-you/apology letter. In the middle of writing it, I thought to myself: *This is getting too strange. Not-worth-it strange. Give him back his apartment. Your friendship with Tommy has cancer. Excise it.* But I'm loyal by nature, loyal to a fault, and I felt I did owe him something. I managed to finish writing my letter and sent it to him that day.

Tommy never mentioned receiving it. Then, a couple of weeks later, the rent checks I'd been sending Tommy over the last few months were cashed—all at once. This effectively wiped out a quarter of my savings. Now I had to get a job. More than that, I knew I had to get out of his apartment.

On the one-year anniversary of my arrival in L.A., Iris got me a meeting on the Warner Bros. lot with director Joel Schumacher, who was looking to cast a film called *Tigerland*. Joel was kind and surprisingly approachable; we talked for almost an hour, mostly about France. Instead of having actors perform dialogue in front of him, he preferred to have a conversation with an actor and go off his gut instinct. I knew going in I was probably too young and wiry for the army-man role he was looking to fill—he wound up going with another young, then-unknown actor named Colin Farrell—but I left the meeting feeling pretty good and even somewhat revived.

It was the last time I'd feel that way for quite some time.

A few months later, Tommy got in touch to say he was coming down to L.A. for yet another business meeting. His calling frequency had cooled considerably and the few times we did talk felt awkward.

Probably the most meaningful conversation we'd had involved rent, which he'd raised on me, claiming that the building had raised it on him.

On the afternoon Tommy was due in town, my phone rang. "My car just explode on freeway," he said, somehow predictably. I heard another person in the car with him saying, "Dude. *Dude!* You gotta pull the thing over, man!"

Tommy had never had any other friends around him since I'd known him—and he hadn't mentioned anything about bringing someone down to Los Angeles with him.

"I'm going to be late," Tommy said, and hung up.

When Tommy finally showed up, he had Jared with him, a thin, curly-headed twenty-three-year-old skater kid from his Jean Shelton class. Jared and I exchanged a look like we simultaneously understood something about Tommy that neither of us wanted to acknowledge.

"I had to get new engine for car," Tommy said, aloofly walking past me. He was behaving like he owned the place. Technically, of course, he did, but he'd never lorded that over me before. Jared seemed a little perplexed, not knowing why he was in this apartment. Tommy had not spoken of Jared to me. Not ever. I began to get the sense that Tommy hadn't really bothered to explain who I was or that I was renting Tommy's place.

"You guys don't look like cousins," Jared said. "At *all*."

So Tommy had told him that much.

"We are cousins," Tommy said, "whether you like it or you don't."

"Right," Jared said, drawing the word out. Soon Jared explained he was staying with an ex-girlfriend in Westwood and it was time for him to go. We were in the middle of saying our uncomfortable good-byes when the doorbell rang. My doorbell didn't ever ring. I hadn't made many friends in Los Angeles. I'd made a couple of acquaintances, but certainly no one who'd spontaneously ring my doorbell. Maybe it was a neighbor? Maybe some solicitor had sneaked through the gate?

Tommy was looking at me in the most peculiar way. His face was getting redder by the moment. Jared was right by the door, so he peered through the peephole. "It's some dude," he said.

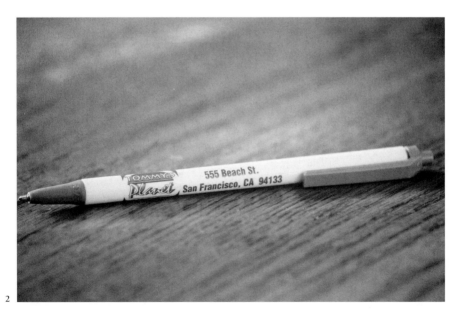

San Francisco, 1998. I had known Tommy for one month.

"My planet will be bigger than everything."

3

4

Blue Steel-ing in Milan, 1995.　　The headshot seen by every casting
director in Hollywood.

5

Tommy channeling the Bard in his demo-reel Street Fashions commercial.

Reenacting the *Rebel Without a Cause* knife fight, Griffith Observatory, 1999.

Tommy and his "big Hollywood thing"—the two-camera setup.

Peter Anway's famous plugged-in grin.

8

Tommy and Raphael Smadja discussing some finer points of cinematography.

9

"All I need is a pink angora sweater and I'm good": Sandy Schklair, *The Room*'s script supervisor.

10

The sound guy,
Zsolt, can't take
any more.

11

Tommy getting
"depuffified."

12

"Oh, hi,
Mark": From
left, Amy
Von Brock,
Safowa
Bright, Philip
Haldiman,
and I watch
Tommy
rehearse.

13

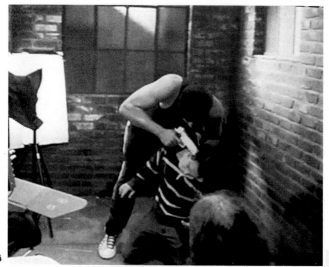

The lost take of the Chris-R scene on the indoor alley set—our first day of shooting.

14

The Rooftop set.

15

Juliette Danielle and Carolyn Minnott share a much-needed laugh during a break from shooting.

16

17

Philip Haldiman and Dan Janjigian. Where's his fucking money?

18   19

Kyle Vogt as Peter and Greg Ellery as Peter's replacement, Steven. Separated at birth? Probably not.

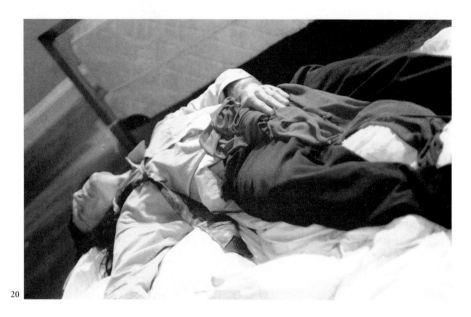

Tommy and the red dress, together at last.

Filming the opening shots of *The Room* on location in San Francisco. From left: Tommy, Todd Barron, Joe Pacella, Zsolt Magyar, and me.

22

Invitation to the premiere of *The Room,* June 27, 2003—a day that would change the face of American cinema.

From left: Carolyn Minnott, Tommy, and Kat Kramer at *The Room*'s premiere.

23

Juliette with the first of many, many red roses to come.

24

Me in my ill-fitted evening wear with Dan Janjigian and friends.

25

The indomitable Robyn Paris.

26

Philip Haldiman, freed from the Charlie Brown shirt, with a friend at *The Room*'s premiere.

27

"This is my life."

28

The billboard over Highland Avenue. Feel free to call for screening info!

29

The crazy cult of *The Room*. From left: Michael Rousselet, comedian David Cross, and Scott Gairdner.

30

Spoons!

31

Meeting fans in Dublin, Ireland.

32

A Tommy impersonator
in San Francisco.

33

A typical reaction
to the film, at
its Copenhagen
premiere.

34

35

Tommy plays football with *Room* fans outside Prince Charles Cinema in London.

36

The Room heats up the South Pole!

Tommy, circa the late 1970s.

37

Tommy in one of his
early San Francisco
shops during the
"Birdman" era.

38

Beach Street, San
Francisco—Street
Fashions headquarters.

39

Tommy returns to Paris, 2012.

40

41

Legends.

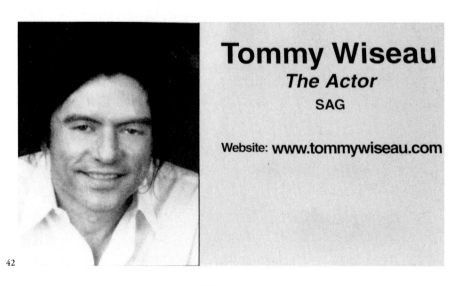

Tommy Wiseau
The Actor
SAG

Website: www.tommywiseau.com

42

The Actor.

Jared moved out of the way and I looked through the peephole myself. It was my neighbor Cliff from the first floor. I'd run into him and his girlfriend earlier that day in the elevator. Cliff was an actor doing a play at a small theater nearby. They'd invited me to see it. I thought it was just pleasantries, but now he was apparently here to present me with my ticket for tonight's show.

"Who is that?" Tommy said, his voice loud and suspicious, which Cliff had to have heard.

Why I didn't simply answer the door, I have no idea. I think I was afraid of what Tommy would have done or said if he'd seen poor Cliff. That's when I realized: Tommy brought Jared here to show me he had a new friend—that he was capable of making a new friend whenever he wanted. But Cliff randomly ringing my doorbell had somehow trumped Tommy's friendship power play.

"Who *is* that?" Tommy said again, more aggressively.

I looked out the peephole once more and saw Cliff frowning and fidgeting.

"Do you know him?" Jared said.

"No," I said cravenly. "Probably a solicitor or something."

Eventually, Cliff gave up and walked away. A few minutes after that, Jared left, too, at which point Tommy was practically shaking. "So," he said, "how's your life? Any stories or experiences to tell?" I could tell he had gone deep into some paranoid, sinister place, and was angry that I'd revealed the existence of the mysterious Tommy Wiseau's Los Angeles apartment. That's the thing with Tommy: Even before he was famous, he acted like he was famous. Maybe that's what, in the end, best explains him. Maybe that's what explains the whole thing.

"Is something wrong?" I asked Tommy.

"I don't know," Tommy said, sitting down. "I guess I don't know anything going on these days."

He started paging through an old issue of *Variety*. At that moment Tommy looked like some hateful thing I'd fished out of a nightmare, all red-faced, veiny, vile, and suspicious. "Look, Greg," he said, folding one leg over the other and still looking at his magazine. "Right now I need quiet because I have a big meeting with Stella Adler tomorrow."

The Stella Adler Academy is a tourist-trap acting school on Hollywood Boulevard. Tommy was obsessed with Adler due to her renowned work with Brando. Tommy didn't realize a few things: (1) You didn't need a referral to become a student at the Stella Adler Academy, (2) the school's lineage could be traced back only vaguely to Stella Adler herself, and (3) Stella Adler had been dead for almost ten years.

"Stella Adler is dead," I told Tommy.

Tommy looked up at me, obviously confused. "I just talked to them few days ago. Jared has a meeting with her and he say I can go, too."

"Okay," I said. "Just letting you know. I hope you have a good meeting with the late Stella Adler."

Tommy looked down at the floor. "Whatever. I don't care." He was, I think, trying not to cry.

Whatever had just happened here, it was obviously way more complicated than a random doorbell ring from someone I barely knew. This was about Tommy's fears about being discovered, about being valued, about being admired, about being lost, about being young, and about being alone.

This moment was probably the worst imaginable time for my phone to ring and for me to learn that I had a callback for *Viking,* an NBC movie about Leif Erikson, the next day. I tried to cover up the excitement I was feeling, but Tommy was not impressed. "You have another audition?" he asked. "How good for you." He kept looking at *Variety* while I did my best to ignore him.

At that moment, I felt like I didn't know Tommy. In the past he'd annoyed me, sure, but he'd also been supportive and often made me laugh. Occasionally I thought that the way he looked at the world was genuinely delightful. But the closer you got to him, the darker he became. He'd never seemed as dark as he did right now, though. There was just so much I didn't know about Tommy: his real name, where he was from, his age, his profession, what he did all day. Tommy, even the Tommy I thought I knew, was a stranger to me.

Cliff's play started in a couple of hours; I could not compound my shunning him at the door with failing to attend. I went downstairs and caught Cliff just as he was leaving, and he gave me a ticket. Back in the apartment, Tommy was chatting on my fax phone with someone. When I walked in he fixed those dead, suspicious eyes on me. That was all I needed to see. "I'm going to see my friend's play," I told him. "I'll be back later."

Tommy continued to talk on the phone as though I hadn't said anything.

I barely paid any attention to Cliff's play. I spent most of it thinking about Tommy's eerie behavior. Why was he always so secretive about everything? Why did he get so angry that Cliff rang my doorbell? Maybe, I thought, we weren't friends. Maybe Tommy had somehow conned me this whole time. That's the thing with con artists. They never tell you their story. They give you pieces of it and let you fill in the rest. They let you work out the contradictions and discrepancies. They let you believe that the things that don't add up are what makes them interesting or special. They let you believe that in those gaps are the things that hurt and wounded them. But maybe there's nothing in those gaps. Nothing but your own stupid willingness to assume the best of someone.

Tommy was still on the phone when I came back hours later, but he ended the call the moment I walked in. That he might have been on the phone all night concerned me. What if my agent had tried to call? What if, even worse, my agent or some casting director had called and Tommy picked up—especially given the state of mind he was in? Would he try to sabotage me? It suddenly did not seem beyond Tommy to do something like that. I hated having that thought in my head, but I couldn't get rid of it.

"So!" he said, once he got my phone nice and hung up. "How was your night? How was your friend's play?"

"It was okay," I said, busying myself by pretending to look for something to eat.

"You know, I talk to your friend, for your information."

I had no idea who Tommy was talking about. Iris? My manager?

"Which friend?"

"This goofy friend you have from San Francisco."

Oh, Jesus. My unicycle-riding film-editor hippie friend from San

Francisco was just about the only person, other than my mom and dad, who ever called me here. This was a man whose distrust for Tommy and his intentions toward me had napalmic qualities. Whenever I talked to him, he pumped me for information about Tommy. He thought Tommy was bad news. Maybe in the mob for a while. Then he thought Tommy was a Serbian warlord. Then he thought Tommy was a pornographer. If the two of them ever got together . . . And now they had.

"You know this guy pretty well, I guess. He has number here; he knows to call number here. He knows you live in L.A. And he knows about me, too."

I knew instantly what had happened. My friend, a straight shooter like no other, had asked Tommy all the forbidden questions—all the questions *I had told him were the forbidden questions*: Where he was from. How old he was. His occupation. Tommy tried to play his usual games, but my friend laid into him and sent him into a psychotic tantrum. Tommy's secret identity was now, in his barbed and sick mind, in danger of being exposed. That's why Tommy liked me, I thought. He saw me as this naive young loner—a non–security risk. The perfect friend for him.

"So you have two friends I don't know about," Tommy said. "This goofy guy and this doorbell guy. Why you involved with such strange people?"

"Tommy, I went to the guy's play as a favor to him. He's a neighbor. I barely know him."

"Oh, wow. I guess I was not invited to play, huh? That's too bad for me." I couldn't win. Whatever I said made me guiltier.

"I go for ride now," Tommy said as he got up and headed to the door. "I don't want to talk now. I go get fresh air—maybe see girl or something. You have audition and I don't want to spoil. We talk tomorrow."

I got into bed with psychic spiders crawling all over me. Was this just a pretext for Tommy to throw me out of here? Had I really done something wrong by talking about Tommy with my friend? Tommy had walked me into a minefield of paranoia and left me there all alone.

When I woke up the next morning I could hear Tommy snoring in the other room. I thought, *You have built a human relationship on a foundation of asbestos*.

I mangled my *Viking* callback, which was held next to a restaurant appropriately called the Stinking Rose. All I could think about was whether I was going to be homeless at the end of the day.

When I got back to the apartment Tommy was once again on the phone. I knew he'd had his meeting with the late Stella Adler at around the time I was forfeiting my *Viking* role. "These Stella Adler people," he was saying to whoever was on the other line, "they're all behind schedule. Not as good at acting as I thought. They don't even understand the subconscious. You know what, I'm sorry. I do my way." He looked over at me. "Well, I have to go now. My *friend* is here." He'd really doused that word in kerosene and set it on fire. For a long few seconds after hanging up he didn't say anything. He was sitting on a chair, not making eye contact, his hands folded in his lap, smiling a hideously false smile. "And how was audition?"

I stared right back at him. "Not good. It was better the first time."

"Oh, come on. I'm sure you did good job."

"Yeah. Sure you are."

He stood up. "Let's go for a spin and talk about stuff."

I was nervous to go anywhere with him. I knew something bad was going to happen if I did. But if I didn't go with him now, it meant the last two years of our friendship were based on my being a stupid, trusting idiot, and I didn't want that to be true. I followed Tommy to his car. A few minutes later he was turning left on Sunset, not saying a word but driving faster than I'd ever seen him drive: the speed limit. Then he floored it. My hands flew out to grip the dashboard. "Tommy," I said. "Slow down."

He veered recklessly around one car, another. "This guy from yesterday at the door—I guess he like you, huh? Best friend?"

"Tommy, what is this really about?"

"And your goofy friend. You talk to him all the time, huh? You tell him all these things." His mouth was set at an ugly angle. He was driving slower now but somehow just as recklessly.

"Tommy, I have no idea what you're talking about."

"Why you talk about me?" His voice was slightly more aggressive.

"I don't even know what—"

"Why you *talk* about me to this *friend*? *Why*? You *talk* about *Jean Shelton*! You talk about *football*! You talk about *acting*! *My place*! *Why do you talk about me?*" He was screaming at the windshield, hunched over his steering wheel, too disgusted to look over at me. *"Why do you talk about me? I thought I trust you, and you talk about me!"*

Now I was scared. Tommy had completely lost control of himself. What was he so afraid of? I knew, then, that this was how Tommy's Planet operated. I wondered if the reason he didn't have any friends was that they all, eventually, wound up here: untethered, lost in space.

"Tommy!" I said. "I don't even know why you're so upset!"

"Why do you do this? Why do you do this?" He wasn't hearing me. He was lost in the orbit of his own rage.

All I had told my hippie friend about Tommy was simple stuff, basic stuff—*fond* stuff, even. I told him that Tommy was always willing to try new things, things he had no prior interest in, like playing football. I described his openness to new experiences. I told him how good Tommy could be, and how kind he often was, once you got to know him. I told him how grateful I was to Tommy that he let me live in his place, that he was the only one to tell me to keep going when everyone else in my life had urged me to give up. *I know you don't trust him,* I said to my hippie friend, *but Tommy really is a good guy, deep down.*

Tommy turned off Sunset Boulevard and pulled over—pulled over on the very street Joe Gillis uses in *Sunset Boulevard* while trying to avoid those loan sharks, after which he discovers Norma Desmond's mansion. But I didn't know any of this at that moment. I didn't know that I was living Joe Gillis's life in twenty-first-century form.

"Look," Tommy said, more calmly, and I knew instantly that he'd been preparing this speech for a while. "I decide I'm moving to Los Angeles to be actor. I just want people to leave me alone. I can't have anyone around at this time. Now is time you find your own place. I cannot trust you. The feelings go away." Tommy held his thumb and forefinger apart and squeezed them shut. That was our friendship now: a molecule's width of nothing.

This felt like a bad dream. Tommy was so oily with menace that all I wanted to do was run. The person whose support had meant so much to me was gone.

I got out of the car and started walking away. Everything I'd worked for, I thought, was done. I'd wound up exactly where my mother had predicted I would. The tears in my eyes proved it.

The next thing I knew Tommy was driving beside me, urging me to get back into his car. "I'm sorry, Greg," he said, gulping the words. "I'm sorry I yell at you. I can trust you. You know that. You can stay in apartment."

That was all this ridiculous tirade had been about. Tommy was still capable of hurting and affecting and controlling me, and knowing that he could do all these things was, to him, the very stuff of relief. Now that Tommy had this dark assurance, all between us was, in his mind, fine. But it wasn't fine. I now knew that everything my mom and friend had said about Tommy was right. There was something twisted and poisonous inside him—something potentially dangerous, even. It was just a matter of time.

I got back in the car and said, "Okay," but I never again looked at Tommy in the same way. I started searching for a new apartment that night.

eleven

"I'll Record Everything"

No one leaves a star. That's what makes one a star.
—Norma Desmond, *Sunset Boulevard*

One afternoon, during the fifth week of production, Raphael appro-ached me on set and said, "We need a line producer. If we don't have a line producer by the end of this week, I'm leaving."

Raphael confessed to feeling "embarrassed" by the blinding ama-teurism of Tommy's project, especially when he had to do his job in front of Birns & Sawyer's owner, Bill Meurer, who'd recently taken to yelling at the crew about the disorder that was now disrupting his busi-ness. Worse, Raphael kept having to do other people's jobs. There was simply no organization. Tommy was constantly hiring and casting and firing and hiring again, all while finding ways to sandwich two jobs into one: I was a lead actor but also the line producer. Sandy was the script supervisor but also the first assistant director. Peter Anway was the Birns & Sawyer sales representative but also, somehow, Tommy's assistant.

Tommy knew Raphael was upset but didn't believe he would ac-tually ever follow through on his threat to abandon the production. After all, Tommy had a line producer: me. So what was the problem? The problem was this: Tommy didn't really know what a line producer was. He didn't know how a film set was supposed to operate. Being a line producer on a chaotic movie shoot is a consuming full-time job, to say the least. The line producer has to run the production, make sure people are paid, help the art department fetch stuff, schedule call times, and do everything else that no director wants to do—and Tommy Wiseau was incapable of doing. To ask a person who is also a lead actor to do these things was self-defeating and ridiculous. I was being forced to rush away from scenes I was shooting, thereby stalling production, so I could order pizza for a starving cast and crew. Raphael was right. We needed help.

Obviously, I understood Raphael's concern, but I also knew what Tommy's response was going to be. Tommy had to feel that all decisions were coming from him. If someone else proposed something, no matter how strong the proposal, Tommy would refuse to take any action. And unless Tommy believed he would directly benefit from an idea, no money would be spent, not under any circumstances. If Raphael needed a line producer, he was going to have to tell Tommy in such a way as to make Tommy feel like the idea was his and not Raphael's—and good luck with that.

Later in the day, on our lunch break, Raphael finally grabbed me in the long-odds hope that I would be able to influence Tommy's decision. "Come on," he said, "let's go tell him."

Tommy, as always, was off eating his lunch alone in Johnny and Lisa's living room set, where he couldn't be disturbed. He didn't like anyone but himself preparing his food plate, especially after the difficult first week of production. He occasionally voiced concerns that someone might spit in his food or drink. Tommy also refused to eat off plastic utensils, which he worried could be poisoned. In other words, he was already well on his way toward developing full-blown wicked-king paranoia. Raphael walked right up to him, with me balefully dragging behind.

"Tommy," Raphael said, taking a deep breath to shift into now-I'm-talking-to-Tommy mode. "Look, it's time we get a line producer."

Even though Raphael had mentioned this to him many times, Tommy looked up with total surprise. Tommy had ninja skills when it came to ignoring things he didn't want to hear or act on. When you're able to see only what you want to see, it's remarkably easy to live in a problem-free world. Tommy directed his metal fork at me. "We have Greg," he said, as calmly as a magician might say "voilà."

"Tommy," Raphael said, "Greg is not a line producer. Greg is acting in your movie, and you can't keep putting this on him."

Tommy set down his utensil and placed his hands on his thighs. His expression became one of great, put-upon affront. "Greg can do job. He has skills. Why are you putting Greg down?"

At this blatant attempt at manipulation, Raphael's hands flew up. "I'm *not* putting Greg down. Tommy, listen to what I'm saying. I need a professional line producer to be here if we want to continue this. If I don't have that, I'm leaving on Sunday." With that, he turned and walked away.

Raphael pointedly refused to bring the issue up again for the rest of the week. Tommy did nothing. When Sunday morning came, Raphael showed up and asked me if a new line producer had been hired. I said no, of course not. "Then I'm not shooting," Raphael said. "Good-bye, Greg. *C'est fini.*" He began to pack up his equipment as Tommy approached him.

"Greg is here," he said to Raphael, who kept his back to Tommy as much as possible while he got his gear together. "Greg is *here*." Again and again, Tommy kept repeating this, with growing anger, while Raphael headed over to Peter Anway to shake his hand and say good-bye. Peter accepted the shake with obvious alarm. They were speaking quietly, so I couldn't hear them, but I did notice that all of Raphael's guys—half the crew, in other words—were now packing up. Crews will almost always follow a respected DP's lead. If he leaves, they leave, too. Tommy noticed Raphael's crew packing up and promptly lost control. He began bouncing around the set, screaming at people, calling them traitors, accusing them of wanting to sabotage his "feature-movie project." They ignored him, which only made Tommy more hysterical.

I was watching yet another disaster unfold on the set of *The Room*. Locating and hiring a group of competent professionals accustomed to working together—and willing to work under Tommy—was not something that could be done quickly or cheaply. This movie, I thought to myself, was dead in the water. At this rate, no production on earth could survive Tommy. I couldn't see any lifelines. In the midst of all this chaos, the actors all bailed and went home.

Tommy was still yelling at Raphael, his wobbling finger outthrust: "You're a very disrespectful person! I'm sorry to tell you, but you're *very* disrespectful! I can't throw away million dollars, hire hundred people, because *you* tell me so!" Raphael, ignoring Tommy, was still circulating around the set, saying farewell to his colleagues. Tommy was following Raphael from a distance, heaving insults at him like rotten fruit. "Very, very disrespectful! You will not sabotage my project! We do my way!"

When he had had enough, Raphael turned to Tommy and said, calmly, "Tommy, I was very open with you. I can't continue to work like this. I gave you until today to hire a line producer and you ignored me. So there's nothing I can do. I'm sorry." With admirable dignity, he waved good-bye to the rest of us and made his way to his car.

"Fine," Tommy said, spinning around to face the remaining members of his production. "Let him go! We don't need this guy. We don't need him."

Raphael was willing to leave without picking up his last paycheck, but his crew was not nearly as accommodating. They wanted to be paid. Now. It was quickly turning into a mob scene, with the remaining crew yelling at Tommy and Tommy yelling back at them. Poor Peter Anway wedged himself between Tommy and the angry crew members, who might as well have been brandishing pitchforks and torches. "Please, guys," Peter said. "Let's all just calm down and talk this through."

Tommy, the most irate of anyone, yelled, "I don't have to talk! Calm down *nothing*! Raphael's disrespectful. It's *his* problem. It's not my problem!"

"Just *pay* us, you son of a bitch," one of Raphael's people demanded. You could feel weeks of frustration burbling up. Some of these guys were plainly prepared to worsen the asymmetrical quality of Tommy's face.

Tommy looked at the guy who called him a son of a bitch, his eyes lidded and heavy. Then, something seemed to reboot in his mind, and he made a big, sweeping, carnival-barker gesture. "Everyone, inside! We have emergency meeting!"

Knowing they had to suffer through Tommy's emergency meeting to get paid, everyone simultaneously groaned as they filed into Birns & Sawyer. The office we wound up in was not large, and the air was suffused with the hot stench of anger, body odor, and bad breath. "Okay," he said. "So here we are. Let's have discussion. We have obviously problem today, but we here to talk. It's America. I'm an American, just like you."

The absurdity of this comment was met with some giggling.

"American with accent," Tommy said, waving away the laughter. "So be it." He looked around. "We like to know who stay today. Because we will continue production. Okay? We are not going anywhere. No one will ruin my movie." His voice, by this point, was slightly quivering. "Production will continue. Cameras will keep rolling."

In fact, the cameras were rolling at that moment. At the beginning of production, Tommy had hired a young Czech kid named Markus— he'd been doing odd jobs at Birns & Sawyer when Tommy found him—to shoot the rough footage for a making-of documentary about *The Room*. Tommy's orders to Markus were to film everything, all the time. Oftentimes Markus stuck his Canon right into people's faces. Sandy, at one point, shoved the camera away and said, "Turn that off or I will." Other members of the production more bluntly told Markus to "stay the fuck away" whenever they saw him coming. Markus revealed this resistance to Tommy, who said, "We don't care what they say. Keep going."

And now Markus, ever diligent, was filming Tommy's emergency meeting. No one much liked that, given the circumstances. "Get your fucking camera out of my face!" one of Raphael's people said.

Tommy noticed this and said, "No!" His outburst momentarily shut up everyone in the room. Tommy pointed adamantly at Markus. "You keep filming. You may film this strike." What no one knew—what I didn't even know at the time—was that Tommy was daily watching all of Markus's raw footage until the wee hours, which went some way toward explaining why he was always so late in the morning. All this time, Tommy had been spying on his own production. So just about every time someone made an unkind comment about Tommy, Markus was there recording. Just about every time someone laughed about

Tommy's acting, which was often, Markus got it. Tommy knew more about how he was perceived on set than anyone was aware. And now he let people know what he knew. He began pointing out crew members in the crowd and repeating back to them some nasty comment they'd made. "This guy," Tommy was saying, "this guy here, with the hat? I know what you're saying. You say I'm bad actor? I say you're bad *crew member*."

Tommy's emotional insurance policy scheme, if that's what it was, worked. The mood in the room softened immediately—whether because people felt bad or guilty or genuinely worried, I have no idea, but there was now enough fragile goodwill between all parties to move forward in a civil manner. "We'll work for you," one of Raphael's people said, "*if* you meet our basic demands."

Tommy said he was willing to hear those demands.

They were: Tommy couldn't keep showing up four hours late. Tommy couldn't take the HD camera home with him every night, because it delayed the already delayed process of setting up in the morning. Tommy needed to pay the crew decently. If the crew stayed for ten hours, Tommy needed to include dinner.

Tommy had heard enough. "Please stop," he said. "Stop this nonsense. Have respect for producers. You guys are flying in the sky."

"Then pay us," someone new said, astonished that these reasoned and reasonable demands could be called "nonsense." "We're done!"

"Yeah," another said. "Just give us our check and we'll get out of here. We don't *want* to work for you."

Tommy kept repeating, over and over, that all this was "nonsense," that in Hollywood this was "how things work." "Be professional," he said. "Stop this crying."

I said, over the arguing, "Tommy, just *pay* them."

Again there was silence. Tommy looked at me, at them. "I'm sorry," he said, "but we don't have enough checks at this time. And I notice you guys, all of you, you say very condescending things in your statements. It's on the camera. Look, we will pay you later. We cannot pay you now."

Uproar. The crowd was closing in on Tommy; his directorial force field was rapidly giving way. "Guys!" Peter Anway said. He was standing next to me, in the back of the room, trying to shout sense into someone, anyone. "Everybody calm down! It's fine." No one acknowledged him. Peter looked over at me, terrified. This shoot was his responsibility. If a fight broke out and Birns & Sawyer got turned upside down, Meurer would likely fire him. The battery powering Peter's famous, plugged-in grin had expired. Tommy was almost certainly going to be assaulted if something wasn't done—even though he might well have deserved it.

Tommy would milk this power position as long as he could. Even if he were physically attacked, he'd refuse to do the right thing. "Tommy has checks at his house," I said to Peter.

"Go get them," Peter said.

I muscled through the crowd and went to Tommy's apartment to grab a handful of Bank of America checks from the huge stack on his living room table. When I got back, everyone was lined up waiting outside Birns & Sawyer. I held up the checks and they cheered. "Thank you," Peter Anway kept saying. "Thank you. Thank you."

Tommy spent an hour writing out checks. His signature, illegible on the smoothest and most lucid of days, was an infuriated slash. After every slash, he handed the check to its recipient and said, "Go inside and make copy. We need a copy!"

A few people stayed on, including Sandy. "We're completely fucked," he told me. "I don't know how long I can do this. I can do it for a little bit longer but I don't know how much longer. Maybe if Tommy gives me a director credit I might stick around."

No chance, I told him. Sandy then told me that a buddy of his was working on a big show—*The West Wing,* I think. This buddy of Sandy's had bags under his eyes from all the work but he was making what Sandy described as "wheelbarrows of money." If Sandy left, we really were done. Sandy helped set up eyelines, blocked scenes, worked on the dialogue, and established a basic through-line of minimal coherence. I knew Sandy needed more money, so I wrote him an extra week's check as incentive to stay and sneaked it by Tommy.

Peter Anway had asked for a few days to go through his contacts in order to find a new DP. When he found someone, Tommy, Sandy, and I came in to Birns & Sawyer to meet him. His name was Graham. Peter described him as a talented young upstart from USC's film school. He'd already directed a couple of music videos and had experience with HD filmmaking. Graham was a thin, pointy-looking guy who was upbeat and eager about learning new techniques in his craft.

Peter floated behind us nervously as we began watching Graham's music-video reel. The title appeared over black. "Oh, wow," Tommy said. "He does the nice thing. Oh, very good job. Wow. Such excellent work." The actual demo reel hadn't even started but Tommy was in full charm mode. That, or Tommy really thought that a blank screen was a display of peerless talent. Graham was obviously finding Tommy's oohing and aahing a little excessive but smiled all the same. When the reel was done, Tommy immediately began going over with Graham what he wanted. Sandy would occasionally interrupt to provide some sanity-based addenda. Whenever Tommy wasn't paying attention, Sandy would pull Graham aside and say, "This movie is—and you'll have to trust me—this movie is going to be absolutely crazy."

"So what do you say?" Tommy finally asked Graham. "This is feature movie. Do you want to do it?"

Graham was still several years away from thirty, and being asked, at that age, to take over photographing a feature film was a big deal, even with someone as wacky as Tommy at the helm. Plus, if Graham took the gig, he'd get to work more with Birns & Sawyer, as well as with high-definition cameras, which few young filmmakers at the time had the opportunity to play with in a professional setting.

"Okay," Graham said. "I'll do it."

Tommy went away after that, leaving Graham with Sandy and me.

"Here's what you need to know," Sandy said. "Greg's the line producer. He's also a lead actor."

Graham began nodding and then, suddenly, stopped. He looked at us both. "What?"

"I've never been a line producer," I said. "I don't even know what a line producer is, technically."

Sandy continued: "That crazy guy you just met? He's the star, director, writer, producer, and one of the executive producers. We don't know who else is producing this turkey because we haven't met them. He has a shitload of money but won't say what he does or where he's from."

Graham looked at Sandy for a moment. "What the heck is this thing about?"

Sandy: "It's not about anything. It makes absolutely no sense."

Graham, slowly: "Okayyyy."

Sandy: "You'll catch on to what's going on here really quickly. People don't *believe* the stories I tell about this experience. Oh, another thing: He *bought* all this equipment."

Graham looked over at some pricey cameras sitting nearby. "It must have a huge budget, right? Nobody buys this much equipment. Is there some big studio behind him?"

"Totally independent. It's cinematic masturbation, basically."

Tommy was walking out of Birns & Sawyer with Peter Anway, holding a sizable box. He'd just spent an immigrant family's yearly earnings on a new lens for his HD camera.

Graham took this in. "I think I got it," he said somewhat jokingly. "This is obviously a huge money-laundering scheme."

At that moment, I had absolute confidence that Graham would be able to handle this movie, and Tommy. Plus, he'd bring into the production half a dozen crew members—a little pocket of the USC film-school mafia.

We escorted Graham to the interior stage. The first thing Graham said was, "This is way too small to shoot in. Plus it needs air-conditioning." Tommy's two-camera 35mm/HD setup proved especially baffling to him. "What is this?" he asked, after looking at the camera mount for a long time.

"Tommy had that made special to fit the two camera formats," Sandy said.

"Why?" Graham asked.

"We don't know," Sandy said.

"How do you even light this set?"

"Poorly."

Tommy approached now, wanting to know what Graham thought about the two-format camera mount. Graham diplomatically phrased his concerns to Tommy, off whom they bounced without making a mark. "This is our place," Tommy said proudly. "Our big Hollywood thing. You see, we are first ones ever in Hollywood to shoot with two cameras, thirty-five millimeter and HD, at the same time."

Graham ran his hand over his mouth. He would be doing a lot of that over the next few days.

We had a week off before filming picked up again, but I had no respite. Amber's and my relationship was going about as well as *The Room*. She accused me of being constantly exhausted, distant, distracted, which I was. We fought a lot, and neither of us was ever wholly right and neither of us was ever wholly wrong. Amber was resentful that the *Room* gig had gotten me out of retail while she was still struggling at her miserable counter job and mired in debt. I couldn't understand her envy. I felt like you'd have to be a wartime refugee to be envious of my current work situation. On one attempted date, she closed the night with "I liked you so much better when you were broke."

On our first day shooting with Crew Number Two, the mood was decidedly more indie, which I realize is quite a statement. This suited Tommy, because it meant he had hardly anyone else his age around. Tommy is often very playful with young people, the younger the better, but people his own age—especially film-industry people his own age—made him prone to fits and tantrums, probably because he felt self-conscious and challenged by them. The problem was that the first crew was the cream of what a production like this could have reasonably expected to score. Crew Number Two had talent, but not nearly as much experience.

Our first day back in production was also the day Raphael came in to pick up his check. He found me during lunch. I wrote the check and brought it to Tommy for his signature. Tommy looked at the check, spotted Raphael's name, and tore it up on the spot. "Absolutely not!"

Tommy said. "He can wait like everyone else!" No one, as far as I knew, was waiting to be paid for anything that day. Raphael didn't see this, thankfully. Tommy then told me he'd tear up every check I brought to him, if necessary. Raphael would not be paid until Tommy was ready to pay him.

I returned to Raphael and told him that Tommy was still pouting. "Am I," he asked, "going to have to come in every day before I get paid?"

"I'll work on it for you," I said. "I'll call you."

The first scene shot with the new crew involved Lisa and her mother, Claudette, talking about Johnny. Carolyn Minnott, who was playing Claudette, welcomed the informal new atmosphere heralded by Crew Number Two. "Do we get to see a full script this time around?" she asked, only partly joking. Carolyn liked to remark that every one of her scenes in *The Room* amounted to the same thing: "You should *marry* Johnny—he's the perfect man! Also, I hate this person and that person. And now I have to go home." This day's particular scene, however, had Lisa admitting to Claudette that she was—in the words of Tommy's original script—"doing sex" with someone else. Also in the original script, this scene opens with Lisa answering the phone to talk to her mother. While writing the scene, Tommy forgot, at some point, that Lisa was on the phone, so he ends the scene with Lisa walking her mother to the door and saying good-bye. It's the most wonderfully surreal thing I've ever read.

On that day, the heat was unbearable. You could cut it with a knife, salt it, eat it, and use it to wipe your mouth afterward. Apparently it was a mere ninety-four degrees in the studio, but it felt like twice that. Tommy had refused to buy an air conditioner for a long time. He finally did, but it broke down immediately.

I watched Carolyn and Juliette rehearse for a little while before going outside to cool down. Some of the younger, newer crew guys were out there doing the same thing. We talked a bit about Tommy, and how eccentric he was, and before too long I was saying, "You haven't seen anything yet. Follow me." I took them to Raphael's old Giggle Tent outside the studio, which had a VCR loaded with unused footage from the first two weeks of filming. I started showing them some of Tommy's greatest acting hits. "Oh my God," one of them said, laughing. "This is *so* terrible."

Another one, looking back so as not to be overheard by anyone, said, "Seriously, Greg. Does he think this is serious? This is real?"

"Completely," I said. "Tommy thinks this is the next *Streetcar Named Desire*."

"What's he planning to do with this movie?"

"Submit it to the Academy Awards." Everyone laughed, but I wasn't kidding. That was Tommy's stated goal.

We heard a commotion outside the tent; it turned out Carolyn had passed out from the heat. Luckily, Juliette caught her. When I got into the studio, Carolyn was sitting on the floor, drinking from a bottle of water. Everyone, obviously, was very concerned—Tommy most of all. *Liability* was the word floating behind his eyes when he asked me to take Carolyn to the emergency room. So Carolyn was helped into my Lumina and I drove her to Cedars-Sinai.

Carolyn was sixty-four at the time of filming and lived in San Clemente with her family. Every day she made the two-hour round-trip drive up from Orange County for filming. She had been making this drive now for months, starting with casting and rehearsals. And she was never late. She'd always wanted to be an actress, but having a family waylaid her aspiration. When her kids got old enough to go to college, she started looking around again, booked a few small parts, eventually became frustrated, and cooled down. She still kept an eye out for opportunities, but they were few and far between. Then, in *Backstage West,* she saw an audition announcement for *The Room.*

Carolyn, too, was a pro. She never complained, did exactly as she was told—even if that included a scene in which her character announced that she had breast cancer with no apparent concern—and delivered one of the more coherent performances in *The Room.* It helped, I think, that Tommy was unusually considerate when dealing with Carolyn. He never barked at her. Maybe this was because she, like he, was trying to fulfill a later-in-life dream of movie stardom. Or maybe she just made him feel younger.

Carolyn was quiet and, I think, a little embarrassed as we drove to the hospital. She laughed when she told me what line she said right before she fainted: "If you think I'm tired today, wait until you see me tomorrow."

I checked her in at Cedars-Sinai. The ER nurse said, "What are you doing at your age, passing out in the heat?"

Carolyn sighed. "I'm working on a movie," she said.

"You poor thing," the nurse said. "Well, that movie of yours should have air-conditioning."

When we returned to the condo set, Tommy and Sandy were having an unusually vociferous argument. It began when Tommy referred to Sandy as his assistant and told Sandy to let him do the "director job," which, quite understandably, made Sandy angry. "No, no, no, Tommy," Sandy was saying. "I'm *not* your assistant. And I'm telling you this scene is just . . . this is ridiculous. It's totally, totally *ridiculous*."

"No, it's not," Tommy said. "It's how I want it."

"That doesn't mean it's not ridiculous!"

When I approached them, Sandy looked over at me with an *all-praise-God-you're-back* expression. Sandy mistakenly believed that Tommy listened to me.

At issue was the fact that Lisa begins the scene talking to her mother on the phone and ends by walking her to the door. Yet, somehow, their entire conversation gets recorded on Johnny and Lisa's answering machine? Tommy was adamant that the answering machine record the conversation, so that, in the next scene, Johnny can find the tape on which Lisa admits she's having an affair. Tommy had been alerted to the rather intractable space-time conundrum the scene created, but he was fixated on having Johnny find the recorded conversation. In the end, Tommy decided to shoot the scene so that Johnny overhears Lisa and Claudette's conversation from the condo's spiral staircase. Then, when Lisa and Claudette leave the scene, Tommy wanted Johnny to proceed to the phone and hook it up to a tape recorder.

I'll start with the most obvious problem: The living room set was fifteen feet across. Johnny would have had as much luck hiding from Lisa and Claudette on the staircase as he would lying at their feet. An only slightly smaller problem was the method by which Johnny sought to record his future wife's future conversations. Bugging a phone generally takes a little more effort than plugging it into a yard-sale tape recorder, and you need a different kind of tape than a ninety-minute Maxell—which Johnny, of course, happens to already have in his shirt pocket. None of it made any sense, but this was what Tommy wanted to shoot. Some crew guys were setting up the coverage shot of the tape recorder when I came in.

"You can't shoot that," Graham told Tommy. "Sandy's right."

Tommy was wholly unruffled by their concerns. "We shoot like this. How we want."

"How *you* want," Sandy said. "*I* don't want to shoot it this way. You don't *need* to have Johnny record anything. You already have him *overhearing* the conversation." It was an undeniable point. Johnny hears his future wife admit she's having an affair. Does he now need proof he has proof?

"I disagree," Tommy said.

In interviews about *The Room,* Tommy always shows an unusual amount of defensiveness about Johnny's tape-recorder surveillance of Lisa. He maintains that Johnny's method is a legitimate way to record telephone conversations. Tommy believes this because, in his personal life, he has taped his own phone calls for years using similarly low-tech techniques. Whenever anyone called him—including me—he put the call on speaker and hit record on the same yard-sale tape recorder he now wanted to film. This was why he always said "I'm listening" whenever I called. He *was* listening. He was also recording. I know all this because I eventually found a huge cache of tapes with hours and hours of phone calls on them, some of which were ours. I confronted him. He denied it at first. When he realized he couldn't deny it, he claimed he'd done this to study my accent, in order to lose his own. I told him that didn't sound like a very plausible explanation, and from then on, I hung up on him if he ever put me on speaker. Then he became paranoid that *I* was taping *him*. Whenever we were on the phone, he would repeatedly ask me, "Does anybody listen this conversation?"

"Fine," Sandy said, dabbing at his sweaty forehead with a handker-chief. "I'm too hot to argue anymore. Let's just shoot the thing." When Tommy walked away, Sandy said to me, "Nobody is going to see this movie anyway."

The first task was to shoot Tommy on the condo set's spiral staircase while he looks down at Claudette and Lisa as they have their conversation ten feet away from him. Tommy wanted to be filmed through the bars of the staircase, which made him look like an imprisoned long-haired Kong.

"This doesn't work," Sandy said, watching the setup from behind the camera.

I overheard Graham say to his cameraman that if someone had told him about Tommy, he would have refused to believe that such a film-maker could exist. Once they got the eyelines set, Tommy went off to makeup for the fifth time that day. Graham started looking around the room. "What's the deal with all these candles?" he asked. "And what's with these red curtains? Why does the CD tower have only three CDs in it? Who on earth decorated this set?" (He might as well have said: "The candles, the music, the sexy dress—what's going on here?")

No one answered Graham, which was all the answer Graham needed. His shoulders sagged as Tommy placed himself on the spiral staircase again. They started to film, but Tommy couldn't stand still. He kept bobbing, moving, and messing up the shot's composition. "Stop moving, please," Graham said.

"I'm not moving," Tommy said.

They tried it again. Again Tommy was moving.

"Please stop moving," Graham said, through clenched teeth.

Eventually, Tommy stopped moving, but now came the acting part. This is what Tommy had to say: "How could they say this about me? I don't believe it. I'll show them. I'll record everything." Yet again Tommy's humble, self-scripted lines proved too much for him. After an hour of blown takes, botched lines, and Tommy's calls for "Line!" Graham asked someone to write the lines down on a large piece of paper and hold them up so Tommy could read them. If you watch this scene carefully, you can see Tommy's eyes scan the impromptu cue card being held up before him. Once we finally got the shot, Graham turned to me and said, "He wrote this, right?"

"He did."

"Just checking."

Now came time to shoot the scene in which Johnny crosses the living room to set up the phone-tap tape recorder, which for some reason had already been placed in a nook beneath Johnny's end table.

Sandy made the mistake of telling Tommy to be cautious not to hit his head on the way down the stairs, which meant that his first ten takes coming down had all the briskness and surety of a grandmother carrying a Ming vase. When they finally got a somewhat usable take of Tommy coming down the stairs, he had to be told to continue walking across the room to the phone, at which point Tommy started making what the crew instantly designated The Face. I knew The Face for what it really was: Blue Steel. Tommy has always been fascinated with models and pretty clearly believes he should be one. In fact, earlier that day, before everything went crazy and Carolyn fainted, I saw him looking at a Calvin Klein ad in *GQ* while getting his second round of makeup done. "You think I could do the modeling?" he asked me, holding the magazine out.

I wasn't sure how honest he wanted me to be. "Sure, why not," I said.

Tommy spent the rest of his time in the makeup chair going from studying the Calvin Klein ad to pursing his lips in the mirror.

Let's explore Tommy's decision to Blue Steel at this particular moment in the story. Johnny has just learned that his future wife is cheating on him. He's devastated and upset, presumably. This was Johnny's time for sobriety and doubt. It was not his time to explode with sexuality.

"What's with the duck-lip thing he's doing?" someone asked quietly, as Tommy vamped his way across the room. "What the hell is he *doing*?"

Simple. Tommy decided to have Johnny respond to the shattering news that his future wife is banging another guy with some Blue Steel.

Later in the day, during close-up shots for Tommy's actual assembly of his tape-recorder wiretap, he gave the most *incredible* Blue Steel I think I've ever seen. Graham, and the people he'd brought in, were stupefied at this point. It was as though they'd been called in to do a simple nature film and found themselves confronted with the Loch Ness Monster.

Getting Tommy back across the room and up the stairs was the most difficult portion of this sequence. Sandy had to talk him through the entire thing. When Tommy looked back at the tape recorder triumphantly, nodding in amazed self-admiration at the genius of his wiretap, Sandy said, "Why are you looking back? Keep going! Don't look back!" Tommy reached the stairs and climbed them at such a glacial pace, it looked as if Johnny had never been in his own house before.

When Tommy finished, he clearly thought that he'd just delivered a master class in dramatic acting. He approached me, smiling. "You think you can do it," he said, "and I can't, huh? Don't worry, but I may be a model, too. I don't know yet. Maybe I'll try it. Maybe do underwear modeling. Maybe design my own underwear. What about that?"

I didn't point out to him that Juliette and Carolyn managed to film their conversation in less time than it took to film Tommy walking across a room—and that included the time it took Carolyn to visit and return from the hospital.

Graham and his crew shot for several more days in the punishing heat of Johnny and Lisa's condo set. Among the scenes they filmed were the master shots of a conversation shared by Johnny and Peter, Johnny's psychologist friend, in which Johnny admits that Lisa has not been loyal to him. As usual, it took Tommy an entire afternoon to get a few clean takes, and Graham was getting less and less patient with him. Graham was particularly unhappy with the moment in which Johnny says, "You know what they say. Love is blind." The best take they had of that line was all mumbly and garbled, and it needed to be done again. Tommy saw this as an opportunity to earn his Oscar. He buttonholed Sandy and said, "Listen, this is very important scene. I want camera very close on my face. Very close. So you can see the eyes. This is dramatic scene for the character."

Sandy was so beaten down by this point that if Tommy had come to him and said, "I want to shoot this scene with unicorns in the background," Sandy would have said, "Yeah, sure. Sounds great."

Graham didn't like the sound of this close-up business, and liked it even less after looking at some of the test shots. "I don't know, Tommy. It's kind of scaring me. You look a little . . . possessed."

Tommy, though, was bothered by something else in the test shots. "Makeup artist!" he said, turning from the monitor. "I need you here. Look at this scene. I don't want to have the lines on my face. See? What is this thing on my face?"

Amy, the makeup artist, looked at him. I'm pretty sure she wanted to say, "That's called reality, Tommy."

"I don't like this puffy stuff," he said, touching the area under his eyes. She got him into the makeup chair and went to work getting rid of the puffy stuff. "Don't pull down on my face!" Tommy said, jerking. "Be gentle, my God." She rolled her eyes and kept doing exactly what she was doing. "Okay. Thank you. More powder now. More powder, please."

Kyle Vogt, who was playing Peter the psychologist, approached Tommy during this depuffification session. He'd made it very clear to Tommy when he was hired months ago that he had a commitment to another project that had priority over *The Room*. Tommy had assured Kyle that *The Room* would wrap before Kyle's other project began. Kyle's project was on the eve of starting, and his scenes in *The Room* were not anywhere close to being finished.

"Tommy," Kyle said, "I have to tell you that this is probably going to be my last scene. I can't work any more on this because of my other commitment."

Tommy's eyes were closed while the makeup artist powdered him. Now they popped open, like those of a sleeping dragon whose treasure had been snatched. In the original script, Peter was one of *The Room*'s most prominent characters, with more scenes than, say, Claudette.

"Why," Tommy said to Kyle, "do you try to ruin my project? This is unacceptable." He was going for hard-hearted menace here, but that proved impossible to pull off when someone was dabbing his face with a small foam cube covered in powder.

Kyle held his ground. "Tommy, I told you about this. You knew about this months ago."

Tommy sat there, sneering and breathing. "You know what," he said, after a moment, "that's fine, you leave, don't come back. We don't need you anyway. It's your loss—you and your stupid Warner Bros. They *spit* on you at Warner Bros."

The project Kyle was leaving for was, in fact, an indie film. Kyle had never said anything about going to do a film for Warner Bros. He worked for Warner Music, though, which a confused Tommy had obviously latched onto. Kyle tried to make things right with Tommy, using reason, but Tommy just sank into silent, powdery sullenness. Eventually Kyle left him alone.

Kyle, like most of us, saw *The Room* as a vanity project intended to promote Tommy and Tommy alone. By this point, he didn't think the film would get finished. It all must have felt very silly to Kyle, especially considering that his previous job was working for NASA at the Jet Propulsion Lab.

Whatever the case, he and Tommy now had to act together. Kyle was obviously upset and off his game, and while blocking the scene he smacked his head hard against one of the spiral staircase's low-jutting stairs. Blood gushed from his head, which caused Tommy to panic once again. Many people have wondered why Kyle blinks so much during this scene, and why he reaches out to touch so many props. The explanation is that he had a concussion and his depth perception was a mess. It's impressive that he was able to perform at all. He does not, however, make a very convincing psychologist.

Tommy claimed to be fascinated by psychology. He once mentioned having seen a psychologist or psychiatrist—he had no idea there was any difference between the two—and suggested it had been a positive experience. He supposedly studied psychology at Laney College and had the relevant textbooks stacked up in his messy apartment, but whether he had actually read any of them, I have no idea. It's worth pointing out that Peter's psychologist wisdom to Johnny ranges from cliché ("People are people") to obvious ("This is Lisa we're talking about?") to terrible ("If you love her, you should confront her"). Peter is one of the most oddly inconsistent characters in *The Room:* his firm and resolute opinions on Lisa change completely depending on which scene he's in. At one moment, he can't believe a woman as saintly as Lisa would ever cheat; minutes later he calls her a "sociopath."

Watching Tommy perform this scene, I wondered what his psychologist or psychiatrist had made of him. I tried to imagine Tommy's mind from the inside out. I saw burning forests, blind alleys, volcanoes in the desert, city streets that plunged into the ocean, barricades everywhere, and all of it lit in the deep-cherry light of emergency.

Graham was growing increasingly upset. The production had needed a generator for weeks now, because every time a piece of equipment ran out of juice, everyone had to wait for its operator to plug it in and recharge. If Tommy had had a generator on set, they could have filmed to their heart's delirious content. The production was losing hours every day due to the lack of a generator, which could be rented for around $200 a day. But the man who was spending half a million dollars shooting an HD film he wasn't going to use could not be bothered with such a peasant's expense. Graham had been asking for a generator daily and Tommy kept telling him he'd work on it.

During the Peter-Johnny scene, everything began to weigh on Graham: the heat, Tommy's flubbed lines, Kyle's excessive blinking, the way the water sounded when Johnny poured it into a glass. He seemed to be losing his mind a little. I think what was actually happening was that he was beginning to understand what it meant that his name was going to be attached to this film. I knew the feeling.

"Let's shoot something outside," he said to Tommy and Sandy after the Peter scene was finished. "Let's get out of this set. It's too hot and I'm going nuts with claustrophobia."

Sandy suggested shooting the rooftop party scene, which takes place near the end of the film. A night shoot, he said, might be nice. Tommy, though, wanted to shoot something else, something inside.

Graham made him a deal: If Tommy got a generator, they could shoot inside again, just as Tommy wanted. Tommy agreed. Graham gave him the number of two good generator places, and Tommy said he'd call.

After a long weekend break, Tommy pulled into the Birns & Sawyer lot to find Graham sitting on an apple box by the Rooftop. Tommy had come on his own, quite tardy of course, saying he had had a "dailies meeting with producers." Graham's crew was there, too, waiting with him. Tommy was supposed to have called about a generator, but I knew he hadn't. Tommy got out of his car, looking agitated, and walked toward Graham, who didn't stand. A box filled with paint towels and paint cans was at Graham's feet.

"Why sitting, not working?" Tommy asked.

"Where's the generator?" Graham replied.

Tommy explained that he'd called Graham's generator people. Unfortunately, they had no generator available at this time.

Graham nodded. He looked exhausted and frustrated—nothing like he had a couple of weeks ago. It was like someone had replaced his young, happy eyes with those of a miserable old crone. Even his hairline looked less robust. It was terribly depressing to be confronted with this good man's emotional and physical degeneration. He'd been such a fun, wry, amusing person to have around the set at first. His problem was that he wanted to make something he was proud of.

Tommy looked around at Graham's loafing, glowering crew and said, "Why is everyone sitting down? Let's move it, come on, let's get going!"

"I need a generator," Graham said, still sitting. He was no longer looking at Tommy. "This day, like all the others, will be hell with no generator."

Tommy stopped and fixed upon Graham a long stare of intense disapproval. "Well, I'm sorry. Generator is not available at this time. I cannot create it for you here. I can't make it out of nothing."

Again Graham nodded. "You never called."

"Oh yes I *did* call."

"No, you didn't. I called them, and they never received a call from you. They told me they had plenty available. You're a liar, Tommy."

"No," Tommy said. "You liar yourself! We call. They say unavailable. So do your job, okay?"

"Do my job." Graham played with the words as though they were little gobs of dough and he was still deciding what to make with them. "How about *you* do *your* job?"

Tommy began to walk away. Suddenly he turned around and pointed his finger at Graham. "Listen to me, young man! It's not my problem. I need to prepare for acting, okay? I don't want to hear your problem."

Graham grabbed a paint towel from the box at his feet and stood with righteous fury. *"Tommy,"* he said. Tommy turned and Graham marched up to him and threw the paint towel at Tommy's feet. This was far more dramatic than it sounds. It looked as grave an insult as some seventeenth-century Frenchman slapping another with a white glove. He stuck his finger in Tommy's face. "You're a fucking liar, Tommy. You're a *fucking* liar."

Peter Anway heard the ruckus and came out immediately.

"Don't raise your voice on me!" Tommy said, pointing his own finger in Graham's face.

Graham knocked it away. "You know what? I fucking quit! You're a fucking liar, Tommy! I quit!" Graham turned and stormed away. He motioned to his crew, who all snapped into action as though Graham were Toulon and they were his puppets.

Tommy had never been confronted in this way before. He'd been yelled at, but not like this. Throughout the filming of *The Room,* Graham was the only person to directly call Tommy out for his lying.

Tommy walked after Graham as he and his crew left. "Keep going, you sissy guy," Tommy said. "You sissy faggot! Keep going! Learn how to walk!"

Graham, to his credit, didn't turn and didn't acknowledge Tommy's insults. He and his crew were gone quickly. Tommy seemed to be hyperventilating, out of his mind. I've never heard the word *sissy* more times than I did in the next minute. This was some of the ugliest on-set behavior I'd ever seen from Tommy. It was despicable. There was no other word for it. He looked like a damaged wraith. He'd clearly lied, and he'd just as clearly been busted for it. It was as if he wanted to sabotage his own project—and Graham's sin was simply responding to Tommy like most of us wanted to.

"You see how these people are?" he shouted. "They're monsters! Pricks! I give them job and they don't appreciate damn thing."

Tommy could tell I was appalled by him. He could lie to himself all he wanted, but he couldn't keep lying to everyone else. How was it that he never seemed to feel any guilt? What kind of a person could do that?

I wanted this episode to end. I wanted the film to be finished. I was actually still rooting for that at this point, because I couldn't bear the thought of so many people working so hard for nothing. "Stop, Tommy," I said. "Enough."

He didn't stop. He was pacing back and forth, snarling and muttering to himself: "They want me to spend money, they want to take my money, they try to ruin my project."

Everyone who didn't quit went home for the day—except for one person. A guy who'd been working the cameras—a guy, importantly, who didn't much care for Graham—now approached Tommy in the Birns & Sawyer parking lot. He was tall, with short, sun-bleached hair and a very laid-back manner. I pegged him as a former surfer now using the onset of his late thirties as motivation to get more professional. "Hey, Tommy," Todd Barron said. "I can be your DP."

Tommy turned and looked at him.

"I'll run it. I'll light the set. I'll do the camera. Just pay me a couple hundred bucks a day. Joe, my camera guy, will stay on with me, too."

Tommy hired Todd Barron on the spot. "Now," Tommy said, "we see how good you are."

twelve

I'm Not Waiting for Hollywood

You can change the people, change the scenery,
but you can't change your own rotten self.
—Tom Ripley, *The Talented Mr. Ripley*

After Tommy's meltdown in the car, weeks went by before I spoke to him again. When we finally did connect he apologized several times for losing control. Although he was still planning his move to L.A., he assured me that I could remain in the apartment. "I don't force you to live there," he said, "but it's your house, too." Thanks to what Tommy described as "issue" with Street Fashions, his imminent arrival kept getting postponed. The delays were fine by me. I'd been scanning the classifieds for apartments in my price range: an exercise in despair.

Around Christmastime I went up to the Bay Area to visit my family for the holidays. As soon as I got there, my feelings of melancholy and doubt about my future almost overwhelmed me. I pondered my options in the face of my dwindling savings and lack of income. I could afford a few more months in Tommy's apartment but barely a month elsewhere. So that was it, then: If I wanted to stick it out in L.A., I needed to get a job as quickly as possible and endure living with Tommy until I saved up enough to move out.

After Christmas, Tommy called me at my folks' place and said he was going to spend his New Year's Eve at the base of the Hollywood sign. I told him that sounded very interesting. Tommy then surprised me by announcing that he'd already moved to Los Angeles. He was, in fact, living in the apartment right now.

"Wait," I said. "What?"

"Oh," Tommy said. "It's very simple. At midnight, I am going to yell, 'Tommy Wiseau is here! I will take over the Hollywood! Year 2000 is my year!'"

"Not the sign thing," I said. "You moved to L.A.?"

"Yes," he said. "It is my time."

Tommy was too proud to admit that he'd be spending New Year's Eve alone, but I knew he was. I wasn't surprised when he started pestering me to come down to witness his Hollywood sign proclamation in person. Instead, I stayed in San Francisco, too depressed to do much more than watch movies all day. Iris had already warned me that pilot season this year was going to be rough. Reality shows had become so popular that the networks were scrambling away from traditionally scripted television like roaches from fluorescent light. Who needed actors when civilians were willing to eat bugs on camera?

When I confessed to my mother that I was going back to L.A. to live with Tommy for a few weeks while I found another place, she braced herself against the nearest firmly mounted object. She'd thought I was now home for good. "I warned you," she said. "I told you! He's always been a weirdo, but now you *know* he's a weirdo—and you're still going back there? Come *on*. Who did I raise?"

This succeeded only in putting steel in my back. When I got *Retro Puppet Master,* I hoped I had kick-started my strenuous climb to regular work. Things, of course, hadn't quite panned out that way. My mom, on the other hand, couldn't figure out why, after doing a movie, I wasn't already a big star. She wondered how much more time and effort this megastardom of mine was going to take. The one thing that managed to cheer me up was a Christmas card from Iris. "You have everything it takes to become a successful actor in L.A.," it read.

One day, right after Christmas, I got a call from my hippie friend who had, in some ways, inadvertently instigated this whole mess by going toe to toe with Tommy on the phone a few months ago. I didn't blame him for wanting to confront Tommy about his bizarre need for secrecy; I knew he was trying to look out for me.

The first thing my friend said: "I just saw a movie you need to watch. Now."

"What is it?" I asked.

"The Talented Mr. Ripley."

I'd seen previews for the film but knew only a little about it. "Really? What's it about?"

"Just trust me, Greg. You need to see this film." My friend, a longtime film editor, was also a self-proclaimed movie snob, so it was rare that he ever got that excited about anything that wasn't *Casablanca* or *Cinema Paradiso*.

A couple of hours later I met my friend at Festival Cinemas in downtown Walnut Creek, where he'd already purchased two tickets. I didn't know what to expect from the film, having never read the work of Patricia Highsmith, who wrote the novel *Ripley* was based on, and having never seen any of director Anthony Minghella's previous films. (I've since rectified this.)

"So why do you think I should see this?" I asked while we waited for the previews to begin.

"Just wait. After I saw it, I couldn't stop thinking about the move you're contemplating."

I laughed. "My move? Why?"

He didn't laugh. "You'll see."

The last decade has brought about a general and much-needed critical rehabilitation of *Ripley,* which was simply ahead of its time. Today a lot of people regard it as one of the best films of the last twenty years. It's certainly among the most beautiful: Italy hasn't looked so good since Fellini. The performances, too, are affecting and powerful. The first time I watched it I noticed all that stuff, yes, but it had far more piercingly personal resonance than that. From *Ripley*'s opening scenes, in which Matt Damon's Tom Ripley vacuums up all the requisite bits of knowledge he'll need to convince Jude Law's Dickie Greenleaf that they were at Princeton together, I knew precisely why my friend was forcing me to watch it. Tom Ripley is someone who wants to belong to respectable society so deeply that he'll do anything. He loves Dickie Greenleaf's life, and this love turns into an obsession with Dickie himself. Tom is so skilled at reading people and situations that he's usually able to get what he wants, but he's utterly incapable of recognizing when he crosses the line into abject creepiness. Those who call Tom on his strangely obsessive social-climbing tendencies are usually punished with violence. In this way, Tom's small, innocent lies become gargantuan, soul-killing lies. Murder becomes the foundation of the life he makes for himself, the life he refuses to let go of. Tom's brotherly attraction to Dickie becomes a spurned lover's rage when Dickie tries to cut him out of his life. When the film places Dickie and Tom in a small boat off the coast of San Remo, both yelling about what they believe their friendship really constitutes, my stomach squirmed in wormy recognition. I simply couldn't believe what I was watching. I couldn't believe how well it captured what Tommy's and my friendship had come to feel like. All of which made me Walnut Creek's least happy and most startled moviegoer when Tom grabs an oar from the boat and beats Dickie to death with it.

I was stunned by the aftermath of this scene: Tom sobbing and cuddling up to Dickie's corpse on the floor of the small boat while bloody water sloshes over them both. It was one of the most intense and chilling things I'd ever seen. I looked over at my friend, who was already staring at me. He said one word over Ripley's desperate weeping: "Tommy."

That night, I came down with the worst flu I've ever had. I couldn't walk, think, sleep, or talk. I was vomiting every thirty minutes for the entire night and didn't get out of bed for three days afterward. By day four, I was so weak I could barely lift my arms. I felt as though I'd been torn apart by microscopic locusts.

My mother tried to convince me not to go back to L.A. She failed. My hippie friend tried to convince me not to go back to L.A. He failed. Patricia Highsmith, Matt Damon, Jude Law, and Anthony Minghella tried to convince me not to go back to L.A. They failed. Now my body was trying to convince me not to go back to L.A. It, too, failed. Two weeks later, against all logic, I was in my Lumina and heading back to

Hollywood. My apartment in L.A. was, at the end of the day, all I had going for me; it was my life raft. If I wanted to keep my dream alive, I had to live on the raft I had, even if this meant that Tommy was, however briefly, my fellow passenger.

The last thing my mother told me before I left Danville was this: "You are at a crucial time in your life. You're twenty-one years old. Don't make the wrong decision. Wrong decisions can take an entire life to undo. You're playing with fire." Even my father thought I was crazy for going back to L.A. He made it very clear, in fact, that my choice meant I didn't have a "normal mind." But if having a "normal mind" meant reporting day after day to a job my heart wasn't in, for months and years on end, then no, I didn't have a normal mind, and moreover didn't want one.

During the drive down to Hollywood, I thought about what could have been driving Tommy's renewed interest in Los Angeles and acting. I'd managed to piece together some of Tommy's acting trajectory. I knew, for instance, that he'd made his first attempts in the late 1980s, when he was commuting to his LACC classes from San Francisco. After that, he'd moved to L.A. and bounced around: Westwood, West Hollywood. He'd most likely begun living in the Crescent Heights place in the early to mid 1990s, which was also when he made his last serious push to become an actor. I'd heard a circa-1994 tape in which an innocent, exuberant Tommy chronicled his darkest acting hours, telling himself to "try acting for couple more months," and repeating to himself, "I believe I have something to offer. I will do it. I really have something. To break me take time. Take really time." By 1995 or so, however, his aspirations had fizzled, thanks in no small part to his no-nonsense L.A. acting teacher Vincent Chase. After that, Tommy left acting behind and retreated to San Francisco. But he kept renting that L.A. apartment during the years that followed, which means his dream never really went away; it was simply dormant. After his San Francisco car accident, Tommy enrolled in San Francisco acting classes. He began Jean Shelton's class, where, for the first time, as I heard him happily say on another tape, "someone pick me" for a scene partner. That someone was me. This random collision ended up changing everything for us both.

I reached the apartment after midnight. My heart was jackhammering in my chest as I neared the door. I entered to find the entire room walled off by thick black velvet drapes hanging from the ceiling. It was like Tommy had turned one side of the apartment into a cable-access television set: Apartment Chiller Theater.

Before I could do the sensible thing and flee, Tommy's large white face peeked out from a gap in his black velvet curtains. "Well, hello, stranger," he said.

I was quiet for a moment. "Hey," I said.

Tommy stepped out from behind the curtains. "You can see there have been some changes in apartment. This is now my private corner. No one is allowed back here. Unless they have special access."

I was more than fine with Tommy's private black-curtained refuge. It was a little Addams Family, maybe, but at least it meant I still had my own space.

I'd been back in the apartment for only a few minutes when Tommy started asking me for my agent's contact info and the name of the headshot photographer I'd used. An image of him crashing into Iris Burton's office—and her driving a wooden stake into his heart—popped into my mind. I saw that he'd prepared a stack of envelopes prelabeled with casting directors' addresses. I had been in the same room as Tommy for five minutes and already I felt suffocated.

He announced that if I decided to continue living in the apartment, my rent would be upped. Instead of paying Tommy less than one-quarter of the mortgage a month (Tommy's story was inconsistent as to whether he owned or rented the place), I was now to pay him half. "You need to learn responsibility," he said. "The school is over." This, too, was fine, since I didn't want to keep living my life in indentured servitude to Tommy. But it meant my already diminished savings were going to run out more quickly than I'd anticipated. I promised myself I would spend the next morning looking for part-time jobs and a new place. Already I could feel that the apartment's old, beloved energy had become warped by Tommy's presence. Tommy may or may not be a vampire, but I can say with surety that, at least in close quarters, he's eminently capable of draining the life and light right out of someone.

While I was unpacking my stuff in my bedroom, Tommy stood in the doorjamb. "You look so skinny and pale, my God," he said. "What happened to you? Are you ghost?"

"I had the flu for two weeks," I said. "Like I told you."

"How much weight did you lose?"

"Ten pounds."

Tommy's hands went to his stomach. "Well, you're lucky! Maybe I should get sick, too, huh?"

"I'm tired," I told Tommy, hoping to convey that it was time for him to head back to his vampire wonder cave. "I'm going to try to get some sleep."

Tommy nodded, and I closed the door.

Tommy stays up very late. I knew that, at the time. When you don't live with someone, *Tommy stays up very late* is a curiosity, a personality quirk, an abstraction. When you live with someone, however, *Tommy stays up very late* swiftly defines the living dynamic. On that first night, Tommy spent an hour on the phone working on his diction with his friend Chloe. He could be heard repeating the phrases she was apparently feeding him ("Yes, I think so," "Where is the nearest telephone?" "I don't agree with you"), all in his valiant ongoing attempt to lose that ineradicable accent of his. The apartment was too small for me not to hear every syllable of every exchange.

"How is my voice tonight?" Tommy would ask Chloe after ten or twelve attempts. "Less accent?" I assumed Chloe's judgment was usually not affirmative, because Tommy would begin the process anew.

After Chloe had had enough and hung up (or killed herself), Tommy busted out some English audiotape course he'd purchased. I listened to the rough *chock* of Tommy pressing the play button. Then: "You think it's good, do you?" Tommy would repeat that: "You think it's good, *do you*?" Then another *chock*, this time of the rewind button being pressed, followed by a whirring sound, and there the phrase was again: "You think it's good, *do you*?" Tommy would repeat it, his intonation so hopelessly wrong. Tommy played and repeated the phrase "You think it's good, do you?" for over an hour. He did it at least eighty times. I know because that's when I stopped counting and put my pillow over my head.

You think it's good, do you? This wasn't even a phrase the average native English speaker would *say*. Tommy should have been learning to say "I'd like a refund for these tapes, please."

I was fast asleep when my door opened and Tommy began doing pull-ups on the bar he'd installed in my doorway, which I'd somehow not noticed. It was 4:00 a.m. After a grunty set of ten pull-ups Tommy dropped to the floor with a thud and turned to pace around the living room like a caveman, after which he hit the chin-up bar again. Once he completed four sets, he closed the door.

This is a nightmare, I thought. Either that, or Tommy was trying to convince me to leave.

In the morning, I hit every service-industry and retail establishment I found on Sunset, Hollywood, and Santa Monica Boulevards. I probably filled out a few dozen applications that day. Near the end of my quest, I found myself in a gay bar that wasn't due to open for a few hours. This wasn't the kind of bar in which hipsters drank elegant potions and talked about the film industry. This was a slightly feral bar with an older clientele and dungeonlike décor.

"I wanted to see if you guys are hiring?" I asked the manager. Well, they needed a bar back, which is the person who carries kegs and boxes of booze around and, per the manager, also occasionally cleaned the toilets. "I can do that," I said desperately.

The man's eyes filled with strangely friendly pity. "I'm really sorry," he said, "but you wouldn't last one night in this place."

At the end of the day I walked four miles to drop off an application to work at a grocery store. I was told that the store didn't have any positions open at the moment but that they'd keep my "stuff" on file. I'd never felt so defeated in my life.

I spent the next few days walking around Los Angeles, hoping that while I was out, my home phone was ringing with prospects. Alas, it wasn't. I did manage to do some constructive things, one of which was load up on literature at the Samuel French Bookshop on Sunset. Then I signed up for two courses at Santa Monica College: the History of Film and the History of Theatre. I'd resisted college for so long and been such an indifferent student in high school, I was a little stunned by how much I wound up loving both classes. I could thank Tommy, at least, for inadvertently making school an enjoyable endeavor.

I spent a lot of time wishing I were more of a partier or a reveler—anything to break up the nights back in the vampire wonder cave—but I wasn't. So while Tommy spent his evenings and nights and *very late* nights trying to lose his accent, I mostly read books with my door closed and my headphones on. One name I came across in several acting books was Jeff Corey, a character actor who'd been very successful in the 1940s. He was summoned to testify before the House Committee on Un-American Activities, a committee he ridiculed during his testimony. Following his blacklisting, Corey became a highly sought-after acting teacher. He'd worked with Gary Cooper, James Dean, Jack Nicholson, Sharon Tate, Leonard Nimoy, Jane Fonda, and, more recently, Shannen Doherty. Corey still ran a weekly acting class out in Malibu, so I made an appointment with him to see whether I could get in.

The day of our meeting my Lumina didn't start, and the bus to Malibu was as grueling as a trans-Siberian train. Tommy offered to drive me to the coast, which typically took an hour. I didn't say anything about Corey or what I was doing in Malibu, for fear that he'd run into the house with an armful of headshots.

We found Corey's house on the Malibu cliffs, which overlooked Point Dume Beach, and I suggested to Tommy that, while he waited, he should take a swim or something. "I don't go in ocean," Tommy said. I tried to convince him that ocean water was actually very good for the body. *Anything*, basically, to keep him from curiously popping in on Corey's and my meeting. "Are you kidding?" Tommy said. "Ocean's not good for you. There are monsters that bite your *ass*."

Tommy parked across the street and left me with these parting words as I started toward Corey's house: "Be careful. The gigolo business doesn't work how you think."

Corey took me to his guesthouse, where he held his classes, and which had a panoramic view of the Pacific as beautiful as any I'd seen. Corey himself was irritable and cranky in the way that only old men can pull off and make adorable. I sensed that Corey no longer had that many eager young visitors, but the man still loved to talk. The first thing he told me was that Bob Dylan lived across the street from him. (I immediately thought, *Tommy Wiseau is blocking Bob Dylan's driveway*.) The second was that Elia Kazan, who had been one of my favorite directors, was a shitty tennis player and an even worse loser. He told me tales about when he'd done *In Cold Blood* and Rod Serling's *Night Gallery* and described working with James Dean on "his walk" the week before Dean was killed. I could take in Corey's charactery face—all white hair and big unkempt eyebrows—and listen to his anecdotes for hours. I remember thinking that if someone were to play Jeff Corey in a film, the only two people who could have pulled it off were Burgess Meredith and Jeff Corey.

After we'd talked for a while, Corey asked me to do a monologue. I did, and it came out sideways. I was, I admit, greatly intimidated by his direction: "Sit with your legs closer together! Come on, young man! Stand up and take command!" My monologue was rough, but Corey had mercy and invited me to take part in his class.

The next morning, for the first time since I'd come back to L.A., Tommy's curtains were slightly open, allowing me the chance to peer into his lair. It was as weird as I'd feared it would be. For a bed, Tommy had placed a regular twin mattress over a half-inflated air mattress, which meant he was sleeping at a tilty thirty-degree incline every night. For pillowcases, Tommy was using old T-shirts. He noticed me pondering these Wiseauvian masterpieces of squalid home décor. "How do you like my new creation?" he asked, as he held up one of the pillows. "This is my new thing." Scattered across Tommy's glass-topped desk were papers, his how-to-lose-your-accent tapes, the tape recorder he'd later use in *The Room,* exercise books, and yoga videos. His clothes were thrown everywhere. Half-empty glasses of water were sitting on the floor, some cloudier than others. Taped to the wall was a piece of paper, scrawled across which was one of Tommy's more mysterious mantras: "I, me, you. Voice. Body. Mind. We all have that!"

That night I started writing a screenplay about a young guy who lived with a lunatic in a house that had been built on a haunted Indian burial ground. I wasn't expecting to sell the thing. It was pure therapy.

A few nights later—January 23, 2000—was the Golden Globes, known to Tommy as "the Golden Globe." I was driving home from school, fighting my way through the limo traffic, and wishing desperately that I were flowing with it instead. When I walked into the apartment, Tommy was hanging upside down from the bedroom doorjamb's pull-up bar like a bat. He was wearing his tank top and baggy sweats with multiple bleach stains. His eyes were closed. Being greeted by this vision of Tommy nearly made me sit down on the kitchen floor and quietly weep. The man-bat spoke: "Take your shoes off. I get sick because of all this bacteria, dammit."

"Bacteria?" I said. *"Are you serious?"*

"Yes I am serious. I get sick because of all this bacteria. Sneezing like hell." This was when I noticed that Tommy was wearing white surgical gloves. So it was official: Tommy had gone Howard Hughes nuts. "From now on," he went on, "you must wash the hands, immediately. Leave your shoes outside. Don't touch my things. I'm sensitive to all this stuff. Have respect." Then Tommy curled up, grabbed the pull-up bar, released his legs, hung on for a moment, and finally dropped to the floor. "I'm starving," he said, wobbling a little as the gathered blood rushed from his brain. "Let's eat something."

Tommy couldn't bear to eat alone. He would suffer through hours of hunger-pain spasms to avoid the solitude. But I liked—even *preferred*—to eat alone. Sitting by myself at the end of a day was a way for me to think and reflect. Since I'd started living with Tommy, it had also become a useful time to *plot*.

"I'm not going out tonight," I said. "It's crazy traffic everywhere because of the Golden Globes."

Tommy shrugged. "Golden Globe? So what. I'm not invited. Who cares. Let's go eat. Go see feature movie. Something different. Find some chicks or something! I'm bored in this apartment. I can't be in cage all day long. Why you keep me in cage? I think I will get married soon."

Tommy was right about one thing: He *was* living in a cage; a self-constructed, curtained cage called Tommy Wiseau's Life. That said, going out and eating was bound to be better than spending another evening in my bedroom while Tommy alternated between English-language mangling and pull-ups. I also knew if I stayed home I'd be tempted to watch the Golden Globes, and that was only going to re-mind me of how distressingly far away I was from the life I wanted.

We wound up at the Koo Koo Roo on Santa Monica Boulevard, which had recently become Tommy's new favorite restaurant. From the moment we walked in, though, Tommy was off. Everything bugged him. The booths, the décor, the light from outside, the clientele, the small portions. ("Is there shortage here?" he asked.) When the server took our orders, Tommy started quizzing him on the chicken: how it was prepared, whether the chickens were clean, how many calories, why it was so expensive. The server walked away when Tommy dared him to find the most delicious piece of chicken they had. At one point, I had found all his goofiness entertaining, or at least tolerable, but now it was embarrassing.

After our interminable dinner, we were standing in front of the Beverly Cinemas trying to figure out what to go see. *The Talented Mr. Ripley* was still playing, and I somehow knew—I *knew*—that Tommy was going to suggest we go see it. If he did suggest *Ripley,* I decided I wasn't going to tell him that I'd seen it a month ago; he'd just com-plain about not having been invited. Tommy scanned the posters and stopped on *Ripley*. I was watching his eyes, and the poster just *snagged* Tommy's attention. Then he turned to me while pointing at the poster. "I want to see *this* movie."

I'd seen several movies with Tommy. He'd always get bored and restless before it was over. Sometimes he got chatty within the first half hour and other times he fell fast asleep after ten minutes. Or he'd shout "Boring!" in the middle of the film. "There's better acting in the Jean Shelton class!" When *Ripley* started, though, Tommy didn't talk. He didn't stir. He was wide-eyed and riveted from the very first scene. For me it was even better the second time, because now I was watch-ing it through Tommy's eyes. I was trying to decide if he was seeing it the way I had. When the scene of Tom beating Dickie to death came to pass, Tommy actually leaned back and clamped his hand over his mouth. When, at the end of the film, Tom asks his beguiled, deceived lover Peter to tell him "something nice about Tom Ripley" moments before strangling him to death, Tommy leaned forward in his seat and sat there with his face cupped in his hands. I kept glancing over at Tommy, thinking, *What's he feeling right now? What's running through his head?* Tom Ripley has to kill Peter, the only person who's ever loved him. Why? Because to get that love he'd had to lie about who he really was.

For the first time since I'd known him, maybe for the first time in his life, Tommy insisted on staying in his seat through the entire end-credits crawl. When the lights came up, Tommy looked devastated. His eyes were wet, his mouth slightly pried open. He had the wrung-out look of a man who'd just come to the end of a long, doomed love affair. The movie had bludgeoned him to within an inch of his emotional life.

I didn't think Tommy was a killer like Tom Ripley, but the movie told me that a tortured person can do horrible things for sympathetic reasons. And Tom Ripley was deeply sympathetic. So was Tommy.

I felt sad walking out of the theater. I realized that when Tommy had gone haywire in the car months ago, he had done so to avoid rejection. He'd decided that to avoid losing someone who potentially understood or accepted him, it was best to get rid of that person preemptively. That way, he could comfortably continue to live his deeply lonely life, consoled by his conviction that others had done him wrong.

Tommy and I didn't talk much until after we got into his car. On La Cienega, some limos were cruising alongside us; the Golden Globes had just gotten out. *Ripley* had been nominated for five of them, including Best Actor for Matt Damon's Tom Ripley and Best Supporting Actor for Jude Law's Dickie Greenleaf. We pulled up to a red light; a limo idled next to us. Suddenly Tommy said, "You know what? I'm not waiting for Hollywood. I can make my own movie."

I looked over at him. I knew better than to say anything right now.

"I can make movie," he said again. "I will make better movie than these fuckers, you watch." He sped up and cut off the next limo for emphasis. "I know they don't want me. I know they don't understand me. Guy with accent and long hair. So I show them. I show them what I can do." Tommy had sent out more than a hundred headshots since he'd arrived in Los Angeles. He did, in other words, exactly what I'd done when I got here. No one had called him back. Not one person.

We returned to the apartment. Tommy drew his curtains and sat down at his desk. He was rubbing his forehead, his eyes as intensely focused as a laser beam. I started to head off to my bedroom but Tommy asked me to stay and talk with him some more. He ran his hands through his hair and slouched over and didn't say anything for a long time. Then he sat up. "You know what? Fuck it, man. I will write my own play. I'll do my own project and it will be better than everybody else. You think this movie we just saw was tragedy? No. Not even close. *I* will make tragedy. People will see my project and . . . you know what? They will not sleep for two weeks. They will be completely shocked. You watch."

I'd seen Tommy angry before, but this was different. For the first time since I'd known him, his anger had a discernible target. He wasn't going to try to please Hollywood anymore. Forget the headshot game, the get-an-agent game, the audition game, the sell-yourself game. He'd make his own rules and create his own project. *Ripley* had planted a mysterious seed inside him. Excited by his own plan, Tommy stood up and pounded himself on the chest. "Listen to me, okay? I'm going to do it all myself. Everything. I'm going to show all these fuckers from Hollywood in their limousines."

He started to pace and furiously describe the play or movie (he kept going back and forth about which one his project would be) he wanted to make, all of it coming to him on the fly. "So listen. Very important information. Are you ready? My movie will have seven main characters. I will play main character. I call him Johnny. He has this beautiful girl, Blondie, and his best friend—this all-America handsome guy. You will play him.

"It all take place in one room, this drama. Everybody is so close and life is perfect, but then girl, beautiful girl, she betray him. She sleep with his best friend. Everybody hurt and betray Johnny. So he become furious! He's fed up with his life, with everybody, and decide to kill himself in front of entire world. Then everyone will see. People will be shocked. It will be big drama. After my creation, people will not sleep for two weeks. You watch. Hollywood want reaction? I give these bastards their reaction."

Not until years later did I really understand what Tommy had done, which was to create his own personal version of the three main *Ripley* characters. This meant he mix-and-matched their characteristics according to his own strange value system, after which he placed them into a warped version of his own life experience. In Tommy's story, the Tom Ripley character is half Lisa and half Mark, while Johnny is half the charismatic Dickie Greenleaf and half the innocent and lonely victim Tom Ripley. It's such a strange interpretation of the story, but it was what Tommy took away from it. Tommy couldn't see what the film was actually trying to tell him about himself.

"I play the best friend?" I asked, still mostly humoring him, never imagining that this scheme would last into the morning.

"I know the name of your character now," Tommy said, looking at me. "You will be called Mark—like this guy Mark Damon."

thirteen

"Leave Your Stupid Comments in Your Pocket"

Sometimes it's interesting to see just how bad bad writing can be.
This promised to go the limit.
—Joe Gillis, *Sunset Boulevard*

"Tommy!" Peter Anway said, all rubbing hands and grinning nervousness, when Tommy arrived on set. "Mr. Meurer is not happy with us right now. Do you understand? He doesn't want to see that Rooftop set when he comes in today."

Tommy always took the Meurer-to-Anway information-transit system seriously. Bill Meurer, in Tommy's mind, represented the Hollywood establishment he so desperately wanted to be a part of. So right away he gathered his (third) crew together and announced, "We don't want to upset the Bill." Now, instead of filming, our job was to disassemble the Rooftop set one piece at a time.

This was the morning of the one-year anniversary of September 11. While we were ripping apart the Rooftop a plane flew overhead. It was a fighter plane of some sort: low-flying, sleek, vaguely wasp-shaped, and traveling very fast. At the sight of the jet Tommy stopped everything. "Okay, everybody," he said. "We have meeting inside. Please follow me."

We all looked at one another. What now? It was blood-boilingly hot inside Birns & Sawyer's cramped studio space, but once Tommy got us all in there, he asked everyone to please be quiet and "remember the American flag." We stood there, doing our best to be quiet. Then someone laughed. Tommy furiously decamped to another part of the studio and returned with a digital timer one of the camerapeople had been using during filming. Tommy set the timer to five minutes and placed it where everyone could see it. "Because you laugh," he said, "we now have five minutes of silence for America. Have due respect." Ten seconds into that five-minute silence, someone else laughed. Tommy reset the timer. "If I hear any laugh," he said, "which is very disrespectful, we do another five minutes. You can laugh the rest of your life. So you be the judge."

It was probably the longest five minutes I've ever experienced. Eyes were glazed and several mouths were trembling, but no one wanted that clock to be reset. Somehow, on our third try, we made it all the way through. The timer ran out to several gasps, and I realized how many of us had been reduced to holding our breath near the end to keep from cracking up.

Tommy followed these five minutes with a little speech: "This prick Osama is the biggest asshole-motherfucker-piece-of-shit who ever lived. He think he can stop America. I'm sorry, Mr. Dickhead Osama, you don't have chance. We are the best country in the world." He then led the room in a chant of "USA, USA!"

Five minutes of reverent silence followed by fist-pumping mania: That was a pretty accurate encapsulation of the patriotism of Tommy Wiseau.

Tommy typically kept his Christmas tree up all year long. Sometimes he didn't remove the menagerie of Halloween pumpkins from his doorstep until the following Halloween, when he replaced all the old, black, rotten pumpkins with fresh new orange ones. Tommy's favorite American holiday was Thanksgiving, but he didn't just celebrate Thanksgiving Day. He celebrated Thanksgiving *Month,* eating a full turkey dinner every day for the next thirty days. I once asked him about this. His explanation: "We live in America. Anything is possible. I love living American life."

I have never gotten the sense that Tommy is mysterious for the sake of being mysterious. Rather, he is an incredibly guarded person trying to be less guarded. But the emotional fortifications Tommy has built around himself are too entrenched. When trying to express the parts of himself he seems to have lost access to, Tommy offers up fantastical, sad, self-contradictory stories. I've heard these stories many times. One of them begins like this:

Long ago, on the far side of central Europe—Communist Bloc Europe—sometime after the death of Stalin, a young boy, T——, is born to a mother who loves him. T—— has a brother and sister; he is the youngest or second youngest. His father is abusive, largely absent, alcoholic, and dead early, or was never there at all.

Seventy-nine percent of T——'s hometown was destroyed in World War II. He inherits nightmares from this ruined landscape, this ravaged country. Life is hard. His family is poor. Sometimes he sees Soviet soldiers, the closest thing he has to reliable father figures.

Very early T—— becomes determined to do something so simple and yet so impossible: travel to America. He goes to the library every day and looks at those few books about America that the Communists have neglected to remove from the shelves. T—— touches the pictures. He *sees* something in them, something he can't fully explain. He knows he belongs there. With the death of Stalin, little by little, things begin to change in his country. By the late 1950s there are Disney movies in the cinema, though his family is too poor to afford tickets. Nevertheless, the gray, bombed-out world around him is replaced by something more glorious, more Technicolor.

One of his first memories is of standing outside a cinema, watching *101 Dalmatians* through a crack in the door. He's chased away, eventually, but that night he dreams of being among those tiny spotted dogs, safe inside Disney's reality. Occasionally, his schoolmates will have American magazines—as precious as food or contraband—and he begs to hold them, just for a moment. He defends America to his peers and teachers who tell him terrible lies about life in the place he loves. For this, T—— is beaten up, picked on, mocked for being a traitor: the scar under his eye derives from one of these valiant early fights. They call him *Americanski, Johnny Americanski,* as he walks home from school. He doesn't have friends. He goes to the Catholic cathedral in his hometown and prays to be allowed to visit America. He cannot confess this sin of wanting to be different, to forsake his homeland, to any priest. He worries he'll be reported. He feels alone.

As a teenager, he sells posters of Marilyn Monroe, James Dean, and John Wayne in the city square. Maybe he sees in one of those contraband American movie magazines a photo of something he'll have a hard time forgetting: John Wayne standing outside what T—— imagines to be a great Hollywood movie studio, Birns & Sawyer. His countrymen buy his posters, of course, but some of them criticize him for selling American propaganda. He doesn't care. In his head, he's left already.

Sometimes he wants to be a movie star. Other times, a rock-and-roll musician. He schemes about how to get to America. He knows he'll have to visit somewhere else first, like West Germany or France. He doesn't much like the sound of either place. Decades later he'll tell a friend, disgustedly, "America is so much better than your stupid France, your stupid Germany." He tries to learn English by reading English-language books at the library, willing himself to understand the words. He makes lists of English words he likes. Maybe he waits with his mother in the bread-buying line, saying words to himself: *Bread. Street. Movie.*

He becomes a young man. He's strong, quick, and wily. His cousin is like him, hates the Communists, and desires nothing more than to escape. They ask around, investigate. They hear of a small French city whose police are said to tolerate illegal immigrants. Someone, after all, needs to do the terrible jobs French people are unwilling to do. He and his cousin scrape together the money needed to bribe the right people and suddenly they're on a bus. It's dark. No doubt there are many people on this bus from other Communist countries, and maybe T—— has the feeling of being involved in some endeavor much larger than himself. He's no longer alone. Other people feel the way he does. This must make him happy.

After a connection in Berlin, he and his cousin get off at Strasbourg, an Alsatian town known for its cuisine. He knows nothing of this. He's told to report for work at a restaurant in the middle of town. He thinks he has known belittlement and cruelty—but he knows nothing.

The work is terrible: unclogging toilets, washing dishes. T——, much later in his life, will refer to it as "black market" work. He eats food from dirty plates when no one's looking. He lives in dark, subterranean spaces. This is not the life young T—— imagined for himself when he boarded that bus. He learns French. The name of the restaurant in which he works is L'Amour, and soon he knows what that word means. It seems like a joke.

His cousin is caught, sent back. T—— is never clear as to why or how this happened. Nor is T—— clear on why he is allowed to stay. Maybe some of the women in the restaurant protect him. He's a hard-working, innocent young man and they like him; perhaps his prog-ress with French especially amuses the women. The chef of L'Amour, though, is terrible to him. One day he chases T—— out of the kitchen with a butcher knife. He calls T—— *"le rat."* What has T—— done to deserve this? He's asked the chef if he can have Sunday off. T—— stops complaining when it's made clear to him that he will find himself back in the wild East, just like his cousin, if he doesn't watch his step. He's frightened. Some nights he weeps upon his dark basement bed-roll. He worries he will never leave Strasbourg. Here he is, in the West, and he's living in terror. To young T——, this makes no earthly sense at all.

With the Rooftop set fully deconstructed, Tommy decided to shoot a final Rooftop scene. No one could believe this. It meant having to build another rooftop set.

The scene Tommy wanted to shoot involved Johnny announcing to everyone at his wonderful surprise birthday party that he and Lisa are expecting a child. There's never a moment in the script where Lisa tells Johnny they're expecting a child, but whatever. No one cared any longer about continuity or making any sense. We just wanted to finish the damn thing. So the crew started building.

Tommy was sick with a cold and his voice was almost cartoonishly froggy. To combat that, he had drunk half a bottle of NyQuil. To com-bat the NyQuil, he'd drunk about seven Red Bulls. As a result Tommy wasn't making much sense. One moment he was weird and peppy, the next he was leaning against a wall for support. Just about everything he said was slurred.

The new rooftop needed no green-screen tomfoolery, since the nighttime birthday party scene was going to be shot against a wall in the Birns & Sawyer parking lot. Tommy wanted candles and Christmas lights everywhere. "Have fancy stuff," he kept saying. "Have style. I want lots of style."

While the crew was putting together the new rooftop, Tommy wanted to shoot my half of the conversation that Mark and Lisa have over the phone at the very beginning of the film. It was supposed to be shot with me sitting in a car, so I suggested we use my Lumina. Tommy didn't want that: not fancy enough. Tommy also didn't want the scene shot in his Benz. Absolutely not. "License plate issues," Tommy said. I reminded him that the shot would be entirely of my profile; you wouldn't even see the car's steering wheel or tires, much less its license plate. Tommy didn't care. He asked around among the crew and learned that one of them drove a big blue Buick. Perfect. The Buick was a prototypically American car, and that's exactly what Tommy wanted. I got into the Buick, which was parked in the Birns & Sawyer parking lot, and prepared myself for the scene, with Juliette standing just off camera doing her half of the lines.

Tommy's dialogue can be genuinely amusing, but now, with all eyes focused on me sitting in a parked car, the lines became curiously difficult to get out. I mean, who tells someone "Oh, hey, I'm very busy right now" when he answers his phone? Who then says the same thing in his next sentence? Well, who else but Tommy? My first few takes were so uncomfortable and terrible that I threw in a few lines that made Mark sound more human. Tommy caught my changes. When I tried to explain why I'd ad-libbed, he didn't listen. "Greg," he said, "say the lines. Don't change anything. It's simple. Mark is Johnny's best friend, what's so difficult?"

Yes, I said. I know all that. How about, I suggested, we give Mark some backstory? Like, say, maybe Mark is an undercover narcotics cop or something, and when Lisa calls him he's on, like, a stakeout. That would explain why he keeps his weed stashed in an Animal Crackers box up on the Rooftop behind a false brick, wouldn't it? I mean, if the guy smokes weed, why wouldn't he just keep it in his apartment like a normal person? A weed-smoking narco might have to be more clandestine than that. Mark-as-narco would also explain why he says "It's clear!" after the whole Chris-R drug-dealer citizen's-arrest thing. "It's clear!" sounded like cop language to me. Tommy heard me out, thought about it, and said, "We don't like this stuff. I'm director. You do the scene as in script." (I had a good laugh when, years later, the people who created the *Room* video game imagined a backstory for Mark that was virtually identical to the one I proposed to Tommy.)

I got back into the car. Knowing Tommy would hate it, yet wanting to disguise my despair, I decided to wear sunglasses for the next couple of takes. As soon as I put them on, Tommy rushed over, saying, "No, no—I don't like this primitive stuff."

In frustration I threw Mark's big prehistoric cell phone down on the seat next to me.

Tommy leaned into the car and looked at me. "You know what? We will not have this, okay? Do you upset me just for kicks?"

In the end Tommy consented to let me wear the "primitive" sunglasses. I still think it's hilariously strange that it's never revealed in the film what Mark does for a living, or where exactly he lives, or why he smokes Rooftop weed, or why he tries to kill Peter, or why he so suddenly turns against Johnny late in the film, or where he and Johnny take Chris-R, or why he does any number of things. He's a character without a head and without a tail. In terms of characterization, Mark makes André Toulon look like the English Patient.

Right after we did this scene Tommy had an idea for yet another new scene. A few weeks before, anticipating promotional stills, Tommy had purchased ill-fitting tuxedos for all the film's male characters. My tux was so unfortunately roomy that I needed a lifeguard to safely wear the thing: I was drowning in Joseph Abboud. Tommy now said he wanted Peter, Denny, Mark, and Johnny wearing tuxedos while playing football. Sandy had objections. First and foremost, this was Kyle Vogt's last available day on set. Didn't Tommy want to use Kyle's last day shooting Peter's remaining scenes? Tommy didn't. Why are the characters in tuxes and playing football? Was it for a wedding picture? A sort of pathetic bachelor party? Tommy didn't know. All he said was that it was a "very important scene." Sandy finally caved, asking anyone who would listen, "What on earth do you say to that?"

Before we played tuxedo football, though, Tommy told me he wanted me to shave off my beard. He wanted Mark to walk into Johnny's condo freshly shaved. He called this a "moment."

I told Tommy that under no circumstances would I shave my beard.

"Listen, I have to tell you, I'm sorry, but you must shave it. Trust me on this." We were standing next to the brick wall outside of Birns & Sawyer, where he wanted to shoot the football stuff. The catering woman walked up to us, handing us both pastrami sandwiches. I told Tommy I didn't want mine; he could have it if he wanted it. Tommy looked at me and said, "I see what you do. You want me to have big stomach. You don't want me to be attractive, so I'm not competition." Tommy was serious about this, I'm pretty sure.

Rather than address that particular lunacy, I sighed and said, "I'm not going to shave." I felt like a different person in my beard. It was also a decent disguise. If *The Room* was ever released, I would quietly change my credited name in the film to Greg Pestermo—or I could take my mom's stage-name advice and go with Greg Paris. Either way, the beard was a key component of my *Room* anonymity strategy.

"No," Tommy said insistently. "You have to shave. Just trust me."

"I never agreed to this."

"But it's much better without! Much younger, much more American."

I thought of Amber, who was in San Diego at the time, and how much she hated my beard. She even kept a pre-beard picture of me in her purse to remind her what I used to look like. A clean-shaven boyfriend might be a nice surprise for her when she got back.

Amy, the makeup artist, went down the street to buy clippers and a razor. Later, as I headed to the Birns & Sawyer office bathroom to rid myself of Beardacus, I was shocked to see Markus, Tommy's spy, following me with a camera. Tommy wanted him to film me while I shaved. That was creepy. Even worse, Tommy wanted to be right next to me, analyzing every pass of the razor, as the deed was done. That was *Single White Female*–meets–Tom Ripley creepy. "Be careful, take your time," Tommy said, as I pulled the razor across my cheek. "Slow down. Don't cut it. Don't cut. Don't cut. We don't rush you." He was directing and recording my shaving. When I emerged, Sandy said, "You've lost ten years!" I hoped not, because that meant I was fourteen.

Walking into the condo set for my big, freshly shaved close-up was almost certainly my low point in the film. If you look at my face in the dailies, you can detect the precise moment in which my dreams of being an actor are summarily snuffed out. Having to caress my own chin as Johnny and Denny ooh and aah over my freshly shaven face was the most embarrassing scene I've ever done or will ever do. I had no idea why Tommy was so anxious to film this scene, until he called me Babyface during one take—the take he wound up using.

The rest of the sequence is just as bad. Not only are the tuxes unexplained, but Tommy had Peter and me arrive one after the other, my doorbell ring coming right on top of his, as though we're emerging from a clown car on the other side of the door. When Tommy said he wanted us all to end the scene doing his ridiculous chicken imitation— flapping our arms, saying "cheep-cheep"—I almost walked off the set. In the end I gave it everything I had, which was nothing. I barely opened my mouth at all; I moved my arms even less. You really do have to admire the comparative gusto with which Philip cheep-cheeped.

A few nights later we filmed Johnny's birthday party scene on the new rooftop. Tommy's line in this scene was to say, "Hey, everybody! I have an announcement to make. We're expecting!" After this, everyone was supposed to file up to him and shake his hand. A very simple scene. But first Tommy had to say his line. By this point, Tommy had come to grips with the fact that he couldn't remember his lines. All day he'd been walking around, looking at the script, saying the line over and over to himself or to anybody who was in close proximity. Unfortunately, all this recitation had been bad for his still cold-strained vocal cords. I guess it was sort of poetically perfect: The one time Tommy had adequately

prepared, his voice was so shot that he couldn't get the lines out.

"Hey, everybody," he said, his voice all trembly and broken. "I have an announcement to make. We're expect—" And then he would cough with tubercular explosiveness.

When Tommy finally felt prepared to give the scene another go, he mentioned that it might be good to have some footballs being thrown around after Johnny makes his announcement—this on a roof, mind you. "No, no, no," Sandy said instantly. "We'll be here all night with that damn football. No more football!"

Byron, a crew guy who more or less appeared out of nowhere to take charge of the dramatic-motivation and second-director aspects of *The Room* (Sandy had by this point given up on helping with anything other than script supervision), also voiced his objections, though not within earshot of Tommy. Byron wore his ball cap backward at all times and carried himself like the South Carolina–bred former marine dude he was, but he was smart and canny, with a big voice, and for some reason Tommy listened to him. Between him and Sandy, Tommy was compelled to give up on having any footballs at Johnny's party.

Tommy finally managed to say "We're expecting!" without expectorating a lung, after which some of the filmed takes were reviewed on the monitor. They looked as hilarious as anything filmed so far. Tommy fretted for a while and decided that the problem was that the party wasn't enough of a "thing." The way the scene was blocked, the shot just opened with Johnny standing there. Tommy didn't know how to create dynamic camera movement—*The Room*'s cameras move around about as much as statuary—so someone suggested we film Juliette from behind, with a dolly shot, as she comes into the party. I'm fairly certain Tommy had never heard of a dolly shot. When it was explained to him what the shot would look like, Tommy loved it.

The crew set up again. The dolly camera follows Lisa very, very slowly into the party; given what it's actually accomplishing, this is an excruciatingly long shot. It's like the Copa scene from *Goodfellas* if *Goodfellas* had been directed by a malfunctioning R2-D2. After the dolly stops and Lisa moves out of frame, Johnny steps up to make

his announcement. No matter how many times he ran through this, Tommy couldn't find his mark when he stepped into the scene. You can see Tommy, in the finished film, look down at his feet to figure out where to stop. Byron had to talk Tommy through the whole thing: "Okay. Start moving. Look up. Nope, you passed it. Go back. Now you're looking into the camera. And you passed it again. Start over. And go. Look up. You missed it again. Don't look at me. Just ignore me and start over. Okay: Go. Look up. And you passed it."

One of *The Room*'s more amusing audience rituals concerns this scene. There's a moment right before Johnny makes his announcement in which he seems to look down and to the right and wave at someone. Consequently, some audiences send a small gaggle of people to converge in the bottom right-hand corner of the movie screen, where they gleefully return Johnny's wave. So what's really going on here? Well, after so many blown takes, Tommy is signaling to the cameraman that he's ready, he's got it, let's roll film, motherfuckers. And yes, a take in which Tommy annihilates the fourth wall by motioning to the cameraman was the best take they got.

I thought about how sad this party scene really was. Having all of Johnny's closest friends and future wife gather together to celebrate his birthday—with a child on the way, no less—was Tommy's dream life. But it was a dream life in line with what he *thought* an American would want. After all, Johnny's life in *The Room* doesn't quite resemble anyone's idea of a perfect life: working in a bank, not getting your promotion, living in a crappy condo, having a future mother-in-law all up in your business. Johnny's life was everything Tommy had no chance of having, on the one hand, but it was also what few people would actually want for themselves, were they lucky enough to design their lives. Tommy didn't know what he didn't know about the dreams of others.

T—— is calling himself Pierre now and often receives compliments on how quickly he's learned to speak passable French. His situation has in many ways improved—he's living in a hostel a few streets away from Strasbourg's Gothic cathedral—but he's still working in a restaurant. One freezing December night the Strasbourg police raid Pierre's hostel.

Drugs are being sold on the premises, but Pierre knows nothing about this. All the same, he's nabbed during the sweep. Of course, he has no papers, and two officers cuff him and bring him to the Strasbourg police station.

They take his fingerprints and sit him down in an interrogation room. The officers are pure French-German Alsatians and, in T——'s mind, embody the worst of both nationalities. They call Pierre an "Eastern invader" while he maintains his innocence. Then he's slapped once, twice, a third time. The police officers are laughing. Pierre can tell they are enjoying this.

The officers put a written confession before Pierre, which they demand he sign. Pierre refuses. More slaps. They strip him to his underwear, leer, and say something sinister about "checking inside his ass." Pierre is shivering now; this interrogation room is scarcely heated at all. One of the men unholsters his gun and hits Pierre on the forehead with the butt. Pierre is crying; he's terrified by the appearance of the pistol. "Maybe we'll kill you and put you out on the street," the man who struck him says. "No one here cares about you, do they?"

"No," the other man says, unholstering his own pistol. "Let's make this more fun. Let's play Russian roulette."

Pierre begins to pray out loud. "God, protect me," he says. "God, protect me."

"God won't help you here," one of them says. "God doesn't help Communists."

Pierre tells the men he's Catholic and is struck again on the forehead for this impudence. His forehead has broken open now; he's bleeding. Pierre makes the sign of the cross.

"Okay," one of them says. With that, he shoves his pistol into Pierre's mouth. Pierre gasps and chokes. His face is wet with tears and blood. He can't stop shivering. The man removes the barrel from Pierre's mouth as roughly as he stuffed it in and shows him that there is, in fact, one bullet in the chamber. Pierre looks down at the man's shirt and sees a name: FREDERIC. The man realizes that Pierre has seen his name. He leans close to Pierre and says, very quietly, "If you say a word about this, I'll kill you and your entire family. Don't worry—I'll find them."

Pierre knows that he would hunt down Frederic, and Frederic's entire family, and make them all pay for this night if he could.

When Pierre describes this story many years later, he will weep. He will say he survived two rounds of Russian roulette, and even maintain that one of the officers fired his pistol into the wall to frighten him, though it's hardly credible that anyone would discharge his weapon in a police station interrogation room.

In the end Pierre is pushed out into the night by the laughing police officers. He stumbles home, bends down to grab a handful of snow to hold against the cut on his forehead. France is no better than some Communist police state. He knows he has to leave France. But how?

He is taken in by an older gentleman. That is all Pierre will say. "Taken in": It could describe a dozen varieties of human interaction. The man lets Pierre use his phone and, sometimes, sleep in his apartment. Then, one night, the older gentleman approaches Pierre, who has just hung up the man's phone. The gentleman is naked and offers Pierre several francs to suck him off. Pierre will later say he took the money, ripped it up, and threw the pieces into the stunned gentleman's face. As Pierre is leaving the gentleman's apartment, he sees an ornate mirror. He bends down, grabs a heavy knickknack from a coffee table, and hurls it at the mirror, which shatters. As with so many of Pierre's stories, it's hard to know precisely what to believe of this or what's really being said or admitted to.

Pierre is broken. He lives on the street for a while, does things for money he will never fully describe or reveal. Then he learns that his uncle Stanley, the brother of his deceased father and a World War II veteran, is living in America. Pierre, desperate, contacts him. Could he come to visit? Please? In a series of negotiations that, Pierre will later say, somehow involved the Red Cross, he convinces his uncle Stanley to sponsor him. First, though, he must make some money. Pierre heads off to Paris and works in a sex shop in the Pigalle district. He sells handcuffs and lingerie and mops up the floors of private rooms. Pierre is apparently written up in a French newspaper by some journalist whose eye he catches. In the article about his struggling, odd, nocturnal life, Pierre will be called the Night Owl. This is just the first time in Pierre's life that he will become known as a strange local fixture in a cosmopolitan city. Around this time, Pierre goes to see a film called *The Rocky Horror Picture Show*. He will say it had no particular impact on him.

His sponsorship eventually comes through. He is free to come to America and stay with his uncle Stanley and aunt Katherine. He heads out to Charles de Gaulle airport with his small bag. Everything important to him is in that bag or within his pockets. Somehow he has a French passport. But how could he? Again: unclear. The customs officials at the airport don't believe that Pierre is French. They demand that Pierre speak good French to them, to prove his identity. "I'm not fucking French," Pierre says—the last words he speaks while standing on French soil.

Once Johnny's big announcement was finally completed, we moved on to filming the debut of a new cast member, whose name was Greg Ellery and who was playing a character Tommy hastily named Steven. ("I have attorney named Steven," Tommy explained.) Steven's lines were all originally intended to be spoken by Peter, Johnny's psychologist friend, but Tommy had lost Kyle Vogt, who was playing Peter. Rather than assign the rest of Peter's lines to other, established characters in the film—Mike or Denny, say—Tommy created an entirely new character, which I think might be the most fascinating artistic decision he made while conceiving and making *The Room*.

The rooftop and interior party scenes in *The Room* are where everything reaches a dramatic boiling point. Lisa admits to having lied about being pregnant. Mark confronts Lisa. Johnny confronts Mark. Johnny and Mark fight. This is the film's dramatic payoff. Everything we've seen until now has prepared us for these moments—and into the film walks a character we've never met. We have no idea what he's doing at the party or why he's so unhappy about Lisa's involvement with Mark. Steven is, in this way, *The Room* personified. You could even say that *The Room* is about Steven or, at least, about *Stevenness,* a condition in which things happen for no clear reason, to an unknown purpose, at a fascinatingly inopportune time. Steven completely saves the end of *The Room* by reminding us how weird it really is.

Steven's first filmed line, spoken to Lisa, was this: "When is the baby due?" Byron, watching on the monitor, said, "That's the worst actor I've ever seen. Who picked this guy?"

As it happened, I did—and Ellery was, in my opinion, lovably entertaining. He was a bit of an oddball, but that was what made him so perfect for *The Room*. For the role of Steven, Tommy had first wanted to hire a Mexican guy who was helping around the set and didn't speak much English. "That's okay," Tommy said. "Give this guy chance. He can be great Steven." We talked him out of that when it was determined this gentleman may not have been an American citizen. We tried and failed to talk Tommy out of having yet another casting call this late in the production, but he was adamant that we find his Steven. Once again I grabbed some headshots from a pile and called a dozen people in. Tommy unwisely decided to attend the casting process, once again held in the Birns & Sawyer parking lot. This is how he greeted all of his potential Stevens: "You just won a million dollars."

Most of the actors said, "Excuse me?"

Tommy shook his head at them. "I'm sorry, if you don't act, you have to leave. Don't interrupt the scene. Don't break the character."

Greg Ellery, however, when told that he'd just won a million dollars, immediately got what Tommy wanted and began to celebrate. (It's possible that he believed he had actually just won a million dollars.) "If you like this guy," Tommy said, "hire him." So I did. Ellery showed up on set a couple of days before he was supposed to, driving a loud Harley-Davidson motorcycle. He quickly developed a reputation. He told one person involved in the production a story that he'd once had a bubble on his leg, a boil or something, and when he popped it, a bunch of teeny spiders came crawling out. So there was that. After his first day on set, he approached me and said, "That Tommy dude is the *director*? All this time I thought *you* were the director of this thing!"

For the interior party scene—which was a continuation of the rooftop party—Tommy wanted lots of balloons and, he said, a hundred extras. I managed to bring in eight extras with the tantalizing guarantee of a hundred dollars a day plus food. Tommy had wanted to pay the extras twenty dollars a day, with no food.

The first party-scene extra to show up was named Piper. Tommy insisted on a nighttime meeting, which is not typical casting procedure. I was waiting for her outside a darkened Birns & Sawyer. I could tell she was slightly hesitant to approach, so I smiled and waved her over. Then Tommy appeared behind me. Piper later told me that the first thing she thought when she saw Tommy was: *Run away right now, Piper, or you're going to be killed.* Piper gradually became more confident that she wouldn't be killed and stayed on. All the party-scene extras were called in like this: at the last minute, at night, and under objectively terrifying circumstances. Several wouldn't stay until I showed them all of Tommy's equipment.

With our measly eight extras—one of them being Amy, our very own makeup artist—the party scene looked pathetic. One of the extras immediately earned Tommy's enmity by stepping in front of him during one of the night's first takes. "Excuse me, young missy," Tommy said. "You *never* cross on camera. Oh, my God! This is Acting 101! So, do not try to steal show."

She looked back at Tommy, stunned he was making such an issue out of an innocent mistake. "What show am I trying to steal?"

Tommy rolled his eyes. "You're not that important, sweetie, for your information."

The woman walked away, muttering. "That guy's got control issues. I think he's scared shitless of women. He's a joke is what he is."

This extra had known Tommy for a grand total of thirty minutes.

We'd been filming for much longer than planned, and under increasingly quicksandlike conditions. I could smell the end, though. In the party reaction shot, which flashes on-screen after Johnny arrives at his surprise birthday party, you can see me staring off into the distance when I'm supposed to be saying "Happy birthday!" with everyone else.

"Okay, Keanu," Sandy said. "Time to wake up!" But performing in *The Room* was, by this point, like drinking the very last dregs of something through a tiny straw: It took a lot of effort and you barely tasted it.

We'd just shot the scene in which Mark confronts Lisa and asks if the baby she's carrying is his. Lisa then slaps Mark, which brings the sparsely attended birthday party to a halt. Johnny intervenes, after which there's a near fight. Now we had to film the moment in which Johnny once again approaches a slow-dancing Mark and Lisa, peels them apart, and demands to know what they're doing. This time, though, there's an actual fight. Why not just have one confrontation? I have no idea. In the final film Tommy separates these two nearly identical moments with a supremely nonsensical establishing shot of a San Francisco skyscraper.

As for the fight scene between Mark and Johnny, we'd already sort of blocked it out with Byron's assistance. They started rolling and Tommy approached Juliette and me. I had never before seen him so lethargic; it looked as though he were sleepwalking. Some of the extras started laughing. I actually heard one of them ask what Tommy was on and could she have some? Tommy didn't see or hear any of this. I've never known Tommy to drink or use drugs, but he did take a lot of (legitimately prescribed) medication, gobble a lot of vitamins, and chug Red Bull around the clock. Consequently, despite his nocturnal schedule, there's sometimes a point at the end of a day where Tommy simply stops functioning. A lot of fans over the years have seen Sleepwalker Tommy at midnight screenings and assumed he's wasted, but he's not. Rather, his brain has simply called it quits for the day and turned over all vital operations to his central nervous system. That's the condition he was in right now.

Byron was demanding that Tommy show him something more during our confrontation—a punch, say, or something resembling a punch—but that wasn't working at all. Tommy kept pulling up handfuls of emotional sand. Not even when Tommy and I started "fighting" did he come to life—not until, that is, I said the line "What planet are you on?" Take after take, Tommy would be somnolent and drooling, but at hearing this line he whipped off his sport coat with fire in his eyes. This wasn't an ad-lib; Tommy wrote the line. But I think hearing me say those words set off a long, painful chain of memories in Tommy's mind, memories about his childhood and, I suspect, much else. It's one of only a couple of moments in the film where Tommy's artistry, such as it is, becomes honest.

Pierre is greeted in New Orleans by his uncle Stanley and his aunt Katherine, an American—the first real American Pierre's ever met. He's overwhelmed with joy and optimism. From New Orleans they travel to the small town of Chalmette, which in terms of culture makes Strasbourg look like Michelangelo's Rome. Pierre wants to go to school, but his uncle explains to him that American schooling is expensive. If he wants to live with Stanley and Katherine, he has to help with money. Through his uncle, Pierre finds work as a stock boy in a Chalmette grocery store called Schwegmann's—another grim, thankless job. During the day he oversees the milk section. At night Katherine helps him with his English.

Shortly after arriving in America, Pierre wrecks Katherine's Cadillac; his relationship with his uncle is consequently strained. In short order Pierre feels misunderstood and out of sorts in Louisiana, and he learns to despise its "rednecks," who often drop by Pierre's grocery store and mock him for his accent. Pierre's Chalmette life is humidity, insects, groceries, rednecks, tense dinners with Stanley and Katherine, saving his pitiful paychecks, and dreams of being anywhere else.

A certain kind of strangeness follows Pierre to Chalmette, however, and he will describe being offered a gold chain by an older man in exchange for sex. Of course, Pierre spurns the offer. When he can afford it, Pierre takes the bus to New Orleans, a city he comes to love, and walks around the French Quarter. On one of these visits, Pierre meets a young French guitarist named Jean Luc. Pierre sits with the young man sometimes, listening to him play, and other times drinks with him in bars around town. They have many "strange experiences," Pierre will later say. Walking down Bourbon Street, surrounded by tourists, Pierre confesses to Jean Luc that he's not fulfilled in Louisiana. Pierre confides in Jean Luc because he, too, is an artist. Pierre's real dream, he says, is to be an actor or a musician. Jean Luc tells Pierre, "If that's what you want to do, you should really be in California."

California. Pierre likes the sound of that word. To Pierre, California *is* America—and Chalmette is a fetid swamp.

"Actually," Jean Luc tells him, "I know the perfect city for you. The perfect city! You should go. You will love life there. As soon as you can, you should go."

"Where?" Pierre asks.

"San Francisco," Jean Luc says.

Unfortunately, Tommy's emotional honesty didn't help him with his lines. Tommy had to say, "I'll kill you! Get out of my house before I break every bone in your body!" But in Tommy's exhaustion-altered state, the line became, "I'll kill you! Get out of my body before I break every bone in your house!"

The first time Tommy flubbed the line, I heard someone mutter, "What did he just say?" But he kept saying it. He didn't even understand the problem. He was transposing the words without even being aware of it.

"Tommy!" Sandy finally said. "Where is this coming from? How many times can you confuse that line? What kind of house do you have, anyway?"

Tommy was blinking, dazed, sullen, running his hand through his hair. He tried it again and made the same mistake. Soon enough, two extras quit. They had better things to do than watch a writer/star/director/producer/executive producer going at his own script with a cleaver. A couple of crew members were press-ganged into being extras for the remainder of the night.

Byron wasn't happy with Tommy's and my fight. It's supposed to be a ferocious struggle between two men over a devilish woman, but we were shooting two guys holding each other's arms and hissing; grade school fights are typically more brutal. That didn't mean that Tommy wasn't hurting me during our takes. He happens to have the most in-sanely powerful hands of any human being I've ever known—pure cyborg strength—and by the end of the night I had bruises all over my wrists and forearms.

After a bunch of takes, Byron had seen enough. "Look," he said, "you guys are fighting like a couple of pansies."

Of the many words you should never use to refer to Tommy Wiseau, *pansy* is high in the upper quartile. On the next take, Tommy caught me off guard and finally went for it. He gave me a hard and unpansylike shove. I fell backward, landed on my can, and for good measure hit the back of my head against the door, which is the take that wound up in the film.

Tempers were short by this point. When it came time for the Steven character to jump in and break up Johnny and Mark's fight, Greg Ellery grabbed Tommy, which made Tommy lose track of his lines. When Johnny turns to Steven and yells, "Shut up! Shut up!" that's Tommy really yelling at poor Greg.

Well past everyone's bedtime, we finally finished this emotionally exhausting sequence. Next up was the scene in which I had to say to Steven, "Leave your stupid comments in your pocket!" The line wasn't remotely sayable. I couldn't imagine even Liam Neeson saying this line convincingly. Tommy gave me a brief reprieve from attempting to deliver the line, however, when he decided that he wanted another scene of me and Juliette kissing.

In the original script, Mark tells Peter to keep his stupid comments in his pocket, but this confrontation does not piggyback on Peter's catching Mark and Lisa secretly canoodling on the couch at Johnny's birthday party. Peter doesn't need to catch Mark and Lisa because he already knows they're romantically involved. But now that the character of Steven had entered the picture, the film needed a moment of discovery, and that moment of discovery had to turn on Mark and Lisa groping each other on the couch. In a way I was impressed: For once, Tommy had accurately identified and worked to solve a plot hole in his own script. The first couple of times I tried to say "Leave your stupid comments in your pocket," the words just didn't come. I felt paralyzed, as though I were apologizing to some future audience. The line seemed a violation of drama, of cinema, of language itself.

Every time I looked at Juliette she could see how hard I was concentrating. This always made her laugh, at which point we had to start all over again.

After one calamitous take, I asked Tommy if we could go with another line. Byron backed me up on this: "Wouldn't 'Shut the fuck up!' work a lot better?" But whenever Tommy was questioned about his script, he doubled down. He wasn't going to let any of us move on until he had this ridiculous line of dialogue in the can.

"The problem," Tommy told me, "is that you're not upset. No emotion. You need to be upset!"

"No," I said. "The problem is the line doesn't work."

"The line," Tommy said, "work just fine."

Byron and I exchanged a long, complicated look of shared misery. Then Byron shrugged. "Guess you gotta give the man what he wants."

I tried it again.

"It's not enough!" Tommy said. "Not enough! Not at all enough!"

As we set up again, this was what I told myself: *If you can land this pointless, nonsensical line, you will be one step closer to the end and forgetting about this whole experience. What are you even worried about? No one's going to see this thing. It's going to sit on a shelf in Tommy's house. It's not going to kill you. They're just words.* Leave your stupid comments in your pocket. *See? Easy.*

"Come on, Greg!" Tommy said when I tried again. "You're not upset!"

"Actually," I said, "I *am* upset!"

"Then *give* me something, dammit!"

So I imagined I was saying the line to Tommy, and then changed all the words in my head: "Leave [Why] your [are] stupid [you] comments [doing] in [this] your [to] pocket [me?]!" On the next take, no surprise, I nailed it. Well, maybe not *nailed* it, but the words came out with real, spitting-cobra force. In some sense, saying the line felt like an exorcism of every terrible *Room* experience I'd had up until that point.

"I'm *not* saying it again," I said, walking away from the camera. "I'm done." A decade later, the phrase I had such trouble wrapping my mind around, much less saying aloud, has at least three Urbandictionary.com entries.

The afternoon after we shot the "Leave your stupid comments in your pocket" scene, Tommy and I arrived on set to find Sandy sitting on an apple crate in the Birns & Sawyer parking lot. He looked relieved; I knew immediately what he was going to say.

"Tommy," he said, standing up. "I'm sorry, but I'm going to have to leave your project. I got another offer, and it's too good to pass up."

Tommy said nothing. He didn't ask Sandy what this other offer was.

"It's with Janusz Kaminski," Sandy said, and waited. Kaminski had been Steven Spielberg's DP for his last seven films and was commonly regarded as one of the greatest living cinematographers. Tommy, I could all but guarantee, had never heard of Kaminski. I doubt he knows who he is even now.

If we lost Sandy, I felt, *The Room* might not be completed. He'd been extremely helpful, and we still had a lot of complicated, important scenes to film. Well, complicated by *Room* standards. Byron had been useful, but Sandy actually got into the trenches with Tommy. The only reason we'd gotten anything even remotely watchable on film was due to his ability to turn Tommy's vision into something slightly less extraterrestrial.

I knew Sandy was relieved to be leaving now, because looming next in line to film were Tommy's love scenes. That, really, was Sandy's choice: Tommy's naked ass or Steven Spielberg's director of photography.

Tommy kept staring at Sandy.

"I'm sorry, man," Sandy said, his hands out. "It's Kaminski. The guy's got two Oscars."

Tommy said nothing.

"I've got to take it," Sandy said, clearly boggled by Tommy's silence. "It's Spielberg. Kaminski shot *Schindler's List*!"

Sandy was right, of course. He had to take it. It would be insane for anyone to tell him not to take it. I'm sure half of the crew wanted to jump in the back of Sandy's pickup and ride off the Birns & Sawyer lot with him.

Tommy, finally, spoke: "So what? I don't want to hear this stuff. Oscar nothing. If you leave, don't come back." Tommy then did to Sandy what he had done to so many people, in so many circumstances: He turned away, made Sandy the enemy, and instantly sought to replace him.

fourteen

Highway of Hell

*If I could just go back . . . if I could rub everything out . . .
starting with myself.*
—Tom Ripley, *The Talented Mr. Ripley*

Tommy had begun to write. Sometimes he spent the whole day on his computer, behind his black velvet curtains, using two fingers to peck out his . . . play? Script? Whatever he was writing, his description of it changed day to day. Occasionally he'd call out things like "Prepare yourself physically and mentally!" or "How many pages does normal movie script have?" or "Tell me not to eat any more of these chocolate muffins!" or "This place is too small! I can't think in this house!" At the end of the day I'd find him sitting at the small kitchen table, looking happy and tired as he quietly devoured a chocolate muffin. "Aren't all these human need strange?" he asked one night. "Human behavior is funny stuff." But he wasn't talking to me. He was talking to his script.

As the weeks went on, the stress of writing wore Tommy down. Sometimes he woke up in the middle of the night, screaming about leg cramps. Other times, when he noticed my irritation with him, he'd say, "Don't try to poison my oatmeal, okay?" I was still looking for somewhere else to live, but not very diligently, largely because my non-sleeping hours were rarely spent in the apartment anyway. I'd booked a gig on *Days of Our Lives* thanks to my ability to do a French accent. The role was a guy named Jules, who claimed to be from France (this was his way of picking up gullible American women) but was actually from Indianapolis. I appeared a couple of times over several months, until Jules was forced to admit he wasn't French at all, after which he was shot to death at a party. *C'est la vie,* as Jules would say.

I was still taking Jeff Corey's acting class. Aside from my being berated by Bob Dylan for blocking his driveway, it remained an enjoyable experience. Sometimes my scene partners would call me at home to discuss rehearsals. Tommy hated it when the phone rang before noon, but if they called after that Tommy could be surprisingly chatty. "Your cousin is so sweet," Rena, one of my scene partners, said to me. It turned out that she'd called one afternoon when I wasn't there and wound up talking to Tommy for twenty minutes. "He's a bit out there, though, isn't he? He asked me a lot of really intense questions about acting." (Tommy's version of this: "I talk to your friend the Rena! We have great conversation. Don't be jealous!") For the most part, though, Tommy was so focused on his script that he hardly seemed to notice anything. As he withdrew deeper behind his velvet curtains, my need to move out seemed less pressing. As long as Tommy stayed focused on his writing project, I figured we could manage being roommates for a little longer.

Then Tommy raised the rent—again. He claimed that it was being raised on him, which was what he'd said when he raised rent on me four months earlier. When I questioned him, he got angry and switched tactics, now claiming that he didn't have enough space. This was a very interesting thing for him to say, given that Tommy's "corner" had steadily expanded to include every square inch of the apartment, save for my bedroom. The kitchen sink was perpetually filled with dirty plates, and the ratio of spoiled to unspoiled food items in the fridge was usually five to one. I made the mistake of complaining about this stuff, and all at once Tommy was fuming.

"I stop you right now," he said. "This mess? You create it all by yourself. You need to get a job, young man. You're not fifteen years old, you know. So if you don't like it, you get your own place. You are a guest in this house!"

And so my search for a steady job and a new apartment began in earnest once again. I attended a job fair sponsored by Santa Monica

College and got called in for a salesclerk gig at Armani Exchange in Beverly Hills but didn't land it. I also interviewed for a bellman job at a fancy hotel called Shutters in Santa Monica. At the end of the interview I was asked, "When can you start?" A few days later I learned that a nephew of one of the managers had been judged the more promising bellman.

The day I learned I lost out on the Shutters gig, I came home discouraged—only to be greeted by Tommy, who was once more pestering me about getting a job. I told him what had happened, hoping he'd extend some consolation.

He didn't. "I don't care about your excuses," Tommy said, turning his back to me as he headed off into his curtained lair. "I don't want all your stress in my head."

Infuriated, I had the most unpleasantly pleasurable fantasy of wrapping my hands around Tommy's neck and squeezing. To drive that thought away, I called to him through his layers of black velvet: "What do you do for money, anyway? I've known you for two years and I've never seen you do anything but sit around."

For a moment, silence. Then: "I drive Mercedes, smart guy, so I must do something right!"

Having cooled myself down, I tried to speak plainly and honestly. "I'm working my ass off here. I go to school, I'm going on auditions, I'm trying to find a job. So I *am* working."

"Okay," Tommy said warily. "I got the picture."

"You've still never said what it is you do."

"I told you," he said. "I do the marketing stuff."

"No," I said. "I don't think so."

"Your thinking is not my problem."

"Marketing for who, Tommy?"

"That," he said, "is none of your business at this time." From behind the curtains I soon heard the familiar Tommy-puttering sounds that I'd grown to loathe.

I headed for my corner of the apartment. "That's fine, Tommy," I said. "I'll pay the extra rent. You just keep lying to yourself." With that, I slammed the bedroom door.

Tommy was shouting at me five seconds later. "Don't you slam your door, young man! Remember, you are guest in this house."

I didn't say anything. Ten minutes later, though, he opened my door and began doing his nightly pull-ups. *As soon as I get a place,* I thought, watching his grave, spectral face go from white to an engorged red, *I'm not even giving you a warning. I'm just going to disappear.*

A few days later, the Armani Exchange on Sunset Boulevard, where I'd fruitlessly dropped off an application months before, called me in for an interview, which ended with them hiring me on the spot. It only paid eight dollars an hour, but it was something.

I returned home to tell Tommy the good news. Unusually, he wasn't there. When he finally returned around six thirty, I casually asked him where he'd been. Tommy played coy for a little while but finally admitted he was taking a cold-reading acting class run by Brian Reise, a fairly well-known acting teacher, whose studio was right down the street. Reise's cold-reading classes—wherein students gather outside, on the corner of Hayworth and Fountain, and have a couple of minutes to do unprepared readings of material they're not familiar with—were popular. I'd drive down Fountain sometimes and see actors of all ages out there, cold-reading for one another.

I was happy to hear that Tommy was taking a class. As far as I knew, he'd had almost no human contact with anyone but me since he'd arrived in Los Angeles eight months ago. I also figured a cold-reading venue was more suited to Tommy's talents. In San Francisco, acting classes could be staid and self-important, at least in my experience. I imagined that Los Angeles's aspiring actors would be more receptive to Tommy's brand of thespian bonkers.

Tommy assured me he was having a great time in the cold-reading class. "I make some friends," he said. "I can make friends, too, you know. You think because you have blond hair, you own the world?" He went on to tell me how his classmates would sometimes start chanting "Tommy! Tommy!" as he got up onstage. L.A. *was* embracing Tommy Wiseau, then. This was good for all sorts of reasons.

Then, another positive development: A guy in my Santa Monica

College film class mentioned that his friend was moving to Barcelona for work and needed a long-term subletter. As it happened, the apartment in question was across the street from Tommy's place. Better yet, all the subletter had to do was pay utilities and forward the guy's mail to him in Spain. And the place itself was gorgeous: a two-bedroom in a colonial-style building with an amazing view of Sunset and lovely gardens in its shared courtyard area.

Now all I had to do was break it to Tommy. He wasn't around when I got home; he was still at his cold-reading class. While I was eating dinner, I noticed that Tommy had, for some reason, left his ID out on the kitchen table, along with a bunch of papers. It was a California State driver's license. Name: Thomas P. Wiseau. Date of birth: October 3, 1968.

That would have made him thirty-two years old. I put the license down. Maybe, all this time, Tommy *hadn't* been lying to me about his age? Was it possible he really *was* in his thirties? If Tommy wasn't lying about this, maybe he wasn't lying about everything else—his meetings, his origins, his work—either. Maybe *I'd* been in the wrong this whole time.

A little while later, I went for a drive on Fountain and noticed a large group of gesticulating Brian Reise actors standing on the corner, talking and laughing and hanging out. Then I saw Tommy. He was standing fifteen feet away from everyone, arms crossed, head down, leaning against a brick wall. He looked about as glum and lonely as a human being could look. I slowed and pulled my Lumina over to the curb. When Tommy glanced up and saw me, he smiled like a kid waiting to be picked up after his first day of school. A heartbreakingly genuine smile. I told him I had a few things to talk to him about later that night.

Tommy didn't seem himself when he came back from class. Or, rather, he didn't seem any of his many selves—not his manic self, not his petulant self, and not his zany self. He appeared, instead, profoundly defeated. This was surprisingly hard to see. I'd never known anyone as invincibly optimistic as Tommy, and I didn't realize how central that optimism was to my understanding of him until it was gone. As hard as our rooming together had been, I didn't feel very good about telling him I was moving out when he was in such a state.

Tommy sat down at his glass-topped desk, leaving the curtains open behind him—always a sign he wanted to talk. "Maybe," he said after a while, "acting is not my destiny."

"Did something happen in class?" I asked.

"Forget class for now. Hollywood won't do shit for me. All these months and no call, no audition. They don't want me. They don't want me to be the next Johnny Dapp."

"Tommy," I said. "I know you don't believe that. Come on. You have your script now; you're writing. You're writing a *lot*. Just keep doing that, keep pushing, and something will eventually happen." It was hard to give that advice, because I didn't believe it myself. But then again, I realized, how was my disbelief in Tommy any different from my mother's disbelief in me? Who was I to know what was best for Tommy?

"Yeah," he said, unconvinced. "Talk is talk. Where is result? I don't need the talk. I need something different."

"Okay. So what do you need?"

He was silent for a moment, thinking about it. He turned to me, still slumped over in his chair. "To be star," he said, "I need to reshape myself. Everything. My acting. I need to fix entire thing."

This sounded ominous. "What does that mean?"

He knew he'd said too much. "Look at you," he said, waving his hand at me. "You go on all these auditions. You do a good job and you get nothing. What does that mean for me? They will not give me chance."

I didn't know what it meant for him. I also didn't know what it meant for *me*. Tommy's loss of faith was so difficult to watch that it took a little of my faith right down the drain with it. "It's not supposed to be easy, Tommy. You've said so yourself."

"Easy nothing," he said. "No one want me. Bottom line."

No, the I'm-moving-out conversation would definitely not be happening tonight. I knew all the years of acting classes and relocating back and forth from San Francisco to L.A. had taken its toll on Tommy. I knew this was at least the third serious effort he'd made to be an actor. I knew that he had hoped it was going to be different this time. Of *course* he'd lost his stomach for acting. By this point, who wouldn't? Most of the people who start down this path wind up at a dead end. The odds of success are so dauntingly low that you have to be a special kind of crazy even to want to court such a fate. Optimism can sustain a young actor, but only for so long.

"So look," Tommy said. "I have certain issue. I have to leave for couple weeks."

"Okay," I said. "Are you going back to San Francisco?"

He shook his head. "No. I have work in the London. Marketing stuff. People need me there. So I go for a while."

London? Tommy claimed to despise Europe. He'd often told me that he'd never go back, not under any circumstances.

Tommy saw the concern in my eyes. "Don't worry about me, okay? And you still have apartment. I keep renting it for now."

I looked at Tommy carefully, trying to suss out the truth behind his statement. But there was so much anguish in his face—he had the eyes of a trapped, dying animal—that I had to look away.

"So take care yourself," Tommy said. "Be good."

"How long are you going to be gone?"

"Several weeks or so." He stood and reached out to close his curtain. "Okay. So I'm tired now. I go to bed. We talk tomorrow maybe."

It wasn't even midnight. This was normally when Tommy started to *wake up*. "Yeah," I said agreeably. "Of course." Tommy's hand was still on the curtain. It looked like he wanted to say something more, but he didn't. When I turned away, he pulled the curtain shut. I had a strong sense that Tommy wouldn't be there when I woke up. He wasn't—and he hadn't left a note. He was simply *gone*.

I was packing up my things to move into my new place across the street when I noticed Tommy had left something out on his desk, I think, for me to find. It was a bulletin board. On it, Tommy had pinned a bunch of his headshots. In the middle of this Tommy collage was a picture of me. Knowing him, this didn't strike me as upsetting or creepy. Maybe it should have, but it didn't. I knew he was trying to figure out what it was that separated me from him. Why had I, in his mind, been accepted by Hollywood and he had not? As though a picture could tell you that. All at once I felt both immensely sad and immensely relieved he was gone. Somehow I knew I wouldn't see him again for a very long time.

To my surprise, I liked working at Armani Exchange; it offered me a sense of normalcy and routine. Before I knew it, I was seeing a completely different side of being young in Los Angeles. One day I was being set up with a rich Lebanese customer's daughter; the next, having a friendly dinner with Joni Mitchell, to whom I had sold a sweater, and her pal. (Joni Mitchell was greatly amused to learn, halfway through our dinner, that I had no idea who Joni Mitchell was. She just seemed like a cool, artsy woman to me.) It was as though not having Tommy around freed up all this trapped mental and emotional energy. I was friendlier, happier, and far more open than I'd ever been. You might say that, for the first time in my life, I was acting my age. And I was so thankful to finally have a job, which in turn made me pretty good at selling clothes. Within a couple of months, in fact, I was personally outselling the entire store's staff. A general manager from Armani in New York came to visit and took me out to lunch. "What are your career plans?" he asked me. At that point in my life, *career plans* wasn't a phrase that often passed through my mind.

While I wasn't expecting to see Tommy again for a while, I was certainly expecting to hear from him. But I didn't. No messages or calls. Weeks passed. It got to the point where I almost forgot Tommy existed—like the last two years had been a strange, sometimes upsetting dream. From time to time I'd go back to the old apartment to do laundry or check phone messages, and in the apartment's silence Tommy would weigh heavily on my mind. Eventually I decided to call him. Tommy always used to tell me, "We're on different highways. You are young, so we see things different. You go your way. I go my way." I never really understood what he meant by that, but I found myself thinking of those words while his phone was ringing. He didn't answer, so I left a message: "Hey, Tommy. Just wondering how you're doing and how London is. I hope you're on a good highway."

Six weeks later, when I was at work, my manager called me over to the counter phone. This was odd—no one had ever called me at work. I heard him say, "I'm sorry, sir? I didn't understand that."

Tommy.

I got on the phone.

"I miss you," Tommy said, his voice shaky. "I miss you very much."

"Tommy," I said. "Are you all right? Where are you?"

"I just wanted to say hello. I know you call me. I appreciate."

Tommy sounded even worse than he had that last night in his apartment; his words seemed more howled than spoken. At least a dozen people stood around me—customers, colleagues, my manager—so I comported myself as neutrally as possible. But my intuition was causing my blood to run as fast and icy as some Arctic floe. "I can't really talk," I said quietly. "Are you around later?"

"No," he said quickly. "Never mind. I just want to call and say I hope you're okay. Not to bother you. I just want to make sure."

"Make sure of what?"

"Just to . . . make sure. Okay. I have to go now."

"Look, I'll try you later, all right?"

And he just hung up. I stood there with the dial tone blaring in my ear—a nontransatlantic dial tone. Wherever Tommy was, it wasn't London.

Tommy's call left me rattled. I went to his vacant apartment after work to see if he'd left a message there, since he didn't yet know I'd moved out. I stepped off the elevator on the third floor of the Crescent Heights building and started walking toward the apartment. I looked down into the aquamarine pool and thought about the first time I'd been there, how *alive* I'd felt. I realized that I missed the Tommy from that time. Not who he was now, and definitely not the life-draining roommate he'd become, but the free-spirited person he'd once been, who could cheer me up without even trying. When I tried to imagine Tommy now, I kept seeing him underwater, beyond reach, drowning.

Inside, the answering machine light was blinking. I hit play and suddenly Tommy's voice began filling up that apartment like a ghost. "I'm in a bad place," he said. "I'm scared." It sounded like he'd been crying. "In your message you talk about the highway. Well, I'm on highway—the highway of hell. Highway of dying. Highway of survival. It really is . . . it really is hell right now. I don't know what to do. Hopefully I can get out from this hell. I think maybe I go like James Dean, end in car. Or I disappear. Maybe I jump off Golden Gate Bridge." He became quiet. Standing in the middle of that dark, vacant apartment, I crossed my arms; I felt a rush of cold air. Then Tommy said: "I don't want to feel the pain. I don't believe in hell. I believe in God. Maybe God help me." He hung up.

I was shaking. I knew what I'd just heard: a suicide message. I called him immediately but he didn't answer, so I desperately urged him to call me back. I told him that I knew something terrible was happening, but unless he told me what it was, I couldn't help him. Whatever Tommy was running from, it had finally caught him. It was holding him down and breathing in his face.

I waited in the apartment, hoping the phone would ring. A few minutes later, it did. "Hey, stranger," he said. He sounded a little more stable. Not much more, but a little. "I cannot talk for long. I get your message. I appreciate."

"Tommy," I said, "what is going on?"

"I cannot tell you. I have problem but I can't talk about it. If something happens, I let you know. Look, it's late here in London. I need to sleep."

I did some quick math and determined that, in London, it was actually 11:00 a.m.

"You're important person to me," he said. "I just want to tell you that." And he hung up.

I wanted to help, but I didn't even know where to go or to whom I should turn. I suspected that Tommy was in San Francisco, if anywhere. I knew he was too proud to admit he was not in London, and maybe he had good reason. After hearing his voice I sensed that he wanted, even needed, space. What was so haunting was that I'd known

Tommy for two and a half years and there was literally no one else in his life for me to call or turn to. As far as I knew, I was all he had.

After I'd been at Armani Exchange a few months, I learned that Barney's New York had sent secret shoppers all over Los Angeles to find the best salespeople in town. When the secret shoppers' reports came back, Barney's offered me full benefits and $47,000—plus commission—to sell women's clothes in their flagship Beverly Hills store. As a twenty-two-year-old unemployed actor, I thought about the offer for maybe a nanosecond before accepting. Barney's turned out to be a viper pit filled with a celebrity clientele, insanely competitive salespeople, and an air of acquisitive materialism as thick as L.A. smog. I was doing roughly as well with sales as I had at Armani but felt profoundly out of place. The most significant thing that happened during my time at Barney's was meeting a young woman who worked downstairs in the makeup department. Her name was Amber, and we started dating almost immediately.

I knew Tommy was still alive because when I'd visited my family over Christmas, I'd reached him on his San Francisco condo's landline. I heard this loud clatter, like he'd dropped the phone before getting a solid hold on it. When Tommy finally, breathlessly said "Hello," I told him I was in San Francisco and that it would be great to see him. "I'm sorry," Tommy said. "I cannot see you. I'm not around." Of course, he hung up.

By the spring I was living on my own, working a full-time job, dating Amber, and not doing much acting or auditioning at all. For a while, Aaron Spelling's production company had me on option for a television pilot, but it didn't come to anything, which was fine. I had a normal, comfortable life, and my acting dream had sort of faded away, just as Tommy had. Amber knew nothing of Tommy, aside from a few complimentary stories I'd shared of him, and those memories felt increasingly distant from the person I was now.

Eventually I left Barney's to take a less remunerative but far happier part-time job at French Connection. Months had passed since I'd last seen Tommy. Iris Burton had told me she was retiring, and I was thus heading into the professional unknown. This was when Tommy finally got back in touch with me, nine months after he'd disappeared.

Tommy left a message on my cell. He sounded as though he'd stabilized and announced he was moving back to Los Angeles, but into a larger apartment on the same floor of his Crescent Heights complex. "You know my style," Tommy said.

I did: black velvet curtains, T-shirt pillowcases, and dirty dishes.

A few days later, Amber and I went on a little vacation to Mexico. As soon as we crossed over the border back into San Diego, Tommy called my cell from his new Hollywood apartment. He sounded upbeat and said he was looking forward to seeing me.

I knew it was going to be strange to see him again. Since he had disappeared, I'd done almost nothing to further my acting dreams. It was almost like Tommy's presence had forced me to stay focused on acting. Amber had allowed me to hide from my dream; she didn't push me and she didn't ask questions about it. She accepted me for who I was when she met me. Which was fine. It was pleasant, comfortable even. But it wasn't who I really wanted to be.

That said, I wasn't sure I was ready to—or even *could*—welcome Tommy back into my life. As much as I'd worried about him and occasionally missed having him around, I knew too well the stress and frustration he was capable of sowing. When Amber pressed, I told her that my friend Tommy was back in town, but before I could explain more, she said, "Great! I'd love to meet him."

On May 7, 2001, I walked from my apartment over to the Crescent Heights building, not at all sure what I was going to find. Tommy had been in a dark, dangerous place, I knew, and part of me was prepared for anything. If I'm being truthful, though, what I found was almost exactly what I'd expected.

Tommy was waiting outside for me in the building driveway wearing baggy blue sweatpants and sunglasses. I couldn't see his shirt because he'd wrapped himself in an enormous and ratty black shawl. His hair was much longer—and blacker, and wavier. As he walked toward me in his Roman sandals (with white socks), I noticed how small and deliberate his steps were. Tommy seemed like someone you'd see standing alongside the road in the middle of nowhere. He seemed lost, ghostly.

He also looked different physically. His face was fuller and his body seemed more muscular; he'd obviously been working out. His stomach, though, was slightly bloated, with a paunch that peeked out from the fold in his peasant shawl. When I got closer to Tommy all I could think was how much heavier he looked; not only physically heavier, but emotionally and even spiritually heavier.

"Bonjour, monsieur," Tommy said, smiling.

"Bonjour," I said, hugging him.

"Look at you!" Tommy said. "You look great. No stomach!"

"Glad to be back?" I asked him.

Tommy sighed and looked around. It wasn't that nice a day: smoggy, a little too hot, a little too glarey. "Los Angeles is Los Angeles," he said. "And San Francisco is San Francisco. I miss San Francisco little bit."

"So you stopped by San Francisco between here and London?"

Tommy smiled. "Let's go eat."

We wound up at Canter's Deli on Fairfax. Tommy still hadn't taken off his sunglasses. He didn't that whole day. Indeed, I wouldn't see Tommy without his sunglasses for weeks.

"So," Tommy said, placing his hands flat on the table, "do I look different?"

I remembered what he'd said to me that last night in the apartment: *To be star, I need to reshape everything.* "You look a little different," I said.

"I make many changes to my life and myself. Now it's time to begin the real work."

This could only mean one thing. "Did you finish your script?"

"I have finished my script, for your information. It is completed. And it is copyrighted. The title is *The Room*."

"Totally finished?"

"Yes. One hundred percent. No one has read it yet. Today you will be the first."

I wasn't able to aimlessly spend time with Tommy as I once had. With Amber in my life, my hang-around mandate was far more limited. Amber was waiting for me right now, back at my apartment. "You want me to read it today? Like, right now?"

"Yes," he said. "We read today. It's very necessary."

"How many pages is it?"

"You'll see for yourself."

"Well, Tommy," I said delicately, "the thing is, I don't really have all day. My girlfriend's waiting for me."

Tommy stared at me through those sunglasses. "You tell your girl you are busy this afternoon. She can wait."

Right after our food came, Amber called me on my cell. I didn't pick up. Ten minutes later she called me again. And again after that. Tommy finally put his fork down and laughed. "Girlfriend is serious, huh?"

I could feel it happening at that moment. I was slipping back into the orbit of Tommy's Planet.

"So tell me about the acting now," Tommy said. "What's happening?"

My mouth opened but I said nothing. I had nothing to say. I was looking at myself literally and figuratively in Tommy's sunglasses. I didn't want to admit that I'd barely thought about acting at all in the last few months. It had just gone away. I almost felt like I owed Tommy for getting me here, and was disappointed in myself for setting my dream aside. "Let's eat fast," I said. "I want to read this script of yours."

"That's the idea," Tommy said.

His new, bigger apartment looked very similar to the old one, minus the black drapes and food-caked dishes in the sink. (Don't worry: A week later they were back.) Tommy sat me down in a chair and said, "You must prepare yourself physically and emotionally for what you are about to read. You will see many reflections of your life in my script. Are you ready?"

"I *think* so," I said, not knowing whether to be amused or terrified.

Tommy went into his second bedroom for what felt like a long time. When he finally came out, he was cradling a Kinko's-laminated script, seventy-four pages long, the title page of which bore the words

THE ROOM in 144-point font size, with three separate copyright notices below it. "Remember," Tommy said, "it is copyrighted." I turned the first slick, laminated page and found a director's-note preamble that began: "This play can be played without any age restrictions. It will work if the chemistry between all the characters makes sense."

I looked up at him. "So you settled on making it a play?"

"Yes," he said. "It's easier that way, for now. And maybe, if you behave yourself, you can direct it for the theater."

I laughed in spite of myself. "Maybe I should read it first."

Tommy sat down in a chair directly across from me, and that's how I began reading: with the script's silent, watchful, copyright-minded author wearing sunglasses and wrapped in a black shawl sitting five feet away.

Even though Tommy wanted *The Room* to be a play, his script opened with an "external shot of an apartment building south of Market Street." From there it pushed into a room that was described as being "furnished simply." An alarm clock rings, and a man "reaches to the clock and turns it off. He sleepily arouses [?] and puts on his shorts and walks slowly to the bathroom." When the man emerges he "smiles tenderly" at the woman with whom he shares his bed. The first line spoken by this woman: "I am not a slave here, am I?" The man responds: "Did you like last night?" The man is named Johnny, the woman Lisa. They proceed to have a fight about the man's imminent promotion, which Lisa accuses Johnny of being overly focused on. Of his promotion, Johnny says, "Old man Donkey lets me know today."

Lisa was a terror: shrill, controlling, greedy, selfish, and vain. She had to be one of the most chauvinistically written characters I'd ever encountered in a script—until, that is, I met her mother, Claudette.

"What do you think?" Tommy asked suddenly. "Do you see the reflections? Don't be scared. This is life. Do you see yourself yet?"

"Let me finish," I said. By this point, I was searching Tommy's script for clues as to what had gone on over the last nine months. There was a lot of dialogue about property and money and "the computer business," very little of which I could attach to anything. There was nothing about being sick, or dying, or desperation—at least nothing beyond the desperation Johnny feels about his relationship with Lisa. Everything in the script seemed so curiously devoid of real emotion. Instead I read one conversation after another that opened with lines like "Hi, Mom, how ya doing?" "Oh, hi! I'm very busy. How ya doing?" and "Hello, Peter, this is Lisa. How are you?" I did spot quite a few small details from Tommy's and my stint as roommates. A lot of the dialogue he attributed to Mark, for instance, who sleeps with Lisa and ruins Johnny's life, was Tommy-altered versions of things that I'd said. Which was another considerable problem: Everyone in the script sounded like Tommy. "You have too much competition in the computer field." "You are not drinking your cognac, dear. It will taste good with pizza." "I heard that, Lisa. Get your pretty little buns in here and help." This last line is almost certainly something Johnny or Mark says to Lisa, right? Wrong. This is something *Lisa's mother* says to Lisa. It was all 100 percent Tommy.

Soon enough, I began connecting the dots. The constant talk about money, about best friends (Johnny and Mark are best friends, but Mark also tells Peter he's his best friend; Michelle and Lisa are best friends; Johnny's other best friends all show up for his party—the whole script was like an advisory warning about the perils of having friends at all), about trust, about fear, about truth . . . Tommy's life study of human interaction had been put into a Final Draft blender and sprinkled with the darkness of whatever he'd been living through over the last nine months. The one thing Tommy's script wasn't about, despite its characters' claims? Love.

I had a sobering, sad, and powerful realization: Our friendship was the most human experience Tommy had had in the last few years. Maybe ever. The happy news was that whatever Tommy had been running from, he'd managed to turn and face it down in his script. Instead of killing himself, he wrote himself out of danger. He did this by making his character the one spotless human being amid chaos, lies, and infidelity. Johnny was perfect. He was a lost innocent, a pure victim. And Johnny's story was the perfect American drama—in Tommy's mind, anyway.

When I came to the last page, Tommy asked me, "So what do you think?"

What else could I say? "It was excellent, Tommy. You should be proud you finished it."

Tommy smiled. "Wow. I can't believe you give me compliment. Do you have any suggestions? Because I think about them."

"No," I said. "I think it's perfect."

Now that the perfection of his script was settled, Tommy sighed in relief. "It's so much work to write," he said. "I work so hard on this, to bring it to the life. And I tell you right now, when people see this play, they will be shocked."

"Yes," I said. "They would be shocked. Yes."

"Can you imagine this," Tommy said, "on the stage, in front of so many people?"

I tried to imagine that. I saw the people patiently waiting for the play to begin, their playbills in hand. The theater would be a twenty-seater in some corner of Hollywood. There'd be a leak in the roof; it would be raining. The actors would be Tommy and, oh, Jesus, probably me, doing it out of pity, and the audience would be made up entirely of my good-sport family and friends and maybe some homeless people who'd been lured in with plastic cups of wine. And the play would begin. Based on what I'd just read, it would either horrify everyone or bring everyone to their knees with laughter. Maybe both. "I think," I said, slowly and diplomatically, "that your play, if staged really well, would be something incredible."

"Really?" Tommy asked, leaning forward.

"Really," I said.

"I think so, too," Tommy said, looking away. "I think it would be so powerful."

fifteen

"God, Forgive Me"

Betty Schaefer: I just think that pictures should say a little something.
    Joe Gillis: Oh, one of the *message* kids. Just a story won't do!
       —*Sunset Boulevard*

Tommy kneeled down in front of the condo set fireplace, made a ponderous sign of the cross, and raised a large silver prop gun to his mouth. He was rehearsing his character's final moment on camera, his most dearly anticipated acting feat: Johnny's suicide.

Here's how *The Room* begins to end: Johnny becomes infuriated by Lisa's behavior at his surprise birthday party, trashes his and Lisa's condo in a rage, somehow gets his hands on a gun, requests divine forgiveness, and shoots himself in the head.

The night Tommy conceived *The Room,* he promised a riveting cinematic experience that would leave people so shaken they wouldn't be able to sleep for two weeks. Now, several years later, Tommy was in that promised moment—and half the cast and crew were trying, with spotty success, not to laugh.

Take after take, Tommy was so focused on capturing Johnny's emotional upheaval that he was floundering out of frame, wincing, crying out, flailing his arms—all this *after* he'd pulled the trigger. Meanwhile, Byron was doing his best to get Tommy to please, for the love of God, stay in frame. Byron's on-set evolution had been interesting. Neither a script supervisor nor a first assistant director, he'd gone from being a stagehand to a surrogate Sandy, coaching Tommy step by step, moment to moment. I was beginning to think of him as *The Room*'s Director of Yelling at Tommy. When Tommy's kneeling degenerated into a lazy slouch, Byron would yell, "Be erect!" Tommy would arch his back obediently. Five seconds later he'd be slouched over again and out of frame. "This is you, buddy," Byron kept coaching. "Come on! This is *it*. Energy, Tommy!" Tommy, though, looked flustered, lost, confused.

Tommy couldn't synchronize his suicide moment with the loud, helpful "Bang!" being yelled out by Byron. Sometimes he'd still be kneeling there after the "Bang!" as though nothing had happened. Amy, the makeup artist, who was standing just off camera, would try to time Tommy's trigger pull with a fake blood squib, which squirted the fireplace behind Tommy with a burst of barely noticeable spatter. This not-so-special effect looked like someone sitting off camera had whacked a ketchup packet with a hammer. Tommy's delivery of his final line—"God, forgive me"—also fluctuated from take to take. In a couple of takes he whispered it, in a couple he said it with no emotion at all, and a couple came out like this: "Why? *Why?* Ahhhhh! God. Oh, my *God*! Ahhhh! *Forgive Me!*" Bang. Blood splatter. Tommy was still kneeling there. Then, all at once, he collapsed.

Byron was behind the camera, glowering under his backward baseball cap, looking more and more like an embattled Little League coach. "Come *on,*" Byron said to Tommy as he showed him how to hold the gun properly. "You can do this!"

By this point, most everyone else had given up maintaining any facade of professionalism. You could see giggling crew members wander into shots. There was no director of photography listed on the slate and no one was keeping track of take numbers—neither of which mattered, as the slate was rarely clear. Scene after scene began with the camera out of focus simply because no one cared enough to check.

This new level of on-set laissez-faireism went unnoticed by Tommy. He was too preoccupied with his own troubles, such as figuring out how to smoothly retrieve his silver prop gun from its box. Why Johnny even *has* a loaded handgun in his condo is a subject of fevered *Room* fan debate. When the time came to film the suicide sequence, Tommy decided to stash the prop handgun in a small brown treasure box, which he then placed at the base of Johnny and Lisa's fireplace—because loaded firearms should always be kept near open flames. For what it's worth, Tommy's original *Room* script contained an even more bizarrely elaborate gun-finding scenario: "JOHNNY GOES INTO THE CLOSET AND THROWS OUT EVERYTHING HE SEES AND FINDS A WOODEN BOX ABOUT THE SIZE OF A SHOEBOX. HE TRIES TO PULL IT OPEN, BUT HE CAN'T. HE THROWS IT TO THE FLOOR BUT IT DOESN'T OPEN. HE KICKS IT, BUT IT STILL DOESN'T OPEN. HE PULLS OUT A PIECE OF METAL [?] FROM THE BOTTOM OF THE CHAIR [?] AND PRIES OPEN THE PADLOCK [!]. HE SUCCEEDS. HE OPENS THE BOX AND TAKES OUT THE GUN. HE IS CRYING."

With the suicide moment finally out of the way, Byron sent Tommy on a condo-trashing dry run. Tommy finally had his chance to let loose, Charles Foster Kane–style, but he didn't do anything other than lope around the set, ineptly pantomiming rage. Tommy normally went full-throttle during rehearsals, destroying everything in sight. But now his idea of going crazy was to knock some fake fruit out of a bowl, lazily nudge a couple of candles over with his thigh, and nonchalantly hurl a television out the window. It was the strangely calm tantrum of an overwrought and exhausted man.

In the film, the thing that causes Johnny to lose his mind and trash his condo is the playback of a recorded conversation between Mark and Lisa. Tommy wrote Mark and Lisa's exchange to include such heartfelt nuggets of passion as "I want your body" and "You are the sparkle of my life." Juliette and I got a kick out of squirting as much Cheez Whiz over these lines as possible while recording them. The interesting thing about Mark and Lisa's phone-tapped conversation is that *The Room*'s audience hears the original conversation they have in real time, on-screen; however, when Johnny plays their conversation back a few seconds later, the recording is different from what the audience just heard—and yes, that difference is actually in the script. It had evidently not occurred to Tommy when he was writing *The Room* to scroll back half a page and cross-check the two conversations, and Juliette and I didn't bother correcting the discrepancy. Tommy had his own way of doing things, and this was the way he wanted it. Todd Barron, the DP who'd replaced Graham who'd replaced Raphael, was especially helpful in this respect, in that he had absolutely no concern for the quality of what he was filming, which kept the production moving very nicely. In that sense, and that sense alone, Todd Barron may be the production's hidden hero.

Once Juliette and I finished recording our mismatched lines, we went back to the set to close out the last scene of the film with Philip Haldiman. The scene in question called for Lisa and Mark and Denny to argue while weeping copiously over Johnny's corpse. It's pretty obvious that I mailed in my performance throughout the entire production, but during this scene I didn't even bother to lick the envelope. Amy, the makeup artist, doused my face with shiny glycerin tears. They didn't help. I looked like an unconvincingly weepy replicant.

When Tommy got enough raw footage of *The Room*'s climactic scene, he hurried to the monitor to watch it. Within seconds he was frowning. Tommy wasn't shy about telling us our performances "didn't cut it." Then again, we weren't alone. Byron pointed out that Tommy's deep breathing was noticeable throughout his entire performance as dead Johnny. The only thing we filmed that day that Tommy felt was at all "powerful" was the footage of him storming down the staircase like a wild animal, sitting in a chair, and crying out "Why, Lisa? *Why? Why? Why?*" like someone trying, and painfully failing, to defecate.

After watching the entire suicide and postsuicide sequence several times on the monitor, Tommy turned to us all and said, "We redo Johnny's suicide in the bedroom set"—as if a different set would fix the problem. There was a collective groan.

I returned to Birns & Sawyer the following afternoon to find a bedroom set in which Tommy Wiseau was preparing to get jaybird naked. This bedroom was maybe the tackiest *Room* set yet: red walls, a Greek church's worth of candles, an art-piece wall fountain, and a king-size bed with a sheer cascade of white mosquito netting draped from its canopy. The only surviving element of Johnny and Lisa's condo was a section of the spiral staircase (now with only one step) that had been relegated to the bedroom's eerily lit corner.

Tommy informed me I needed to shoot a second love scene in the newly built bedroom set. I argued with him for a bit but eventually gave in; this, like fighting a great white shark, was not a battle man was meant to win. (Ten years later, I've never once watched any of my *Room* love scenes without either leaving the theater, fast-forwarding, or closing my eyes.)

As bad as I felt about doing another love scene, I tried to put it in perspective by considering poor Juliette's situation. She was being asked, once again, to expose her breasts on camera, and for what? The love scene Tommy wanted to add fit nowhere in the film. I didn't trust Tommy's motives in wanting to see young people—whether in casting or rehearsals or while filming—make out in front of him so frequently. Juliette, in an attempt to make things more comfortable, suggested playing an Alicia Keys song. Tommy's response: "We are not here to promote other people's work."

After shooting Lisa's tryst with Mark, Juliette had to film her love scene with Tommy. This took several days. A lot of productions close their sets during love scenes. Not Tommy's. He *opened* the set, asking every member of the production to come in and "help out with lighting." It started to feel like Tommy didn't want the love-scene-shooting process to end. He delayed things for no reason and stayed naked far longer than was necessary. (When Tommy, wearing a towel, watched some playbacks with Todd Barron, he pointed at himself on the monitor and said, "Look at all these muscles.") He made no secret of the fact that he was enjoying his physical contact with Juliette, who was obviously suffering between takes. I think half of the guys on the crew had to suppress every chivalrous impulse they had during filming to keep themselves from pulling Tommy off her—especially during the shot in which Johnny appears to be im-pregnating Lisa's navel. In the end, Tommy was so pleased with the footage he shot of his love scene that he felt compelled to use it all in the final film, even going so far as to add an additional Johnny-Lisa love scene using recycled footage. Tommy assumed this would go un-noticed by audiences. It did not.

In the love scene's final shot, Johnny gets out of bed and walks bare-assed to the bathroom. Tommy thought long and hard about his deci-sion to show his ass. "I need to do it," he told me. "I have to show my ass or this movie won't sell." Yes, Tommy dedicated an entire scene to his ass. He drew inspiration from the example of Brad Pitt, who unveiled his own rear end in *Legends of the Fall*. Tommy's butt is visible in the love scenes, of course, but there's never a full-on unmitigated ass shot until he walks to the bathroom. Tommy insisted on doing numerous takes of this moment; it felt a little bit like he was *aiming* his ass at us, like the whole scene was an excuse to moon us over and over again. "Unwatched" has never interested Tommy. Not as a human being and not as a performer. I've never seen anyone more comfortable being naked around people who resented him.

Tommy stopped shooting only when Byron demanded he end it. "We can't stop," Tommy said, "until we know we get it."

"Tommy!" Byron responded, somewhat desperately. "We *definitely* got it."

With the love scenes in the can, Tommy was free to reshoot his presuicide trashing, this time in Johnny and Lisa's bedroom. Tommy had one final chance to really show us all what Johnny's desperation looked like. But he remained an oddly lethargic room wrecker. He trashed a cheap dresser, for instance, by lackadaisically pulling its first two drawers off their runners and casually tipping it over. Yet, amazingly, Tommy's sleepwalking bedroom rampage didn't come close to being the craziest part of his performance.

The Room's original script tells us that Johnny, in the middle of going nuts, finds a "sexy nightgown" and, moments before killing himself, does something highly inappropriate with it. To quote the script itself: "HE REACHES IN AND PULLS OUT MORE OF LISA'S CLOTHES AND THROWS THEM ON THE FLOOR. HE LIES ON THE CLOTHES, UNZIPPING HIS ZIPPER. HE IS BREATHING HARD AND WRITHING WITH PELVIC

THRUSTS. WHEN HE FINISHES HE SITS UP AND PICKS UP
THE GUN." I'd read the script several times, but never in a million
years did I think Tommy would actually try to film this. Who has sex
with his future wife's clothes moments before shooting himself?

When Tommy initially decided to film the suicide sequence in the
living room set, he foreclosed the possibility of including the sexy nightgown in Johnny's presuicide activities. (A quirk of Tommy's script is
that only occasionally does it indicate where or when a scene is supposed to take place or include any location notes or specifics. There's no
"EXT. GOLDEN GATE PARK—DAY," say, or "INT. CONDO—
NIGHT." All of this is to say that deciding where to film various scenes
in the *Room* script was basically guesswork.) Now that Tommy was
reshooting Johnny's suicide scene in the bedroom set, the "sexy nightgown" was back in play in the form of Lisa's red dress.

The cast and crew, who'd never seen a full script, weren't at all
prepared for the moment in which Tommy, writhing around on the
bedroom floor, grabbed Lisa's red dress, held it to his crotch, and
proceeded to simulate sex with it. "Wait," someone nearby me said.
"What is he . . . is he . . . Oh, dear God. He is. He's really . . .Oh,
God." Everyone knew they'd just witnessed one of the most genuinely perverse moments in the history of American cinema. Equally
bizarre was the fact that Tommy has Johnny *smell* the dress after his
presumable orgasm. You know you're in trouble as a dramatist when
a character blows his face off and it's the second-most memorable
thing in the scene.

Tommy, to his credit, had at long last come through on his promise.
After watching this dress humping, no one was going to sleep for *at
least* two weeks.

The emotional aftermath of Tommy's dresscapade was hardly an
ideal time for the makeup artist to swoop in and start painting Tommy
with blood for the second half of Johnny's suicide sequence, but that's
what had to happen. The blood the makeup artist used to simulate the
contents of Johnny's skull was water dosed with sugary red food color-
ing. Tommy demanded that someone paint a little blood trickle coming out of the corner of his mouth, even though a man who'd stuck a

gun between his teeth and pulled the trigger would display a drastically different level of oral trauma. I couldn't believe Tommy would skimp so much on the blood effects. This was the payoff of the entire film, wasn't it? No one wanted an authentically re-created head wound, but *Kool-Aid* blood?

Tommy kept going on about needing pools of blood everywhere, even in places that didn't make sense. The effect Tommy wanted, it appeared, was: *Dude, I'm dead. Look how dead I am!* As one commentator on the film eloquently noted, Johnny's death sequence "is effectively a teenage boy's self-pitying fantasy of how, if he killed himself, everyone would regret how mean they had been to him." Tommy wasn't lying in blood; he was wallowing in it.

There was one big change-up during this scene. Peter Anway, concerned that the production might never end, had decided to call in an acting coach named Diane to help speed things along. Diane was essentially hired to replace Sandy, as Byron had proved "too aggressive" for Tommy. Diane was smart, sensitive, and determined to help. Before we got ready to film the scene in which Lisa, Denny, and Mark grieve over Johnny, she took us all aside and started telling us what she felt was at stake in the scene. I stopped her, politely, and asked that she follow me to the room where Tommy kept the dailies. The dailies guy was sitting there eating a sandwich. "Hi," I said. "Could you show Diane some footage from the living room suicide dailies?"

Without saying a word, and without pausing from the ongoing destruction of his sandwich, the dailies guy fired up the playback machine. Diane's expression started in a place of benign expectation, corkscrewed into abject shock, and mainlined into something like existential confusion. Then she started to laugh. "So," I said, "that's where we're at."

The only thing worse than shooting a terrible scene you have no interest in performing is shooting a terrible scene you have no interest in performing for the second time. By this point I truly resented Tommy, which made it even harder to feign heartbreak over the death of his asinine character. Cue the return of the glycerin tears.

During a break, Tommy hauled me aside and said, "Look, I need you to deliver something here. This is touchdown. Very important scene. Your chance to be big actor. I need you to do crying thing."

"Yeah, sure," I said, barely listening to him.

Tommy didn't go away. In fact, he came closer. "You know what I need from you, right? Remember this day in the car? On Sunset, when I say everything was over with apartment and friendship? Your face was so aggressive. So *emotional*. This is type you must show for camera."

In other words, Tommy was asking me to relive one of the most sadistic experiences he'd ever put me through in an attempt to wring some authentic tears from me. He was just as adamant that Mark lean down and kiss Johnny's large, white, lunar forehead—which is a strange gesture for someone who's been porking the dead man's future wife to extend.

In the end, this mournful, dreadful, exhausting, and ridiculous scene ended up taking three days to shoot. Thanks to Bill Meurer's demand that we stop filming on the Birns & Sawyer lot, this concluded Los Angeles production of *The Room*. All that Tommy had left to film were San Francisco exterior shots, none of which would involve any actors, scenes, or dialogue.

Only three crew members offered to help Tommy shoot in San Francisco: Todd Barron; the sound guy, Zsolt; and Joe, who was Todd Barron's assistant camera operator. Tommy had gone from a fantastically wasteful yet still somehow low-budget thirty-person crew to a guerrilla-style three-person production. In talking over the logistics, Todd Barron brought up the fact that Tommy would need to get San Francisco shooting permits. "Permits *nothing*," Tommy said in disgust. "I have certain resources. San Francisco is my city. We film anywhere we want. Let them stop us."

Shortly before leaving, Tommy hit Birns & Sawyer yet again for provisions and wound up dropping some serious coin on long-distance lenses for both his 35mm and HD cameras, expensive filters, more Arriflex lighting equipment, carrying cases, and a fancy new Canon still camera. After purchasing all this, Tommy called me and announced that it was time to pick up my new car—on one condition, which was that I join his three-man crew in San Francisco.

This didn't seem like a big deal at the time. I love the Bay Area and had been thinking about visiting home to recover after filming anyway. So I agreed. There was another Tommy catch, however, which was that Tommy planned to pick out my car for me. Tommy, I learned, wanted to buy me an SUV, for the transparent reason that he needed a large vehicle to transport all his freshly purchased equipment to San Francisco. I wished Tommy could do something, anything, that didn't feel so creepily calculated.

At a car dealership on La Brea Tommy picked out the SUV he wanted within thirty seconds of arrival. The sales guy was ecstatic to find a customer so bizarrely determined to buy. Everything was going well until the man asked Tommy for identification. At this, Tommy crossed his arms and stepped back. "I'm businessman," he said. "No identification necessary."

The sales guy tried to roll with this unanticipated punch. "Okay," he said. "I respect that. But I can't sell you a car without seeing some identification."

"You should accept check," Tommy said.

"Sorry," the salesperson said, smiling politely. "It's company policy. We need to see identification."

Again Tommy refused. I pulled Tommy aside and said that showing one's identification was a pretty reasonable request.

"No," Tommy said. "They play games here. I'm businessman. I don't have time for this bullshit."

"Tommy, you can't drive off in an expensive car after leaving a personal check. What if it bounces?"

"Check will not bounce. Who are you kidding?"

"Okay, but *they* don't know that."

Tommy walked back over to the salesperson and made him a "revised final" offer, which was that Tommy would consent to a *cashier's* check and allow the salesperson to look at but not handle his driver's license. The salesperson, no longer amused, told Tommy that this was not going to happen.

Tommy threw up his arms. "You know what? I have to leave now. Final offer. You want to make money or not?"

"Sorry," the sales guy said. "We don't have a deal."

From there we headed to a slightly seedy dealership in Santa Monica, where the salesperson agreed to accept a cashier's check with no questions asked. I dropped Tommy off at his house and went to pick up Amber in my brand-new SUV, figuring it would be a fun surprise for her, if nothing else. She'd just returned from San Diego and I wanted us to have a nice dinner together before I took off for San Francisco. She liked the car but, beyond that, didn't have much to say to me. Over the last few months, it felt like we had become two boats figuring out how to navigate the same narrow waterway. Later, at her favorite restaurant, Amber started crying. When I asked what was wrong, Amber looked up at me with hopeless eyes and said, "Greg, I can't do this anymore."

I knew Amber and I weren't going to be together forever; we were always better friends than romantic partners. But Amber knew me better than anyone, and had been with me through every painful twist and turn of the last year. We'd outgrown each other, but still her letting me go hurt more than I would have thought.

I dropped Amber off at her place and returned home. When I walked into my apartment, the phone was ringing. I half hoped it would be her. It was, of course, Tommy. "We need to get ready for San Francisco! We leave tonight! Your girl can wait." I packed and left for Tommy's.

When he answered his door, Tommy looked at me and said, "What happened to your face? Your eyes are all red. My God."

I took three steps into his house and collapsed on the first soft piece of furniture I saw. I realized I'd felt happier and freer with my beat-up Lumina and a three-figure bank account. "Amber and I just broke up," I told Tommy.

Tommy said, "Oh," and paused. Then he waved it away. "Don't worry about this. You'll have dozens of girls. She'll be jealous." Tommy's Planet had a strangely simple emotional economy.

Tommy whipped out the new still camera he'd bought earlier that day and started snapping shots of me. "Look at your eyes! My God. Somebody is so sad tonight! How much did you love her on scale from one to ten? Can you smile little bit or is this all end of the world? You are not smiling at all. Greg, what is the problem?"

"Tommy!" I said, covering his lens. "What do you *think* is the problem?"

"Hey," Tommy said, setting the camera aside, "let's talk about it, then. Oh! I have good idea. Why don't we do scene in San Francisco? We can use your emotion. You can talk about your girl in this scene. Talk about Johnny's problems with girl and his life. This will make you feel better, trust me."

I just stared at him. I couldn't believe he was actually suggesting this. "No. We're not going to shoot a scene about Amber in San Francisco."

Tommy sat down next to me. "No, you see. It will help. Let's write scene now. Don't be so sad." He gave my knee a cheer-up smack and stood. "All right? We do scene now."

A scene? I was so drained of energy and motivation that I said nothing as Tommy left the room to fetch his laptop. Upon his return he handed it to me; Final Draft was open on his screen. Tommy began pacing in front of the sofa. "Okay," he said. "So maybe we're in coffee shop, talking about life and women. Right? Johnny and Mark talking. So let's talk. What happened to you with your girl tonight? I'm listening now."

I thought about this question. What *did* happen, anyway?

"Wait!" Tommy said. "I've got idea! Write this dialogue down: 'Relationships never work. I don't know why I waste time on it. Girls are so difficult. They spend long time in bathroom.'" Tommy made an insistent gesture that I type. I did. I didn't much like what I was typing, but I typed it all out.

With that, Tommy started describing other ideas for San Francisco scenes. One took place in a flower shop and involved Johnny buying a dozen red roses for Lisa. The other involved Johnny and Mark playing football and jogging in Golden Gate Park. I started to wonder if Tommy was even emotionally capable of finishing *The Room*. Maybe his real plan was to keep filming it forever—or for as long as people kept typing out his ideas for him.

We left for San Francisco at 10:00 p.m. On the way up, Tommy drank a six-pack of Red Bull, sang along to three rounds of Richard Marx's "Right Here Waiting," and was asleep and drooling on his own shoulder by Fresno. The ride's remaining three hours were still and silent. Just a few more days, I kept thinking, and I could finally stop worrying about money for a while and go back to focusing on what I came to L.A. to do in the first place. My debt to Tommy was paid. My spirits began to lift a little. By 1:00 a.m., we were crossing the Bay Bridge. Of course, that's when Tommy chose to wake up. Vampire trick.

sixteen

Don't Be Shocked

Don't you take the past and just put it in a room in the basement and lock the door and never go in there? That's what I do. And then you meet someone special and all you want to do is toss them the key. Say, "Open up, step inside." But you can't because it's dark. And there are demons.
—Tom Ripley, *The Talented Mr. Ripley*

Our first scheduled exterior shot was a city view from a Sausalito harbor, located just over the Golden Gate Bridge. Todd Barron, Joe, Zsolt, and I were all staying at an Embassy Suites; Tommy slept at his condo on Guerrero Street. Remarkably, Tommy showed up at our hotel that morning, upbeat and exactly on time, which, if I'm not mistaken, shook Heaven itself from its cloudy foundations.

The crew followed us to Sausalito. As I drove over the Golden Gate Bridge, Tommy gazed out the window. "On this trip," he said, nodding slowly, "you may find out several secrets about me. Don't be shocked."

At Sausalito Harbor, Tommy took to pep-talking Todd Barron, Joe, and Zsolt as they set up for the first exterior: "We want big feature movie quality. We need fancy San Francisco buildings. The long shots. *Really* shoot nice way, okay?" They shot the cityscape quickly and packed up for the next location, which was a peak overlooking the Golden Gate Bridge.

We parked at the top of the mountain and set up. Tommy paced behind Joe and Todd Barron as they started shooting, saying things like, "You need to really do good job here, okay? We need entire bridge. We may need to do two to three shots."

"Yep," Todd Barron said as he looked through the camera's eye-piece. But Tommy persisted, oblivious to the fact that he was walking in and out of their shot. "No Mickey Mouse stuff here," he said.

Joe—a funny, brusque New Yorker by birth—was the only crew member, aside from Zsolt, who'd lasted the duration of the *Room* shoot. He'd always been professional, but it appeared his patience was about to expire. Joe inhaled, exhaled, and turned to face Tommy. "Tommy. We know what you want. We're getting it for you. You *need* to back off while we're shooting. We can't do *anything* with you getting in the way."

Tommy took a step backward. "My God, Joey, you so aggressive! I call you Joey from now on, okay?"

Joe almost smiled. "Yeah, Tommy. Okay." With that Joe went back to doing his job.

Zsolt and I were watching all this transpire from a distance of fifteen feet or so. "How could Tommy have ever had a real job?" Zsolt asked me in his thick Hungarian accent. "He's unable to understand such simple things." Then Zsolt turned to me. "Has he ever even told you where he's from?"

Pierre arrives in San Francisco on a Greyhound bus from New Orleans. The ride has taken several days, and Pierre is still unable to believe how big this country is. Either immediately or shortly after arriving in San Francisco, Pierre starts calling himself Thomas.

Thomas carries his two black suitcases off the bus. He is wearing a beret; his shaggy dark brown curls have been tucked up into it. He also has with him a check from a local bank in Chalmette, Louisiana, for $2,011—his wages from the grocery store—but he is unable to find a bank willing to cash it. Someone at some point told Thomas about lodging at the YMCA on Leavenworth Avenue. He checks into it immediately.

San Francisco is the first city Thomas has seen that feels like home to him. "My city": That's how he will always refer to San Francisco. It's almost as if the city's been *waiting* for Thomas to arrive; San Francisco is in the middle of a glorious cultural rebirth wrapped up in a socially calamitous urban-blight collapse. In 1978, there is probably no better place for a deeply peculiar person to be.

Thomas wanders around the city for two days. He loves the Embarcadero area, Chinatown, the Wharf, but it's Alcatraz that captures his imagination. It reminds him, in its severity, of something the Soviets might have built. To him, Alcatraz is scary and dire and secret. He visits the old rock several times.

Thomas needs work. After a week he picks up the *Chronicle* and hunts the want ads. One catches his eye: a man is looking for someone to sell yo-yos on the Wharf. He calls the number in the ad from a pay phone in Union Square. The man refuses to give Thomas his name but tells him to meet him at a coffee shop near Fisherman's Wharf the next day.

At the Wharf coffee shop, an older man with a clean-shaven head walks in and sits down across from Thomas, who is by now quite scared. The deal the man proposes is this: Thomas will sell the yo-yos for him to tourists at an ambitious markup and receive a small percentage of the profits. Thomas agrees to middleman the yo-yos. He later claims to have done so well for himself that he eventually began to wonder, *Why don't I sell my own yo-yos?*

And so Thomas, through means unknown, buys a gross of yo-yos and toy birds directly from the supplier, severing his business arrangement with the bald man. The toy birds Thomas sells are popular in Europe—particularly at the Eiffel Tower—but they are not commonly seen in America. Day after day, night after night, Thomas throws his toy birds into the seaside air; they sail up, circle around, and dutifully return to him. Thomas becomes so skilled at throwing these little avian boomerangs that tourists routinely applaud. He's making money, so much money that he moves to his own apartment in the Tenderloin. At night he sometimes hears gunshots, but so what? In what other country could he have come so far, so fast? He's grateful to America; his love for the place grows.

Thomas earns a Wharf nickname: the Birdman. He changes his legal name to Thomas Pierre Wiseau, taking the French word for "bird," *oiseau*, and swapping out the *O* for the *W* of his birth name. Thomas Wiseau. Thomas Bird. Thomas the Birdman.

Thomas's story grows increasingly murky after his legal name change. He lived harshly, he will later say. Totally day-to-day. Other times he will claim to have been making so much money that he carried bags of bills home to the Tenderloin every night. Part of his story involves an Italian restaurant on the Wharf he claims had mob connections. According to Thomas, one day he tried to use its bathroom but was thrown out because he was not a paying customer. Instead of getting mad, Thomas decides to apply for a job there. He's turned away. It becomes a game: Every week he applies for a job at the restaurant and every week he's turned away. Then, one day, a busboy quits in the middle of a busy shift. The restaurant's manager, panicking, looks outside and sees the Birdman doing his act for a crowd of tourists. The manager sends a runner out to communicate the following message: *We've got a job, Birdman, starting immediately, if you want it.*

Yet again Thomas proves himself to be a ferociously hard worker. When he's not bussing tables he's working the Wharf. Or so he claims. This is how, according to Thomas, he quietly, and improbably, amassed his first fortune.

Then he meets two people who will have a fateful impact on his life. The first is a young woman he spots while bussing tables, whom he will later describe as "so beautiful" that he walked into a door and hit his head the first time he saw her. On Valentine's Day, Thomas makes sure he has roses for her; on her birthday, he gives her a toy bird. Eventually he will give her a $1,500 platinum diamond engagement ring. They move across the bridge, to Sausalito, where Thomas does various jobs— hospital worker, city supervisor—before achieving lasting success as a full-fledged "retail man." He is immensely happy for the first time in his life—until, that is, the woman betrays him ("multiple times," according to Thomas), which drives him into some unspecified breakdown and results in a panic-filled move back to San Francisco proper.

What parts of these stories are true? What parts of these stories are *plausible*?

Sometime after his breakup, Thomas meets Drew Caffrey, who becomes a father figure to him. It is through his connection with Caffrey

that Thomas opens up a booth in an indoor marketplace beside the reputedly mobbed-up restaurant. From his humble stall, Thomas now
sells pleather jackets, trinkets, toy birds, key chains, jewelry, and clothing he claims to have designed. He's not some transient, Wharf-loitering
Birdman anymore. He has business cards now; they list his address as
Wharf Park Shops, Jefferson Street, Number C. Setting up a booth like
this must have cost Thomas money. He must have needed a vendor license. Did Thomas get these funds from Drew Caffrey or simply reach
into one of his "bags of money"? Did the reputedly mobbed-up restaurant have anything to do with his access to Chinese junk suppliers?

Soon he moves his small operation into a large building on Beach
Street—an actual retail space. Somehow, Thomas eventually comes to
own this entire building. From where does a junk-peddling, pleather-
pushing, self-described "little kid" earn the money to buy an optimally
located building in such a short period of time? Where does he then find
the money to knock down the old building and to build on its foundation a new, steel-accented, four-story headquarters? Thomas maintains
that the secret to his string of startling successes was—and continues to
be—his shrewd ability to identify new markets and new things to sell.
Perhaps Thomas P. Wiseau really is some kind of business savant. As
in all things, the simplest explanation is probably the right one. However, this is a man whose skin Occam's Razor cannot cut. The enigma
of Thomas P. Wiseau is that there *never seems to be a simplest explanation*.

Thomas will later say, cryptically and often, that Drew Caffrey was
central to his inimitable rise. When asked how, though, Thomas cavils,
saying only that Caffrey was kind, smoked a pipe, wore a cowboy hat,
and taught him "many things about life."

Street Fashions is so successful that Thomas buys more properties.
One building is on Sutter, another on Dore. The self-described "King
of Levi's" sells jeans with missing belt loops and botched stitching. Even
so, Street Fashions opens up more stores, one of them on Haight Street,
registered to something called TPW Corporation. Years later, Thomas
will sell the Sutter Street building for $2.9 million. A fortune—an em-
pire—founded on yo-yos and toy birds.

Tragically, in 1995, one of Thomas's buildings—the one on Dore

Street—burns down in a fire that spreads to nearby buildings, and in this blaze, a man gruesomely dies. Thomas submits a video to his insurance company detailing his damages. This video is tastelessly scored to classical music, includes local-news footage of the burned man's death announcement, and contains testimony from a material witness who affirms Thomas's damages and good character. When this witness stops praising Thomas, the cameraman eggs him on to continue: "Anything else you can say good things about Thomas?" Thomas, of course, is the cameraman. The material witness, who for some reason wears a white lab coat, is Drew Caffrey. It all seems like a small, strange movie.

Years later, Thomas will memorialize Drew Caffrey, who died in 1999, by crediting him as not only an executive producer of *The Room* but also as its San Francisco casting director. What purpose do these false attributions actually serve? Thomas will never say.

One day, Thomas admits to Caffrey that his real dream is not to be a successful retailer or real-estate tycoon. Sure, that is certainly nice, but it's not his real dream. Thomas's real dream, he says to Caffrey, is to be an actor. No, a *movie star*. "Well," Caffrey says, "if that's the case, make sure you put yourself front and center. Be the star. Make *yourself* the star. Don't think about anybody else."

Long after Thomas has started going by Tommy, he will describe this as the best advice he has ever received.

We got some but not all of the exterior shots Tommy wanted on our first day in San Francisco. While going over the following day's schedule, Tommy surprised us all by saying, "So I have idea for couple scenes. In the first, maybe Johnny and Mark talk in a coffee shop. Then maybe they play football. Simple stuff."

Todd Barron looked alarmed by this news. "You mean," he said, "like *acting* shots?"

"Yes," Tommy said.

"Do you have a script?"

"Don't worry about the script at this time. Just do your camera stuff. We take care of this."

Until now, I hadn't truly believed that the postbreakup therapy session Tommy conducted for me would ever find its way into *The Room*. Among other quandaries, where would Tommy find, at the last minute, a coffee shop that would allow us to film, or the extras that would be needed to fill in the background? But to my shock, Todd Barron, Joe, and Zsolt all warmed to Tommy's proposed scenes immediately. I suspect they saw it as a way to get paid to spend more time in a great city, with San Francisco's own Willy Wonka guiding them.

By eight o'clock the next morning, we were trolling for parking spaces near an already bustling Fisherman's Wharf. "Why are we filming here?" I asked Tommy, scanning vainly for a parking spot, while the crew trailed close behind. "This is the most difficult place to park in the city."

"You have to trust me, young man," Tommy said. "I have resources." He directed me toward a bank of private spots on Beach Street. That's when I noticed the sign hanging above the corner building: STREET FASHIONS USA. I recalled seeing the logo in Tommy's condo and remembered him saying that he'd done marketing for Street Fashions years before. Two massive American flags—so massive I suspected they could be seen from space—were snapping in the wind on the building's rooftop. The four-story building contained other businesses, including a little joint called Pizza Zone. A dingy banner that read CONSTRUCTION SALE hung over a Bunyan-size plastic blue-jeans statue affixed above the door's entrance; both banner and statue looked like they had been up for quite a while.

After we entered, the first thing I noticed was the staircase. It was the same staircase on which Tommy had Shakespeared in the demoreel commercial that scored him his SAG card. The second thing I noticed was that Street Fashions felt more like a warehouse than a store. I don't remember seeing any cash registers or anyone working there. There was, however, merchandise on display, and a lot of it. Why would a retail store in one of the most heavily touristed parts of the city not be open on a weekday?

Tommy started up the stairs to the second floor, which was being used as some kind of storage space. "We shoot Alcatraz from roof," he told us. Tommy was clearly familiar with this building; I assumed he'd called in beforehand for approval to use it. Tommy pressed the button for the elevator on our left, which would take us to the rooftop. When it opened an older man walked out. I thought he might be the store's owner or manager—until he engaged Tommy. The man, it transpired, had a question for Tommy: Could he maybe sublet his space for a little while? Tommy and the man discussed the matter only briefly, but during the discussion, it came out that the man was one of the building's tenants—a successful landscape architect—who was paying $8,000 a month for his space. Tommy nonchalantly told the guy, "No problem. We talk. Call me."

I thought, *Wait. Does Tommy manage this building? Does he* own *it?* I'd known him for four years and he'd never mentioned owning a building. This was premium San Francisco real estate.

We reached the spacious rooftop, which offered a gorgeous view of Alcatraz and a panoramic vista of greater San Francisco. It was so perfect that I couldn't help but wonder why we hadn't used it to shoot *The Room*'s Rooftop scenes. Those scenes could have been shot here, with a small crew, in a few days—sparing Tommy tens of thousands of dollars. Todd Barron, Joe, and Zsolt set up and shot the Alcatraz footage that eventually wound up in *The Room*'s opening credits. After that, they began shooting footage from every angle on the roof. These shots would later be composited onto Tommy's green screens. They filmed from the beginning of a sunny morning until deep into a foggy afternoon, thereby accounting for why the weather in the Rooftop scenes is so consistently inconsistent from one shot to the next.

I wandered over to the flagpoles from which the massive American flags were flying. "For your information," Tommy called over as I looked up at them, "those are the largest American flags in San Francisco." Something had been engraved at the base of each pole: TPW. So he *did* own this building. Only Tommy, a man of supersize patriotism, would buy two flags, and only Tommy would make sure they were this big. Was owning this building one of the secrets he'd alluded to in the car ride to Sausalito? If so, what was next—that Tommy really *was* the Zodiac Killer?

The next morning Tommy and I arrived at Beach Street's Flag Central some time before the crew. Tommy unlocked the door to Pizza Zone.

"You see?" he said. "I told you. I have resources. We can use this for coffee shop scene." It was clear to me by now that he owned the entire building, so I wasn't really surprised when Tommy walked directly to the register, pulled out the cash drawer, and stashed the entire thing in a cabinet. "People's fingers, you see, like money," he told me. "Before you know it, it all disappears."

The night before I'd put out a quick casting call on some San Francisco acting websites, requesting headshots and résumés. By midnight I had the extras. Shortly after Todd Barron, Joe, and Zsolt arrived, the extras began trickling in. I was surprised to see the actor Tommy had called in to play the coffee shop's cheesecake-pushing proprietor: a woman named Padma, who was Tommy's old scene partner from his Stella catastrophe in Jean Shelton's class.

Tommy was determined, much to everyone's puzzlement, to film every extra placing an order. "You," he said, pointing to a brunette, "get a large peanut butter cup with extra whip cream." He acted as though he'd conceived some masterstroke of cinema verité. "You need to say your orders with enunciation. Proclamation! And remember: Be yourself." Even the normally unflappable Todd Barron was baffled by this. "You don't need to hear everyone's order, Tommy," he said. "Let's just get one."

"No," Tommy said. "You don't know San Francisco, my friend. We need impression of very busy coffee shop."

Joe stepped forward and pointed out that sitting through thirty seconds of complete strangers ordering food did nothing for the scene. Tommy wouldn't hear any of this. "This is real life," he explained. "What do you expect? You want to be fake? Not me. I hate fake stuff."

Forty-five minutes later, the coffee shop scene wrapped and we were on our way to Pacific Heights—Tommy's dream neighborhood—to find, and shoot, the exterior of Johnny and Lisa's home. Tommy wanted a mansion exterior, which made no sense at all. At various points in *The Room* it's strongly implied that Johnny and Lisa live in an apartment building; Denny and Mark apparently live in the same building; and all the characters appear to share access to its rooftop. But Tommy wanted a lavish mansion and eventually spotted the place he wanted to shoot.

Todd Barron again brought up the need for permits, especially in a neighborhood like Pacific Heights.

"It's no problem," Tommy said. "This is different territory. San Francisco is not Los Angeles. We shoot. Sa-sa-sa-style. We leave. Don't be so conservative, my God."

We set up, prepared the shot, and were about to start filming when a police cruiser pulled up and asked what we were shooting and to see our permit.

"We just shooting video," Tommy explained to the passenger-side cop. "It's very simple thing."

"Okay," the cop said. "You still need a permit or you can't film here."

"This is not professional stuff," Tommy said. "It's just the video thing."

"Sir," the cop said, his expression turning dark and authoritarian, "show me your permit or you're going to need to leave."

"I'm sorry," Tommy said, "but I disagree with you on your statement."

At this point Todd Barron, Joe, Zsolt, the makeup artist, and I began briskly packing up everything that had a lens or a cord. Tommy continued to needlessly restate his case as we got into the cars and drove away.

Tommy eventually settled on a quieter street in the Marina, right off Lombard. Tommy's pick for Johnny and Lisa's condo this time was a handsome town house duplex, which made at least slightly more sense than a mansion. He urged everyone to set up while he changed into his favorite dark, baggy suit. Moments later Todd Barron was filming Tommy as he walked along the sidewalk in front of the building. I wondered if its occupants were going to come out and ask Tommy why he was grabbing their newspaper and ascending their stairs. Joe and Zsolt manned each side of Todd Barron's camera, trying to hide it from passersby. I'd been given lookout duty, but I also had to get into my hideous costume, which came courtesy of Street Fashions: a pair of running pants two sizes too big, a long-sleeved T-shirt, black tennis shoes, and a dorky visor.

The next shot placed Tommy behind the wheel of his white Mercedes-Benz C280—the car he'd been driving when I first met him—as he pulled into the town house's driveway. As he was turning, Tommy narrowly and harrowingly avoided being killed by an oncoming city bus. When we told Tommy how close he'd come to dying, he said he didn't notice any bus. "Don't worry about bus," he said. "Worry about *scene*. Now let's get a shot of me and Greg coming home from jogging!" He and I got into his Benz. Todd Barron and Joe rolled film. Tommy pulled up to the town house and we climbed out. Cut, print—another shot successfully in the can. I was astonished by this burst of ruthless efficiency. Could this be the same man who had taken an entire afternoon to say "I did not hit her!"?

The next stop was Golden Gate Park, where we began shooting Tommy's and my jogging and football-throwing scenes. In the finished film I begin this sequence wearing my ugly visor but it disappears by the second shot. That's because, almost immediately after we started filming, the wind tore the visor off my head. I was about to chase after it but Tommy stopped me. "Forget this primitive hat," he said. "You look like parking lot man." I let the visor go, and, with it, any last lingering chance at maintaining continuity.

From there we went to the Polo Fields—to the exact spot, in fact, where I had played soccer with Tommy years before. The first few times we ran into frame, Tommy dropped the football when I threw it to him. "Throw me ball correct way, dammit!" he said. He dropped the next pass, too, and then accused me of trying to make him look bad on film, as though Tommy's remarkable case of alligator hands were my fault. On the next run I gave him a soft, floating lob, which he also dropped. "Dammit, Greg! Why you throw this tricky stuff?" His anger was getting uncomfortably livid. On my last attempt, I threw the ball to him as softly as possible, saying, "Catch this," in French.

Tommy's eyes turned into grim, warlike slits. "No French!" he said. "No French words, dammit!" The crew watched in awe as Tommy abruptly charged and tackled me. Tommy was vehemently opposed to the inclusion of any foreign languages in his movie, and he hated it when other people knew he spoke a language other than English.

Tommy kept his rather awkward tackle of me in the film. It looks playful on-screen, but it was anything but in reality.

Principal photography on *The Room* was a single location away from being complete. The last task was to find a flower shop willing to host a film shoot for several hours with no warning. Tommy told us he had a flower shop in mind at the intersection of sixteenth and Dehon Streets, a few blocks from his condo. We found its two owners sitting and chatting. Tommy's tantalizing offer: He would give the women twenty dollars in exchange for a dozen roses and their permission to film in their flower shop for the rest of the afternoon. I didn't expect them to go for these terms, but to my surprise the women looked at each other and said, "Sure! Why not?" Tommy was so pleased that he announced he would *let* the women play themselves. Then again, Tommy *needed* them to play themselves, because he didn't have any extras.

Todd Barron came into the store and found Tommy saying, "I want people! I want life! We can't just have empty store!" He then turned to the makeup artist and charmed her into extra duty. (She's the woman browsing through gift cards in the finished film.) It had been a harried, frantic couple of days and Tommy was now buzzing ferociously on energy drinks. "I'm losing my mind!" he kept saying as the crew set up. Tommy was back to being the hilarious, fun-loving, easygoing San Francisco weirdo I'd first met. Todd Barron had his camera ready. Tommy stood next to him, sugar-stoned and chattering away: "Make sure you get this thing. Details, Mr. Cameraman. I want to have these flowers also in shot. And make sure you get the girl looking at cards. Very important. Also, when I enter, give me good tight close-up. The more lights the better."

Todd Barron looked through his eyepiece, breathing himself into some refined Zen state. "You are missing roses," Tommy said to him. "We must have better close-up also when I put sunglasses on my forehead." Todd Barron stopped what he was doing, turned to Tommy, and said, "Just get in the damn shot." It had taken until the very last location of the very last day, but Tommy had finally rattled the single most laid-back man on the crew.

Tommy rehearsed walking in and out of the flower shop at least ten times while the owner memorized her few lines of dialogue. "We have moment-to-moment acting in my film," he said to her. "Words are secondary!" Truer words have perhaps never been spoken. The dialogue Tommy composed for the flower shop scene, which flies back and forth like some sort of postmodern "Who's on First?" sketch, has the super-compressed density of experimental verse:

Hi

Can I help you

Yeah can I have a dozen red roses please

Oh hi Johnny I didn't know it was you here you go

That's me how much is it

That'll be eighteen dollars

Here you go keep the change hi doggie

You're my favorite customer

Thanks a lot bye

Bye bye

The flower shop owner, I think, deserves some kind of Neo Oscar for selling what might be the scene's funniest line: "Oh, hi, Johnny—I didn't know it was you." You didn't know it was him? Who did you think it was?

Tommy did the scene several times. No matter how badly he messed up his dialogue, he immediately headed over to Todd Barron and asked, "How this come out?" He wanted to watch playback after every take.

It wasn't until one of the very last takes that Tommy noticed something none of us had, which was the tiny pug dog sitting on the counter. The little guy hadn't moved at all since we'd come in. Not once. He just sat there, motionless. When Tommy finally noticed the dog, it was in the middle of a take. Going with it, Tommy patted it on its tiny, wrinkly noggin and said, "Hi, doggie," and walked away.

We watched the scene on playback. It was perfect. To paraphrase the Dude, the estimable hero of *The Big Lebowski,* it really tied the scene together. In fact, this might be Tommy's most candid moment in the entire film—and the clearest evidence of the lovable and endearing side of his personality. *Hi, doggie.* It was warped, accidental genius.

Before running the scene one final time, Tommy wanted to talk to the flower shop owner about her dog. "So cute," he said, as he petted the dog. "Hopefully he doesn't bite me, my God."

I think the owner somehow misinterpreted this as Tommy wanting the dog out of the next take. "Well," she said, "he's actually really old now. He just sits around. He won't bother anyone. He kind of rules over this counter."

Tommy nodded, smiling, still gazing down at the motionless little dog. "So is it real thing?"

The flower shop owner looked at Tommy uncertainly. "I'm sorry?" she said, after a moment.

"Your dog," Tommy said, unfazed. "Is it real thing?"

The woman kept looking at Tommy, probably trying to figure out whether this man who'd taken over her store was really asking if her dog was real. Did Tommy think it was a robot? An android pug of some kind?

"Yes," the woman said finally. "My dog is a real thing."

With that, we ran the scene a final time, after which filming for *The Room* officially wrapped. That night we all celebrated at a restaurant called Tommy's Joynt. Yes. That was its name. After four months of filming, *The Room* was finally in the can.

I stayed in the Bay Area for the next week to decompress and visit family. Tommy was also staying in San Francisco ("For business," he said) and a few days later asked if I could help him move some stuff with my SUV.

When I went to pick Tommy up, his condo was more chaotic than I'd ever seen it. Among the bags of trash and clothing were piles of photos and papers, some of which had been scattered across his coffee table. Tommy was in too good of a mood to bother apologizing for the mess. The moment I walked in, he said he had something to show me. With that, he vanished into another room.

I picked up one of the pictures and saw a younger, smiling, fresh-faced Tommy with the Street Fashions USA logo superimposed above him; I figured it was an old promo card. I also noticed an ID tag from a

1993 Las Vegas retailer convention and, next to that, a TPW Inc. business card, with his name misspelled: THOMAS P. WISAU.

Tommy came back into the room holding up a VHS tape: "This is surprise for you! At first I thought I was not going to show you, but then I change my mind. So here you go! Your present."

"What is it?"

"We watch," he said, "and you find out."

It was the first rough cut of *The Room*. I now learned that Tommy had asked his editor to piece together footage of the movie as it was being filmed. That meant this rough cut didn't have any of the San Francisco footage. It also wasn't yet sound-synched, dubbed, or instrumentally scored, but it was something to behold all the same. Tommy had used placeholder music (Journey, Sade, and Bon Jovi) as a temporary soundtrack. The first Johnny-Lisa sex scene, for instance, was backed up by Bon Jovi's "Always." In fact, the scene ran for the exact duration of the song, which is six minutes—twice as long as in *The Room*'s final cut.

At one point in the film, I glanced over at Tommy, who was beaming. He was filled with such joy and pride. This movie and moment was his, it belonged to him, and I wanted to let Tommy savor it. I imagined him enjoying many future solo screenings in his living room, staring at the television, smiling like he was now, and being, in that moment, the movie star he knew he could be. This was his glorious $6 million home movie.

Right before we left, Tommy handed me a copy of the rough cut to take home. "Watch with your family," he said. "Your mother will be shocked."

After loading up my car with merchandise from the Street Fashions USA on Beach Street, Tommy directed me to a store on Haight Street, fifteen minutes away, to unload. It was another Street Fashions location.

"As you can see," he said as he unlocked the door, "somebody is powerful person." It appeared Tommy was having a liquidation sale. All the merchandise had been thrown carelessly onto the shelves. He'd posted homemade SALE signs on the windows. He'd even placed a sky-tracker spotlight outside the front door. "I'm changing business," he said. "I think I do movies now."

I returned to my folks' house that evening, rough cut in hand. My brother David and his girlfriend, who were living in Sacramento, had come to visit for the night. After we'd caught up, David looked at me knowingly. "So," he said, "guess how old Tommy is?" My brother and I had a long-running debate about Tommy's real age, which continued even after Tommy's driver's license had appeared to confirm that he really *was* in his early thirties. ("There's no way," my brother had said, "that Tommy's only seven years older than me.")

It turned out David's girlfriend had a friend with state government connections. According to public record, Tommy was born much earlier than 1968. It was nice to know David and I weren't crazy, but after I considered the lengths to which Tommy had gone to conceal his age, my feelings turned a bit heavy. Suddenly I saw Tommy in an even sadder light. Was there *anything* about himself that Tommy actually accepted? I hoped that, in some way, completing *The Room* would help him begin to embrace who he really was.

With popcorn popped, my family and I settled in to watch the film. Within the first few minutes, everyone was laughing so hard they could barely breathe. "Greg," David said, "this is . . . It's incredible. Imagine playing this in front of a packed house. They think they're going to watch some intense, dramatic movie—and then *this* comes on. You could retire off this thing!"

"I have to show this to my friends," his girlfriend kept saying, over and over again. My mother absolutely lost it when Tommy says to Lisa, "In a few minutes, bitch." My father—a dear, restrained, altogether good-hearted man who enjoys the daily newspaper's crossword puzzle, *Seinfeld,* and going to bed at 9:00 p.m.—was laughing so hard he had to take off his glasses every few minutes to wipe the tears from his eyes. Not a scene transpired without someone crying out: "Wait!" "Rewind." "Pause!" It was striking to see my family loving this cinematic abomination as much as they were. The room was filled with laughter from beginning to end—huge, bright, joyful laughter. We finished watching it at 1:00 a.m. Our cheeks hurt, our stomachs ached, and we felt closer to one another than we had in a long time.

Although I didn't know it, my family in Danville, California, had become *The Room*'s collective Patient Zero. Their response to *The Room* was a powerful indicator of what this film would do on a much larger scale.

It was not until June 1, 2003—eight months later—that I discovered that any other audience would ever have the chance to see *The Room*. I received an invitation from Wiseau-Films cordially inviting me, and a guest, to the world premiere of *The Room,* taking place on Friday, June 27, 2003, at 7:00 p.m., in Los Angeles.

seventeen

This Is My Life

So they were turning after all, those cameras.
Life, which can be strangely merciful, had taken pity on Norma Desmond.
The dream she had clung to so desperately had enfolded her.
—Joe Gillis, *Sunset Boulevard*

I think it's time we all moved on.
—Dickie Greenleaf, *The Talented Mr. Ripley*

By the time premiere night rolled around, it had been a long time since I'd spoken to Tommy; he'd vanished into the postproduction minutiae of *The Room*. The last time I had seen him was at his editor's studio in Burbank, shortly after the film wrapped. I'd been called in to dub some of my dialogue due to the fact that the sound had been improperly recorded for most of the film. Tommy also insisted on recording dialogue for a PG-rated version of *The Room,* which he hoped would be suitable for prime-time television broadcast; lines like "manipulative bitch" became "manipulative witch." He didn't seem to consider that a much bigger roadblock to his prime-time broadcast version of *The Room* might be its eleven minutes of sex scenes.

My visit with Tommy and Eric Chase, the film's editor, in Burbank made clear that their working relationship was that of two mountain goats repeatedly butting heads. Tommy's mantra during the editing process: "I repeat, nothing will be cut." Nevertheless, a portion of every editing session involved Eric trying to convince Tommy that various scenes either needed to be shortened or lost entirely. "This slows down the film," Eric would say of one scene. "No, it doesn't," Tommy would respond. "This scene has no relevance to anything whatsoever," Eric would say about another scene. "Yes," Tommy would counter, "it does."

Eric was troubled by the lack of continuity. He struggled to make it clear to Tommy that editing couldn't solve every problem. But Tommy saw no problems. The biggest issue was the inclusion of the Lisa-Mark love scene Tommy insisted on wedging into *The Room*'s last fifteen minutes, which resulted in a small time warp that no editing tricks could convincingly account for. "How," Eric asked Tommy, "am I supposed to edit this? Lisa says she's getting ready for 'the party tonight.' Then it's night, and there's no party. Then it's day, and she's still getting ready for the party! And you want a love scene thrown in there?" Tommy's response: "Yes. This is the way I see it."

Eric's greatest battle was trying to convince Tommy to lose the scene in which Johnny bares his naked ass. Eric's reasoning: The shot scared his wife. Tommy refused. The one battle Eric did manage to win was convincing Tommy to trim three minutes from Johnny and Lisa's first sex scene. With the exception of the alternate Chris-R alley scene, Johnny's living room death, and all of the HD camera footage, everything else Tommy shot was somehow squeezed into *The Room*'s final edit.

This "everything stays" mentality extended itself to Tommy's Wiseau-Films production logo, which plays before the movie proper begins. Tommy had had two logo sequences designed. The first was a speck of silver light morphing into a shiny silver *W,* which then explodes into a spinning Wiseau-Films globe. The second option was another, slightly different Wiseau-Films globe that also forms out of the nebular emptiness of space. Tommy had trouble choosing between the two logos. While only one plays in the theatrical cut of the film, both run—one right after the other—on the DVD version.

Another duel Eric lost involved *The Room*'s opening credits. Eric was unable to convince Tommy to follow traditional auteur protocol and list all his credits on one screen: *Written, Produced, and Directed by Tommy Wiseau.* Instead, Tommy elected to dedicate a separate screen to each of his duties. *Executive Producer: Tommy Wiseau; Writer: Tommy*

Wiseau; Producer: Tommy Wiseau; Director: Tommy Wiseau. Tommy's scent is all over the film before it even begins.

Tommy's style proved more fitting for the next item on his pre-premiere *Room* to-do list: guerrilla marketing. On April 1, 2003, the good people of Hollywood awoke to find Tommy's face plastered on a billboard on Highland Avenue, a few blocks down from the Kodak Theater, where the Oscars are held. The ad featured a cropped version of one of Tommy's favorite headshots of himself: lowered face, pursed lips, and eyes filled with furiously blank focus. It was terrifying. Beneath Tommy's mug was the film's tagline: "Can you really trust anyone?" I'm not sure I've ever seen a movie billboard that did less to communicate what the movie it was ostensibly advertising was about. Tommy's billboard could have been an ad for an industrial film about the dangers of radon or some experimental foreign crime caper. The one thing the billboard probably wasn't selling was what the movie actually was: an earnest love-triangle melodrama.

"We do no different than big sharks," Tommy would say. After all, he'd studied closely how the big sharks designed their billboards. They featured language like *Only in Theaters* and *Now Playing* and had MPAA ratings and logos belonging to Dolby Digital and Kodak film. So Tommy's billboard contained the same information and corporate heraldry. It read *Now Playing* and *Only in Theaters* despite the fact that it wasn't playing in *any* theater. This made the billboard's one decidedly non–big shark touch—a *Room* screening RSVP hotline (which was Tommy's home phone number at the time)—rather touching. The *Room* billboard was Tommy's most impressive and costly bit of marketing. Most studios book a one-month billboard run for their major releases. Tommy's billboard didn't come down until *five years later,* during which time it became an odd Hollywood landmark.

His other marketing attempts were just as bold. Tommy, for instance, impetuously phoned Paramount Studios to inquire about distribution for *The Room.* He was told to drop off the film at the Paramount lot for their consideration. It normally takes two weeks for a studio to respond, but Tommy was summoned back to Paramount to pick up

The Room within twenty-four hours. He was unbowed by this. "Well," he said, "they lost. I just do myself."

Rejection seemed to fill Tommy's tank with rocket fuel. After the Paramount debacle, Tommy hired a publicist named Ed Lozzi and kicked off a full-scale publicity campaign. Tommy then tried to reserve Grauman's Chinese Theatre for *The Room*'s premiere. No dice. He did, however, successfully secure a four-wall distribution deal—a process by which a studio rents a movie theater for a period of time and receives all of the box office revenue—with Laemmle Theaters. *The Room* would premiere at the Laemmle on Fairfax and Beverly (which had recently become a $2.75/ticket theater), followed by a two-week run at a Laemmle theater in the Valley. Why pay to keep *The Room* in theaters for two weeks? Because having a film play for two weeks in theaters was a prerequisite for all films submitted to the Academy Awards, which had always been Tommy's ultimate goal.

The media blitzkrieg announcing *The Room*'s imminent premiere included late-night television commercials, local print ads, and a JumboTron that ran a *Room* trailer above Sunset Boulevard for weeks. Tommy's self-scribed promotional material claimed that his film had "the passion of Tennesee [*sic*] Williams" and cited nonexistent critics from nonexistent outlets. This was *Entertainment Today*'s rave: "Wiseau is multi-talented and mysterious, since he is a true Cajun from New Orleans. . . . This electrifying drama is about love and ultimate betrayal." And here was praise courtesy of something called *Beverly Hills 90210*: "If you've been missing Tennesse [yes, *sic*] Williams films, the 'new Williams' is a ragin' Cajun."

Tommy didn't leave a restaurant or restroom without depositing a *Room* postcard. Some of my friends, including Amber and even Don, called me to talk about Tommy's bombardment of *Room* advertisements. Between local TV, news publications, the JumboTron, eating establishments, lavatories, and the billboard, Tommy had Los Angeles covered. *The Room* was everywhere.

• • •

On the evening of *The Room*'s premiere, I put on the closest thing to black-tie attire I had: the oversize shirt and pants from my *Room* tuxedo. Then I drove over to Tommy's house.

When I arrived, Tommy was pacing in his driveway, talking on his cell phone, his white tuxedo blouse unbuttoned halfway. He looked agitated, sweaty, and vaguely debauched. Next to him was a rented van and boxes of gift bags full of promotional *Room* swag: soundtracks, T-shirts, and a making-of photo book. As I approached, he hung up and finished loading the last few boxes into the van. He saw me notice the silk girdle circling his midsection and mistakenly assumed I disapproved. "So what?" he said. "I have to keep my stomach tight! I won't have big stomach because you tell me so."

I laughed as I reached down to pick up a box. "Be careful," Tommy said. "I do lifting. I don't want you to hurt your stitches." It took a moment, but I eventually figured out what he meant by this: Tommy had convinced himself that I'd undergone cosmetic surgery on my stomach. A decade later, I'm still confused as to why exactly he believed this.

As we loaded the last boxes into the van, Tommy's mind was churning out even more fantastical theories: "We receive phone calls. I think I suspect something, you know what I'm saying? These phone calls is not normal. It's obsession, if you really think about it." Translation: Tommy suspected the hang-ups on his answering machine were either famous people or jealous studio executives. He hadn't seemed to consider that these hang-ups were more probably curious people calling the RSVP number he'd recently plastered on a billboard in the middle of Hollywood.

Tommy and I went inside to grab the last of the boxes. His house was practically empty. "I wasn't going to tell you," he said, "but I have new house now. In very exclusive neighborhood." Tommy also told me that he'd closed all of his Street Fashions stores and bought a building in Los Angeles. He wanted to create his own private Paramount Studios.

We were in the limo by 5:30 p.m. Tommy taped *Room* posters on each window before climbing aboard. The limo rolled out of Tommy's driveway and started heading in the opposite direction of the theater, over Laurel Canyon, toward the Valley. "Where are we going?" I asked.

Tommy poured a can of Red Bull into a champagne glass. "We have very exclusive guests coming," he told me. "So behave yourself." Tommy was anxious and grew increasingly so, taking more frequent sips of Red Bull the closer we got to the Valley. He clearly wanted to impress his mystery guests.

The limo turned onto Magnolia Boulevard and made a right into a small private lane before stopping in the driveway of a handsome town house. Two women of a certain age, one blond and one redheaded, both done up in old-school red-carpet-ready attire, emerged. Tommy got out of the limo and waited for them door-side. Both women were overtaken with excitement at the sight of Tommy, hugging and kissing him. As the women ducked into the limo, Tommy introduced us. Karen, the blond and older of the two, was the widow of director Stanley Kramer, who is most famous for directing *Guess Who's Coming to Dinner* and giving Marlon Brando his first film role in *The Men*. The other woman was Karen and Stanley's daughter, Kat, who'd been named after her godmother, Katharine Hepburn.

As the limo headed back toward Hollywood, Kat, who was wearing an impressively red hat, began telling me all about the fun she'd had with Tommy over the last few months. "I introduced Tommy to De Niro and Faye Dunaway," she said, and laughed. "I don't think he knew who they were at first!" I later found out that Kat was referring to an AFI tribute to Robert De Niro that she'd attended with Tommy. I had no idea how they'd met but found the pairing interesting nonetheless. I knew Tommy's dream had always been to be like Brando. And here he was, on the way to his first movie's premiere, with the widow and daughter of the director who gave Brando his start. It was a long-shot connection, but to Tommy this must have seemed like fate.

Tommy, whose nerves had finally calmed, told the driver to turn onto Hollywood Boulevard for an impromptu pit stop in front of Grauman's Chinese Theatre. As the limo idled, Tommy grabbed an armful of *Room* paraphernalia, sprung up through the sunroof, and began shouting, "Hey, everyone! You're invited!" Then he started launching *Room* T-shirts and invites to anyone and everyone passing by. Soon enough a crowd of excited tourists had gathered around the limo. Tommy was now swinging a *Room* T-shirt in a helicopter motion above his head, saying, "Come to feature movie premiere!" The limo, mercifully, started moving and Tommy threw the T-shirt into the crowd. "You're all invited!" He descended back into the limo, smiling. "Okay," he told the driver, "time to go to the Fairfax!"

Tommy got his publicist on the phone. "Ed," he said, "I need you to make sure spotlight is shining! Make sure there's big line out front. Lots of people! We want a line or we don't pull up." Tommy had told his publicity team to fill every seat in the theater. Okay, I thought. Let's assume they did that. The thought of Tommy sitting among an audience expecting to be shown a serious drama was not, to say the least, a comforting one.

The limo pulled up to the theater, but in Tommy's mind there weren't enough people outside to merit stopping. So we went around the block. It was a busy Friday evening: This was a serious commitment to traffic endurance. We passed by the theater again and again Tommy told the driver to go around the block. On our final approach, I saw most of the cast waiting outside, behind red velvet ropes. "Stop!" Tommy said.

The *Room* posters taped on every window allowed everyone in the cast and crew to guess who was sitting inside that limo, but Tommy didn't want to get out quite yet; he instructed the driver to stay in his seat and leave the limo idling. "We need to build the anticipation," Tommy explained to Kat and Karen.

Outside, I saw Dan Janjigian and Don standing with Scott Holmes, Philip, Robyn, Carolyn, Greg Ellery, and Juliette. A few members of Tommy's various crews were there, though neither Sandy nor Kyle Vogt had been invited because, in Tommy's mind, they'd abandoned him. Scattered among the cast and crew were family members, friends, and a whole mess of people to be filed under miscellaneous, all of whom Tommy's publicist had recruited.

Tommy finally opened the door of the limo and stepped onto his red carpet to actual cheers. Tommy kept his shades on and did his best to impress Kat by strolling past everyone in an aloof manner. I headed directly toward Philip and Scott, both of whom were yelling "Gregorio!" Don came over and greeted me with a friendly smile. "Digging the long hair, man," he said as we walked together into the lobby. "By the way, did Tommy hire escorts?"

"Not that I'm aware," I said, watching what appeared to be an Elvis impersonator entering the theater in front of us. Once inside, I could guess what had probably happened. It appeared that Tommy's PR people had called a character casting agency—more than one, from the looks of things. That's how they'd filled the seats. They might as well have requested the entire citizenry of the Island of Misfit Toys.

The first five rows of the theater had been reserved for the cast and crew. I took an aisle seat, which I hoped would allow me to quickly duck out during the love scenes. Kat sat to my right, with Tommy next to her. Juliette, Philip, and Don were in front of us. Right after we sat down, Don turned around and said, "Oh, by the way—I checked online. This is going to be on your IMDb for the rest of your life." I offered Don a courtesy laugh, after which he went back to munching his popcorn.

Ed Lozzi, Tommy's publicist, a beefy guy in a tan sport coat, stepped to the front of the theater, microphone in hand. He briefly introduced Tommy to the audience before inviting the auteur himself to take the stage.

Tommy stood up. He did not look well. In fact, he looked petrified. Big beads of flop sweat had gathered on his forehead and he made no effort to mask his discomfort as he approached the stage. He kept his sunglasses on. This was the first time I'd ever seen Tommy nervous. He was completely devoid of the bravado he'd always had in front of an audience. His hands trembled as he raised the microphone to his mouth. He paused for a moment, too overcome to speak. When he tried, there was only a faint stuttering sound. The audience became very still. Then, at last, Tommy managed to say something: "This. This is my movie. This is my life. I hope you learn something and discover yourself." He made a hang-loose sign with his free hand. "Be cool," he mumbled, before handing the microphone back to Ed. On his way to his seat, Tommy stopped, put his hand on my shoulder, kneeled down, and said, "I'm happy you're here. I could never do project without you."

The Room's premiere was testament to Tommy's unrelenting drive and determination. He'd inflict his vision on the world whether the world wanted it or not. He was a movie star whether the world saw it or not. In getting here, Tommy had sometimes been destructive and sometimes cruel. But how could I—how could anyone—not be moved by Tommy, who'd fought so hard against the unforgiving confines of his star-crossed life? *The Room,* I already knew, was a lot of things. A bad film, a funny film, a bizarre film, a glorious film, a vain film, an absurd film, an incompetent film, a powerful film, a fascinating film, a disastrous film, an independent film, an inexplicable film, and finally, a brave film. Sitting there in the theater, I let myself feel proud of Tommy, who believed his movie was a first-rate emotional drama that contained all his most profound ideas about life. In that regard, *The Room* was Tommy, and *is* Tommy—a man who remains the grandest and most sincere dreamer I've ever known. This is, ultimately, what redeems his immensely conflicted and complicated darkness. In the end, Tommy made me realize that you decide who you become. He also made me realize what a mixed blessing that can be.

Although I knew Tommy's film wasn't going to be received the way he wanted it to be that night, I hoped he'd be able to recognize how incredible this experience really was. When I looked over at him, I couldn't help but see a vision of the young boy who peered through a movie theater's cracked door in Eastern Europe, newly in awe of life's possibilities.

Tommy removed his sunglasses and glanced back at me. He had tears in his eyes. He smiled, nodded, and turned toward the screen. It wasn't often that you got to see a man whose dream was literally about to come true, but then the lights went down, and I couldn't see him anymore.

Acknowledgments

Richard, Marie-José, and David
Tom Bissell
Jim Rutman
Heather Schroder
Trish Todd
Molly Lindley
John Hughes, RIP
Brad Pitt
Jonah Hill
Paul Rudd
Kristen Bell
David Wain
Tim Heidecker and Eric Wareheim
Justin Long
David Cross
Patton Oswalt
Paul Scheer
Michael Rousselet
Scott Gairdner
David Nelson
Elias Eliot
Justin Robinson
Clark Collis
Entertainment Weekly
Kate Ward
John Cassaras
Alex Pardee

George Gross, Ned Martin, and Alec Gross
Ashleigh Erwin
Greg Deliso
Anthony Remedy, Fionn Kidney, and Una Mullally
Gregory Lynn and Paul Vickery
Tom Ranieri
Gavin Hogg
Paul Collins
Roger D. Hodge
Adrienne Miller
Gideon Lewis-Kraus
Dan Josefson
Rob Auten
Trisha Miller
Juliette Danielle
Dan Janjigian
Kyle Vogt
Greg Ellery
Robyn Paris
Philip Haldiman
Carolyn Minnott
Scott Holmes
Marcus Winslow Jr.
Patrick Jagaille
Anthony Minghella, RIP
Billy Wilder, RIP

About the Authors

Greg Sestero is an actor, producer, and writer. He was born in Walnut Creek, California, and raised between the San Francisco Bay Area and Europe. He is fluent in both French and English. At the age of seventeen, Greg began his career in entertainment by modeling in Milan for such designers as Valentino and Armani. He went on to pursue acting, and appeared in several films and television shows before costarring in the international cult phenomenon *The Room*. Greg's many passions include film, sports, nutrition, animals, and traveling. Greg now resides in Los Angeles.

Tom Bissell was born in Escanaba, Michigan, in 1974. He is the author of several books, including *The Father of All Things* and *Extra Lives,* and his work has been awarded the Rome Prize and a Guggenheim Fellowship. More recently, he cowrote the script for *Gears of War: Judgment*. He lives in Los Angeles.